The Place of the Hidden Moon

EROTIC MYSTICISM IN THE VAIṢṆAVA-SAHAJIYĀ CULT OF BENGAL

EDWARD C. DIMOCK, JR.

WITH A NEW FOREWORD BY
WENDY DONIGER

THE UNIVERSITY OF CHICAGO PRESS/CHICAGO & LONDON

The University of Chicago Press, Chicago 60637
The University of Chicago Press, Ltd., London

Paperback edition 1989
Printed in the United States of America

98 97 96 95 94 93 92 91 90 89   5 4 3 2 1

Library of Congress Catalog Card Number 66-13865
International Standard Book Number 0-226-15237-5

Library of Congress Cataloging-in-Publication Data

Dimock, Edward C.
The place of the hidden moon : erotic mysticism in the Vaiṣṇava sahajiyā cult of Bengal / Edward C. Dimock, Jr. : with a new foreword by Wendy Doniger.
p.   cm.
Includes bibliographical references and index.
ISBN 0-226-15237-5 (pbk. : alk. paper)
1. Sahajiyā. 2. Sex—Religious aspects—Vaishnavism.
3. Mysticism—Hinduism. I. Title.
BL1287.84.D56 1989
294.5′22—dc20   89-36881
CIP

♾ The paper used in this publication meets the minimum requirements of the American National Standard for Information Sciences—Permanence of Paper for Printed Library Materials, ANSI Z39.48-1984.

Few men are both teachers and scholars, combining intellectual rigor with sympathy, learning with understanding, an appreciation of beauty and the mysteries with an uncompromising recognition of the necessity of knowledge. One such man was

ARTHUR DARBY NOCK
(1902–62)

This book is dedicated to his memory

Contents

Foreword

This book, first published in 1966, inspired a whole generation of Indologists—my generation—who aspired to emulate it in a number of ways but never, I think, matched it. Certainly I would never have been able to write my first book about Śiva until *The Place of the Hidden Moon* had created a space for that book within the whole new world of possibilities that it introduced for the study of Indian religions. It seems to me, too, that a number of important books written in the last two decades owe their conception, their style of approach, and sometimes even their central idea to *The Place of the Hidden Moon*. The most obvious works of this sort are books about Krishna (John Stratton Hawley's book on Krishna the butter thief, David Kinsley's *The Sword and the Flute* and *The Divine Player*, the translations and interpretations of Surdas by Kenneth Bryant and by John Stratton Hawley) and books about Krishna and Radha (the book of essays about Radha as the divine consort by John Stratton Hawley and Donna Wulff, David Kinsley's book on Hindu goddesses, Barbara Stoler Miller's translation of the *Gita Govinda*, and Lee Siegel's book on sacred and profane dimensions of love in the *Gita Govinda*).

But there are many other books on subjects more broadly related to *The Place of the Hidden Moon* that are, I think, less obviously, but no less profoundly, indebted to Dimock. This list would include not only all the books that have been written since 1966 about the Indological topics of religion in Bengal, literature in Bengal, and Tantrism in general, but books on subjects that extend far beyond the borders of India: books about erotic mysticism, about love, about sex, and about the relationship between love and sex, not just in India but in the world at large.

For this is one of the few books in the field of Indology that combines the kind of meticulous scholarship that great Indology requires—the painstaking translation and analysis of hundreds of obscure, difficult texts—with the kind of elegance and humor that has generally been the privilege of a few gifted scholars of Western literature: scholars like A. E. Housman, Gilbert Murray, and T. S. Eliot. The scholarship is certainly here; this is the most reliable and indeed altogether the best book I know on all of the many Indological subjects with which it deals, some of them major topics in Indian religion: the life of the saint Caitanya, the tradition of the mad Baul singers, the aesthetic theory of *rasa*, the *bhakti* tradition of the love of God, the doctrines of Tantrism, the origins of the figure of Radha, and the worship of Krishna. But the elegance and humor are there too, and these are the qualities that make this book the best book I know on spiritual and carnal love (or sacred and profane love) in general, on love in union and love in separation, on the difference between poetic and doctrinal attitudes to love, between married love and adulterous love, and between European and Indian attitudes to sexual love, spiritual love, and the love of God. It is rare indeed to find that a work that was once a doctoral dissertation, and that still bears the doctoral scars in the form of some fairly technical discussions of abstruse textual problems, can still be not only as readable but as generally humane, as broadly meaningful, as this book is.

Dimock's treatment of Tantrism, unlike the many other books on Tantra that are all seriously flawed in one way or another, steers triumphantly between the Scylla of obscenity and the Charybdis of pedantry. For Tantrism, and the sexual aspect of Hinduism more generally, was until very recently a great embarrassment to Indology, stirring conflicting passions and getting caught on the hooks of various political agendas. The reputed obscenity of Tantric texts (and, indeed of certain Vedic texts and certain Hindu temple carvings) simultaneously attracted and repelled early European Indologists. To the extent that they were attracted, they might titillate themselves either positively, in the "noble savage" genre of Victorian envy ("How free and happy these Hindus are with their sexuality" and "You're a better man than I am, Gunga Din"), or, the shadow side of the same coin, censoriously ("Listen to the terribly, terribly dirty things that these wretched barbarians write about and do, as I relate them to you in luscious detail"). On the fringes of Indology, novels and, later, films, exploited this same perspective with its cast of half-caste fallen women (the John Masters-Merle Oberon-Ava Gardner scenario) in the sultry jungle atmosphere of the approaching monsoon. This tradition lives on in David Attenborough's recent film version of *A Passage to India*.

A more accepting but equally prurient, superficial, and Eurocentric approach to Tantrism (even more Eurocentric when practiced by colonialized Hindus) was manifest in the wave of lavish and often limited-edition art books published in the 1950s (including, notably, an edition by Grove Press). These books lumped together, quite promiscuously, erotic temple sculptures of a religious character (or, at the very least, those set in an erotic context), erotic miniature paintings, some of a religious character (notably paintings of Krishna and Radha) and others of a far more secular (indeed, sometimes downright pornographic) character, and Tantric *mandalas* whose sexuality was blatant but remained entirely misunderstood. There were some exceptions to this general trend—the works of Devangana Desai and Philip Rawson, in particular—but by and large the coffee-table books carried the field.

On the other hand, to the extent that they have been repelled by the Tantras, few serious scholars have been willing to touch them. The one major exception, Sir John George Woodroffe, published a great deal of his work under the uneasy pseudonym of Arthur Avalon, while under his own name he tended to edit, moralize, and even bowdlerize to the point where the texts became largely unreadable. This latter device—hiding behind a shield of unreadable pedantry—was the one adopted by most of Avalon's successors. In a nervous attempt to gain respectability for their subject, scholars of Tantrism, like frightened giant squid, emitted an almost impenetrable cloud of ink in the form of highly technical language, nontranslations that left most of the terminology in Sanskrit (or, occasionally, in Latin, the *lingua franca* for subjects too frank for English), and topheavy commentaries that parroted the apologetic stances of Indian scholars themselves. Thus the five "m"s, which might best be translated as five "f"s (*mansa*—flesh, *matsya*—fish, *madya*—fermented grapes [wine], *mudra*—frumentum [parched grain], and *maithuna*—fornication), are quickly said to have *only* the esoteric meaning that Indian commentaries do, indeed, attach to them—but only as an embarrassed afterthought. Such academic books on the Tantras date them, list them, explain their terminology, argue about their history (an interesting argument, for Tantrism, like syphillis in the European tradition, is always said to have originated in one of the countries on your border), but never tell you *what they are about*.

The Place of the Hidden Moon is the only book I know of that tells you what Tantrism *feels* like, tells you how these texts make a brilliant attempt to resolve powerful and fascinating tensions in the religious lives of men and women. It tells you by setting the Tantric texts not only in their particular geographical and historical context, but in the far broader context of Indian attitudes to love, to sex, and to God, and by exploring the many combinations and permutations of their triangulation. It achieves its goal by drawing not only upon Indian religious texts of all periods, but upon Indian love poetry (which no previous study of Tantrism had ever done, to my knowledge), and equally important, upon contrasting and not-so-contrasting European sacred texts and European love poetry. Like all genuine attempts to understand another religion, this work is necessarily comparative, self-aware, acknowledging its author's original stance in European culture and moving consciously out of that starting position in order to enter into Indian culture.

Finally, and perhaps most important of all, Dimock achieves his understanding of the relationship between love, sex, and God by infusing his scholarship with his own personal, religious, and poetic understanding of love, sex, and God. As this turns out to be a truly original and profoundly conceived understanding, it makes this book a landmark of humane scholarship in the true sense of the word—a book that helps us to understand what it might mean to be a human being.

Wendy Doniger
June 1989

Note to the 1989 Edition

I am, needless to say, delighted that the University of Chicago Press and its consultants think that there is enough in this little book to warrant bringing out a paperback version. I am particularly grateful to my good friend and valued colleague Wendy Doniger, not just for her active role in persuading the Press that a reissue might be of use to scholars and students in the field, but for enhancing the new issue with a Foreword. I also take the opportunity to record here my gratitude to Stella Snead of New York, the photographer whose work appears on the cover of the book.

There is much in *The Place of the Hidden Moon* that has been superceded in the twenty-three years since it was first published. In the past few years four students at the University of Chicago alone have done work in the area of Bengali Vaiṣṇavism which surpasses, extends, or modifies my own: Tony K. Stewart, whose excellent dissertation *The Biographical Images of Kṛṣṇa-caitanya: A Study in the Perception of Divinity* (1985) is, I hope, soon to be published; David Haberman, whose study has been published (1988) by the Oxford University Press under the title *Acting As A Way of Salvation*; Neal Delmonico, whose dissertation *Sacred Erotic Rapture: The Foundations of the Ujjvalanīlamaṇī of Rūpa Gosvāmin* will be submitted in 1989; and June McDaniel, whose work on religious madness is to be published in 1989 by the University of Chicago Press under the title *Madness of the Saints: Ecstatic Religion in Bengal*. There are many other scholars who have dealt with Bengali Vaiṣṇavism or the Tantra, or some combination thereof, in this country and in Europe: names such as Varenne, Padoux, Wayman, Bharati, Lorenzen, Kinsley, Capwell, Salomon, Wulff, Arraj come to mind. And the matter has not been left untouched by Indian scholars, who are too numerous to mention.

Because of the ideas and study of these and other scholars, it would perhaps not be unfair to say that my own sophistication has increased somewhat. If I were to write the present book today, it would be a very different one. And yet, reading it through for the first time in many years, I find that I still accept most of the views expressed, and in general stand by my arguments. There is one area, however, of which I am no longer so sure.

One of the most acute commentators on things Vaiṣṇava over the past several years has been my old and dear friend Professor Joseph T. O'Connell, of St. Michael's College of the University of Toronto. He and I have had some occasion to discuss in public several of the points

I tried to make in this book, in particular the way in which I have connected the names of various devotees of the Vaisṇạva school to its Sahajiyā branch (I suspect there would be an objection to my calling it a "branch"), and in some ways I think he is justified in his criticism. The reader might be advised to be cautious when going through the list of names in the chapter entitled, "Caste, Women, and the Sahajiyā Movement," for often the evidence is flimsy or circumstantial.

Professor O'Connell takes particular exception to my including the great *bhakta* Rāmānanda Rāya among the names of the Sahajiyā Vaiṣṇavas. His arguments against such inclusion are detailed in an article entitled "Were Caitanya's Vaiṣṇavas Really Sahajiyās?—The Case of Rāmānanda Rāy," appearing in Tony K. Stewart, ed., *Shaping Bengali Worlds, Public and Private* (East Lansing: Asian Studies Center, Michigan State University, 1989), and, in a longer version, in J. T. O'Connell and H. A. Sanyal, eds., *Caitanya and the Vaiṣṇavas of Bengal* (Calcutta: K. P. Bagchi, forthcoming). His first criticism is of the use of the term *sahaja*, as it is applied to Rāmānanda. O'Connell contends convincingly that it should be interpreted as meaing that Rāmānanda was a "spontaneous" or "natural" Vaiṣṇava, and I think he is right. On his two other points, however (the peculiar *sādhana* practiced by Rāmānanda, and Rāmānanda as critical in the development of the theory of dual incarnation), I shall stand my ground.

I stand it with deference, however, for I am well aware that some scholars and friends on both sides of the ocean look upon certain observations I have made as approaching offense to a dignified living religious tradition. I can assure such scholars and friends that I mean no affront now, and meant none when the book was first published. My respect and veneration for the extremely subtle and rarified theology of orthodox Vaiṣṇavism will, I trust, be clear when my translation and commentary on the *Caitanya-caritāmṛta* of Kṛṣṇadāsa, which is now ready for the press, appears.

E. D.
June 1989

Preface

MUCH OF THE MATERIAL in this book was first presented as a part of my doctoral dissertation to the Department of Sanskrit and Indian Studies at Harvard University in 1959, and some parts of it have subsequently appeared in various articles and papers; my brief chapter on the Bāuls, for example, reuses some part of the material which was first published in an article entitled "Rabindranath Tagore—'The Greatest of the Bāuls of Bengal,'" in the *Journal of Asian Studies* in November, 1959. I am grateful to the editors of that journal for their permission for this reuse. Some portions of the third chapter were used in an article entitled "Doctrine and Practice among the Vaiṣṇavas of Bengal," which appeared first in *History of Religions* (Summer, 1963) and later in *Krishna: Myths, Rites, and Attitudes* (Honolulu: East-West Center Press, 1965) edited by Milton Singer; I thank the editors and publishers of these publications for their kind permission to reprint those sections here. I am also grateful to the Macmillan Company of New York for permission to quote "Solomon and the Witch," from *The Collected Poems of* W. B. *Yeats* (1952).

Since 1959 I have spent little time working on the Sahajiyās, but an occasional bit of data such as the manuscript *Sahaja nāyikā-ṭīkā*, insofar as I have been able to decipher it, is the result of sporadic work since that time. I have been working, however, on the *Caitanya-caritāmṛta* of Kṛṣṇadāsa Kavirāja, a text that is a product of more orthodox Vaiṣṇavism but one that the Sahajiyās consider important to their own particular doctrine. As a result, certain of my interpretations and conclusions have changed somewhat from those presented in the dissertation, as has the order of their presentation.

I do not feel that this is a finished study. The Sahajiyā writings themselves are obscure, unsystematic, and to make matters worse, written in a language that is deliberately confusing—for their doctrine is esoteric and thus to be hidden as much as possible from outsiders. I have attempted certain conclusions and left others for the reader to draw on the basis of the data presented; I think, for example, that the data indicate certain interesting and general things about syncretistic processes in Indian religion, but I have not attempted to make this an overt theme of the book. I have merely tried, as far as it has been possible for me to do, to provide information about a religious system which I find intrinsically interesting. The information does not always fall neatly into as systematic a pattern as one might wish.

There are gaps in my knowledge, which will be obvious, and my hope is that someone in the future will undertake to fill them and to present us with a complete and definitive study of the Vaiṣṇava-sahajiyā cult. I also feel, however, that some of the material that I give is relevant to the study both of Vaiṣṇavism and of the ancient Tāntric tradition in the history of Indian religion, a matter that deserves much closer examination and attention than scholars have so far given it. At least I have been encouraged to feel so by Mircea Eliade, my most respected colleague at the University of Chicago, who has urged me toward its publication.

I hasten to add that this is not the only book on the subject in English. There are two others, Shashibhusan Dasgupta's *Obscure Religious Cults as a Background to Bengali Literature,* a part of which deals with Sahajiyā schools and thought, and M. M. Basu's *The Post-Caitanya Sahajiyā Cult.* To both of these studies I am greatly indebted. At some points I find myself in respectful disagreement with one or the other of them, but I have had frequent occasion to draw upon them, not only for their thoughtful opinions but also for textual references to sources to which I have not personally had access. Both writers have taken full advantage of the extensive manuscript collections in Calcutta to give long texts from valuable Bengali manuscripts. These texts and the writers' interpretations of them have been invaluable to the present work.

For the rest, I have drawn largely upon the printed texts that are available, some in anthologies, some in good and annotated editions from the Baṅgīya-sāhitya-pariṣad in Calcutta and from Calcutta University, and some printed by the so-called Bat-tola presses of the city; the latter books are in general poorly printed and rarely edited, but in many cases they are the only printings available, and in some cases the only printings ever made. Despite their shortcomings, they are extremely valuable. But the scholar who makes a full study of the Sahajiyā cult will have to go to the manuscripts, which will be difficult work: not only are the texts themselves obscure, but the hands which wrote many of those that I have seen seem to have had no compunction about perpetrating amazing linguistic atrocities. Dasgupta in his *Obscure Religious Cults* (p. 131) says that there are about two hundred and fifty "manuscripts of small texts" in the library of Calcutta University which deal with the Sahajiyā cult, and about an equal number, some of them being common with those held by the University, in the library of the Baṅgīya-sāhitya-pariṣad. The Asiatic Society in Calcutta also owns a large collection, and the number of manuscripts in private libraries is indefinite but almost certainly huge.

Rather than clutter further an already cluttered text I may well mention here the details of some of those Sahajiyā texts upon which I have drawn most heavily. The first is the *Vivarta-vilāsa* by a writer named Ākiñcana-dāsa. The book is long for a Sahajiyā work, about 170 pages, and comes fairly close to a complete, though veiled, outline of the Sahajiyā belief. The VV is a kind of commentary on the great *Caitanya-caritāmṛta* of Kṛṣṇa-dāsa, and states that its purpose is to reveal the true (i.e., the Sahajiyā) meaning of Kṛṣṇa-dāsa's work. The author of the VV was a pupil of the famous

Vaiṣṇava-sahajiyā guru Rāmacandra Gosvāmi, which would put the time of writing of this text sometime toward the late middle of the seventeenth century.

The *Āgama-grantha* was written by Yugalera-dāsa and is a text of average length for a Sahajiyā work—about 27 pages. It is a doctrinal work in the form of a dialogue between Śiva and Pārvatī, with Śiva expounding the Sahajiyā doctrine. This text also dates from the middle or late seventeenth century. A similar work, of about the same length, is the *Ānanda-bhairava* of one Prema-dāsa. It is constructed as a dialogue between a man and a woman, in a story-within-a-story fashion. Most of its stories are obscure allegories and treat sketchily a variety of subjects ranging from the creation to the proper varieties of sexual-religious culture. If its author is the Prema-dāsa who wrote the *Caitanya-candro-daya-kaumudī*, the work can be dated very early in the eighteenth century (Sukumār Sen, *Bāṅgālār sāhityer itihāsa,* I, 664). Another similar work is the *Amṛta-rasāvalī* of Mathurā-dāsa, who was a pupil of Mukunda-dāsa. This work is also about 30 pages long and is also an allegory dealing with the physiological and psychological makeup of man. This is the latest of the four and is dated by Sen (*BSI*, I, 419) as B.S. 1199 (A.D. 1793).

But of all the sources for the Sahajiyā doctrine, perhaps the most important are the padas, short poems of twelve or fourteen lines. Many of the Sahajiyā padas, called *rāgātmika-padas,* bear the signature "Caṇḍīdāsa," although their real authorship is a hotly disputed question. There are several collections of these padas. Among the best is that published by the Baṅgīya-sāhitya-pariṣad, but others include the two-volume *Dīna-caṇḍīdāsa,* edited by M. M. Basu, and *Caṇḍīdāsa padāvalī.* There are also one hundred Sahajiyā padas by various writers in M. M. Basu's anthology *Sahajiyā sāhitya.*

Of all the debts I want to acknowledge, perhaps the greatest is to Professor Sushil Kumar De. Dr. De has not only written the definitive work of Bengal Vaiṣṇavism, a model of erudition and graceful prose entitled *The Early History of the Vaiṣṇava Faith and Movement in Bengal,* upon which I have drawn unashamedly and gratefully, but was instrumental in my beginning the present work by urging me to examine the seventeenth- and eighteenth-century phases of the Vaiṣṇava movement. In Calcutta in 1955–57, in Chicago in 1961 when he was lecturing at the University of Chicago, and again in Calcutta in 1963–64, he gave me freely and graciously of his time and vast knowledge.

I owe a similar debt to Professor Sukumar Sen of Calcutta University. Not only has Dr. Sen written with rare authority on a wide variety of subjects in the language and literary history of Bengal, including in his works by far the best history of Bengali literature, the multivolume *Bāṅgālār sāhityer itihāsa,* but it was largely his encouragement and direction which saw me to the completion of this volume. Many of the matters treated in this book were discussed in well-remembered hours in his home and office in Calcutta, and whatever insight the book may contain is in large part due to him. He gave me not only encouragement and direction, but many needed books from his personal library; for this also I am grateful to him.

There are many other scholars and friends on both sides

of the world to whom I owe more than my words can say. Among them I include Dr. Charlotte Vaudeville of the University of Paris, who read through about one hundred pages of a draft of this book while she was at the University of Chicago in the spring of 1963 and helped me greatly with her comments and criticisms: I hope that some of the material presented here will provide a Bengali counterpoint to her own work on the Nātha cults in northern and western India; the late Dr. Shashibhusan Dasgupta, then head of the Department of Bengali at Calcutta University, to whose books my indebtedness is noticed in the text, but whose help through conversation and in having microfilmed certain manuscripts in the library of Calcutta University's Department of Bengali, I wish gratefully to acknowledge here; Professor Amiya Chakravarty of Boston University, for being one of the readers of my original dissertation and for the encouragement of his feeling that it contained material which was worth publishing; to many colleagues and friends at the University of Chicago, for providing and stimulating thought on such matters as that treated in this book, and among them especially Professor J. A. B. van Buitenen, who read my dissertation and who commented helpfully on parts of the present revision presented as an informal paper to a group of colleagues loosely constituting a friendly seminar, and Professors A. K. Ramanujan and Norman Zide, for their help through those same discussions.

In the dedication of this book, I have tried to describe a teacher and a scholar. Another of the men I had in mind is Professor Daniel H. H. Ingalls of Harvard University. From the beginning of this study, and in fact from the beginning of my serious study of India, he has been to me more than one has a right to expect of a guru and a friend.

No preface is complete, and correctly so, without the acknowledgement of the help given in the chores connected with the preparation of the book. Volumes have been written, and will continue to be written, without the help of people to relieve the writer of a thousand distracting things and of such responsibilities as that of supplying decent copy to the printer. But few will deny that such help saves considerable strain on the time, nerves, and attitude of the writer. In my case, my thanks are to my wife Loraine, for assuming wholly the very considerable burden of five small children in India during the rewriting of this book; to Miss Lena Samuel of Rangoon and Calcutta for her aid with the typing chores and the office work of the regional office of the American Institute of Indian Studies in Calcutta in 1963–64; to Miss Judith Aronson, Administrative Assistant of the South Asia Language and Area Center of the University of Chicago, for her assistance in innumerable ways; and to Mrs. Bonnie R. Crown of the Asia Society, for constant encouragement.

The research for the book was begun under a grant from the Rockefeller Foundation in 1955–57 and continued in 1963–64 with the support of the American Institute of Indian Studies and the Committee on Southern Asian Studies of the University of Chicago; to these organizations I am of course grateful.

The day, coincidentally, is Holi, the festival of Kṛṣṇa and the Gopīs. As I write, groups of *kīrtan* singers, covered from head to foot with red and yellow and purple color, are passing under my window, joyously celebrating the love of Rādhā and Kṛṣṇa; perhaps they are celebrating love itself. To explore this very matter is, in a way less dramatic and more dry, the purpose of this book.

Calcutta.

A Note on Transliteration

THROUGHOUT THIS VOLUME, I have tried to be consistent with the system of transliteration of the Sanskritic languages accepted by most scholars. Bengali, however, is peculiar in certain respects. Neither in Bengali script nor in pronunciation is there a distinction made between the Sanskrit bilabial or labiodental spirant "v" and the bilabial stop "b." Where "v" occurs intervocalically in Sanskrit, "b" occurs in Bengali, both in speech and writing. Where "v" occurs as the second member of a Sanskrit consonant cluster, "b" occurs in Bengali writing, and in Bengali speech the effect is to double the first member of the cluster. Thus, what is usually transcribed Navadvip (the name of the city) would be pronounced [nɔbɔddip]. There is no present need to go into detail about such peculiarities, of which there are several. I mention this one in order to point out two things. First, at some risk of error and as much for æsthetic value as anything else (Nabadbip not only looks awkward but is an inaccurate representation of Bengali pronunciation, whereas Nabaddip is an inaccurate representation of Bengali orthography), I have tried to preserve "v" where that symbol and the sound it represents occur in Sanskrit. Secondly, I have broken this rule when a place or personal name is well known in English: Rabindranath Tagore is not Ravīndranāth Ṭhākur to his English readers; the English spelling of his name was his choice, and we should not Sanskritize him against his will.

Abbreviations

Publication data are included in the Bibliography.

BRK—*Bhaktiratnākara* of Narahari Cakravarti.

BSI—*Bāṅgālār sāhityer itihāsa*, by Sukumār Sen; references are to the first edition, unless otherwise specified.

Bhāgavata—*Bhāgavata purāṇa*; references are to the Murshidabad edition, unless otherwise specified.

CBh—*Caitanya-bhāgavata* of Vṛndāvana-dāsa; references are to the Gauḍīya maṭh edition, unless otherwise specified.

CC—*Caitanya-caritāmṛta* of Kṛṣṇa-dāsa Kavirāja; references are to the Rādhāgovinda Nāth edition, unless otherwise specified.

CHI—*Cultural Heritage of India.*

CM—*The Chaitanya Movement*, by Melville Kennedy.

DBhS—*Durlabhasāra* of Locana-dāsa.

HBV—*Haribhakti-vilāsa* of Gopāla Bhaṭṭa.

IHQ—*Indian Historical Quarterly.*

IL—*Indian Linguistics*, publication of the Linguistic Society of India.

ITB—*Introduction to Tantric Buddhism*, by S. B. Dasgupta.

JAOS—*Journal of the American Oriental Society.*

LWW—*Love in the Western World*, by Denis de Rougemont.

NV—*Narottama-vilāsa* of Narahari-dāsa.
ORC—*Obscure Religious Cults as a Background to Bengali Literature,* by S. B. Dasgupta; references are to the first edition, unless otherwise specified.
PCSC—*Post-Caitanya Sahajiya Cult,* by M. M. Basu (Bose).
RKB—*Śrīrādhār kramabikāśa—darśane o sāhitye,* by S. B. Dasgupta.
Skk—*Śrīkṛṣṇakīrtana* of Baḍu Caṇḍīdāsa.
SPP—*Sāhitya pariṣad patrikā,* journal of the Baṅgiya sāhitya pariṣad.
SS—*Sahajiyā sāhitya,* edited by M. M. Basu (Bose).
VFM—*The History of the Vaisnava Faith and Movement in Bengal,* by S. K. De; references are to the first edition, unless otherwise specified.
VSP—*Vaṅga sāhitya paricaya,* edited by D. C. Sen.
VV—*Vivarta vilāsa* of Ākiñcana-dāsa.

The Place of the Hidden Moon

1) The Vaiṣṇava-sahajiyā Synthesis

1. POETRY AND DOCTRINE

LOVE SACRED AND PROFANE. Students of India sometimes wonder that the culture of that land can entertain two such seemingly opposed views of love in religion as that expressed on the one hand by the admirably athletic and frankly sensual figures on the temple friezes at Konarok and Khajuraho, and on the other by the amorous but somewhat less obvious religious lyrics of the Vaiṣṇavas; or, on the one hand, by the lusty Śiva of the village poetry, who, like Zeus, "knew exactly what he wanted and set about efficiently to get it, without wasting time in introspection,"[1] and on the other by the austere Śiva of the Purāṇic texts, who is not

[1] Maurice Valency, *In Praise of Love, an Introduction to the Love Poetry of the Renaissance*, p. 16.

only indifferent to the lady's charms, but goes so far as to burn up the god of love when the latter tries to tempt him from his meditation. We westerners have of course the same dichotomy in our own views of love. We have on the one hand what Maurice Valency calls "the healthy zest of the primitive and uncomplicated lust" of Zeus (and that of Zeus's successors, Don Juan and the concupiscent hero of some modern detective fiction), and on the other hand the courteous and romantic love of the knight and troubadour (and their successor, the hero of the modern western). But we are not used to encountering the dichotomy in our religious thought.

We have, or think we have, a pretty clear idea of what sacred love is, and what profane love is: sacred love is spiritual or sacramental, and profane love is carnal and non-sacramental. And we consider these to be mutually exclusive categories. The idea of a divine being seeking forthrightly to satisfy his lust, whether it be Zeus taking the form of a bull or Śiva taking the form of a Muslim sentry in order to facilitate his rape of Pārvatī, is faintly disturbing. Since this particular combination of sacred and profane presents a paradox we cannot accept, it is all passed off as the product of a primitive mentality. And yet, with almost perfect equanimity, we read the most carnal imagery of Bernard:

> A completely refined soul . . . has but a single and perfect desire, to be introduced by the King into his chamber, to be united with him, to enjoy him.[2]

We can accept this because we think we know that St. Bernard does not really mean it, that he is using a mere image

[2] *Sermones de diversis* 8:9; quoted in Valency, *op. cit.*, p. 22.

of the relationship of the soul to the Christ, and especially because in the image it is the soul that seeks gratification, not the Christ. Still, it cannot be denied that this image and hundreds of others like it in the poetry of the Christian mystics partake of both the spiritual "sacred" and the carnal "profane."

I am inclined to agree in principle with Balthazar, who says in *Justine*, the first novel in Lawrence Durrell's *Alexandria Quartet:*

> Historians always present syncretism as something which grew out of warring intellectual principles; that hardly states the problem. . . . It is the national peculiarity of Alexandrians to seek a reconciliation between the two deepest psychological traits of which they are conscious.

Although it is possible to sympathize with Balthazar's pride in Alexandria, I suggest that the search for the reconciliation of which he speaks is not an Alexandrian but a human peculiarity, and that consciousness is not a prerequisite of the search. One attempted reconciliation with which we shall be dealing throughout this book is, to put it exceedingly baldly, that between the spirit and the flesh, as it was formulated by the Vaiṣṇava-sahajiyās. The attempt takes place, essentially, in two areas: in poetry and in doctrine.

POETIC EXPRESSION. In the notes to his book of translations of the poems of St. John of the Cross, John Frederick Nims, after quoting García Lorca to the effect that "metaphor links two antagonistic worlds by an equestrian leap of the imagination," goes on to say:

> Absorbed chiefly in the love between man and the supreme object of his desires, [the poet] may have wondered: what image

for this ultimate delight? The poet's equestrian leap took him to the image of human love, as in the *Song of Songs*.[3]

The leap did not have to be too equestrian. The essential problem of poetic expression is the communication through image and symbol of those intuitions and perceptions that often lie beyond consciousness and that cannot be expressed by what is often called "denotative language."[4] As Elder Olson says, symbols "cause us to entertain ideas remote from, or totally outside of, ordinary experience, by the extension of ideas we already possess."[5] The image of human love is, in Olson's terms, a "natural symbol"; for what more apt image could there be in all human experience to express transcendent joy and the silent, unknown place of St. John? Or what more apt image could there be to express the longing of the soul for God than that of the longing of the human lover for the beloved? Or what more apt image to express religious rapture than that of sexual pleasure? The story is that Rāmakṛṣṇa was asked to describe his religious experience. The ultimate state, he said, was an incommunicable state, beyond pleasure and pain. But the penultimate state was one in which it seemed that all the pores of the skin were like female sexual organs and intercourse were taking place over the whole body.

I suppose it might be said that human love has two essential phases or characteristics, union and separation, and that the one is always latent in the other. And one of the beauties of almost any well-used sexual image is that it can call both

[3] John Frederick Nims, *The Poems of St. John of the Cross*, p. 121.
[4] See, for example, Paul Tillich, *Systematic Theology*, I, 123.
[5] Elder Olson, *The Poetry of Dylan Thomas*, p. 10.

separation and union to mind. In Bernard's image, the soul "desires" to be united with the Christ, and this statement emphasizes that the two are separate. It is this aspect of the image which is most usual to Christian, and I might add to orthodox Vaiṣṇava, poets, although the pain of separation always suggests the joy of union. For love in separation is pure love, spiritual love. How this view came to prevail in Christian poetry is of considerable interest and relevance.

It is De Rougemont's opinion that "the condemnation of the flesh, which is now viewed by some as characteristically Christian, is in fact of Manichaean and heretical origin."[6] To the Manichaeans there are two creations. God is love, and the world is evil. Thus God could not have created this dark planet; this was rather the work of the Rebel Angel, of the Demiurge, of Satan. The creations of God are souls, which are good and full of love. To seduce them, Satan showed to them "a woman of dazzling beauty, who inflamed them with desire." And thus inflamed, the souls followed Satan and the woman out of heaven and were trapped in the material bodies they now wear. But still the fundamental spirits are in heaven, close to God, awaiting the Redemption, waiting for Christ to restore the world of love. The anguish of man is thus the anguish of fallen angels, separated from their true selves, confined. A Manichaean hymn says:

> I came out of light and the gods,
> Here in exile am I, from them kept apart . . .
> I am a god. Of the gods I was born
> But now I am made to know pain.[7]

[6] Denis de Rougemont, *Love in the Western World*, p. 75.

[7] The hymn called "Soul's Fate"; quoted by De Rougemont, *ibid.*, p. 56.

The soul by its nature longs for reunion with its true self, with God, as the particle of light seeks reunion with the light. But Dibat, passion, seeks to keep it trapped within dark matter. And thus arises the perpetual struggle between the body and the spirit, between passion or carnal love and true love or longing for God. And what is true love between the soul and God, love in separation, is also true love between man and woman.

It has been suggested, as Maurice Valency points out, that love is an invention of the eleventh century.[8] Although this is debatable, at least on grounds of the persistence of the species until that time, it is nevertheless true that it was about then that the Manichaean heresy appeared in France as the Church of Love, the Cathars; and with it appeared the troubadours, who have left us the whole paraphernalia of romantic love, which is "true" love, love in separation. The troubadour sang with moving ambiguity for his far-off lady: a real woman, or God, or both?

When the days are long, in May,
It pleases me—the song of birds, far-off.
And when I can no longer hear the song of birds,
I remember a love . . .
And then I go, adverse and sad, with lowered head,
and not the song of birds,
nor scent of aubepine,
pleases me as does the frozen winter.

I hold him truly as truly Lord
by whose good grace I shall see my far-off love.
But for one good deed which I recall

[8] *Op. cit.*, p. 1.

I recall two wrongful things which I have done.
And she is far from me.
Ah! Could I become a pilgrim on the earth,
that my staff and slavery
would be contemplated by her lovely eyes.

Both sad and joyous would I separate myself from her
if ever I could see my far-off love.
But when? Our countries are so far. It's true:
there are roads and passages from here to where she is,
but I have not the strength . . .
What is to be is that which pleases God.

Never shall I rejoice in love, if I rejoice not
in her love. For woman more gracious and more gentle
I have never known. So pure is she, and tender,
that I could wish to be a captive there,
in the country of the Saracens.

He speaks the truth, who calls me avid and desirous
of that which is apart. There is no joy
to please me more than this possession.
But to my vow it is an obstacle. For he who held me
at the font bequeathed me this:
that I should love, that I should not be loved.[9]

Later poets also, like Petrarch in his poems to Laura, deliberately chose an inaccessible object for their devotions, thus paralleling their Christian belief. Or, closer to our times, Coventry Patmore writes, in his "A Farewell,"

It needs no art,
With faint, averted feet

[9] A song of Jaufré Rudel, in Alfred Jeanroy, *Anthologie des troubadours*, p. 22.

And many a tear,
In our opposed paths to persevere.
Go thou to East, I West.
. . . .
But, O my Best,
When the one darling of our widowhead,
The nursling Grief,
Is dead,
And no dews blur our eyes
To see the peach-bloom come in evening skies,
Perchance we may,
Where now this night is day,
And even through faith of still averted feet,
Making full circle of our banishment,
Amazed meet;
The bitter journey to the bourne so sweet
Seasoning the termless feast of our content
With tears of recognition never dry.[10]

If true love is love in separation, its logical extension is love apart from marriage; besides, in marriage there is always a touch of the carnal. The song of the troubadour, says De Rougement, "quickens with noble emotions love outside marriage; for marriage implies no more than physical union, but 'Amor'—the supreme Eros—is the transport of the soul upwards to ultimate union with light" (p. 68).

Although, as far as I know, it is questionable whether or not such things as Courts of Love actually existed in medieval Europe, it is a charming fancy that, history aside, has a good deal of relevance to our present discussion. Row-

[10] Coventry Patmore, "A Farewell," quoted in Herbert Read, *Collected Essays in Literary Criticism*, 2d ed., pp. 321 ff.

botham describes the Courts of Love in this way, quoting Jean de Nostradamus:

In [disputes between troubadours and ladies on subtle questions of love,] if they could not come to an agreement, they referred the matter for decision to the illustrious lady presidents who held open and plenary courts at the Castle of Signe and other places, and these gave judgements which were called the judgements of Love.[11]

One of the most famous of all decisions is said to have been taken by the court of the Countess of Champagne in 1174 and is as follows:

We declare and affirm, agreeably to the general opinion of those present, that love cannot exercise its powers on married people. The following reason is proof of the fact: lovers grant everything, mutually and gratuitously, without being constrained by any motive of necessity. Married people, on the contrary, are compelled as a duty to submit to one another's wishes, and not to refuse anything to one another. For this reason it is evident that love cannot exercise its powers on married people.[12]

Whether or not this conclusion is as evident as the Countess and her ladies seemed to feel is not at the moment the point; nor would it be relevant to do more than note that there has been a good deal of speculation as to whether or not the troubadours and others carried all this to its logical conclusion. It is relevant to note that at this point Christian

[11] John Frederick Rowbotham, *The Troubadours and Courts of Love*, p. 225; the quotation is from De Nostradamus, *Vies des plus celebres*, p. 15.

[12] Rowbotham, *op. cit.*. p. 249, quoting from André, *Livre de l'art d'aimer*, fol. 56.

poetry and Christian doctrine come into direct conflict; for of course to the Church, union in marriage is a sacrament. The conflict might be summarized thus:

	Christian Poetry	*Christian Doctrine*
Sacred	love in separation	sacramental union
Profane	sacramental union	love in separation

The reader might reasonably be asking at this point, what has all this to do with the Vaiṣṇavas and Vaiṣṇava-sahajiyās in India? In the light of the decision said to have been taken by the Court of Love in Champagne, it is of interest to note that it is reported in texts almost contemporary with the great sixteenth-century Vaiṣṇava revivalist Caitanya that he loved a story which went like this:

> There were two young people, very much in love, who each day lay together in the flower-grove behind the palace. The girl's father was the king, and one day he discovered their tryst, and forced their marriage. Their bed of flowers turned to thorns, and their love faded away.[13]

This proves, the texts go on to say, that true love cannot exist in marriage; true love, sacred love, is love in separation. And the orthodox Vaiṣṇavas, like the Christians, expressed this by a poetry of separation, though again with erotic overtones suggestive of the joy of union:

[13] The story is told in a great many texts, including the *Kārṇānanda* of Yadunandana-dāsa and the *Vivarta-vilāsa* of Ākiñcana-dāsa. M. M. Basu (*Post-Caitanya Sahajiyā Cult,* p. 50) notes that "the source of the story seems to be a Sanskrit verse quoted in the *Caitanya-caritāmṛta* (II:1), [from] *Kāvya-prakāśa* (I:4), *Sāhitya-darpaṇa* (I:10) and from the *Padyāvalī* (386)." The *CC* text says that Caitanya recited the verse with emotion while he was dancing. The Sanskrit verse in question expresses the same sentiment, but has in its detail only the most tenuous of connections with the story above.

O my friend, my sorrow is unending.
It is the rainy season, and my house is empty.
The sky is filled with seething clouds,
the earth with rain,
and my love is far away.
Cruel Kāma pierces me with his sharp arrows:
the lightning flashes, the peacocks dance,
the frogs and waterbirds, drunk with delight,
call constantly, and my heart is bursting.
A darkness fills the earth;
the sky lights restlessly.
Vidyāpati says:
"How will you pass this night, without your lord?"[14]

The reasons for the idealization of love in separation in Vaiṣṇava thought are in some ways reasonably similar to those in Christianity. The *Bhāgavata-purāṇa*, the basic text of Bengal Vaiṣṇavism both orthodox and Sahajiyā, was written in the ninth or tenth century and is in many ways an enigma. It is not specifically theological and systematic and so has in it the seeds of heresy. It is a text of poetry and says to the Bengal Vaiṣṇavas two basic things. The first is that separation of lovers is the best illustration of the proper attitude of the worshiper toward God, because it draws the mind away from the satisfaction of the self ("Married people . . . are compelled as a duty to submit to one another's wishes"), because it increases the desire for the be-

[14] *Vaiṣṇava-padāvalī*, ed. Khāgendranāth Mitra, Sukumār Sen, Viśvapati Caudhurī, and Śyāmapada Cakravartī, p. 91. The poem appears in other places (see, *Vaiṣṇava-padāvalī*, ed. Sukumār Sen) with the signature "Śekhara." It is a very erotic poem, although the erotic overtones are for the most part carried by symbols that are cultural; for example, the rainy season is traditionally the lover's time, and separation at this time is doubly poignant.

loved one (a troubadour writes, "the farther off I am the more I long for her"), and because intense and selfless desire for God is to the Vaiṣṇavas a saving grace. Kṛṣṇa, separated from the Gopīs, the cowherdesses of Vṛndāvana who love him, sends his messenger Uddhava to them with these instructions:

> I, chief among the objects of their desire, am far away from them; they are stricken with the grief of this separation; they are overcome with grief, thinking of me. . . . Had their souls been left to themselves alone, it would not have been long before they would have been destroyed in grief.[15]

Again, according to a later text, which embellishes a story from the *Bhāgavata:*

> Kṛṣṇa, attracted by the Gopīs, brought them into a forest. When they had all arrived there, Kṛṣṇa asked them why they had come with him. They all replied that they were filled with love for him; and they began the [rāsa] dance. But during the dance Kṛṣṇa disappeared from them, for into the minds of all the Gopīs had come the thought "he is mine," and in the thought "he is mine," parakīyā [i.e., true love in separation] cannot remain. . . . But when longing again rose in the Gopīs' minds, Kṛṣṇa again appeared to them.[16]

The second thing the *Bhāgavata* text states is the awkward but incontrovertible fact that the Gopīs were married to other persons at the time they fell in love with Kṛṣṇa. A great deal of thought has been given to explaining this, and we shall examine in detail some of the intriguing intelluctual

[15] *Bhāgavata* 10:46–47. See Thomas Hopkins, "Vaiṣṇava Bhakti Movement in the Bhāgavata Purāṇa" (doctoral dissertation, Yale University, 1960), p. 114. I am also grateful to Dr. Hopkins for much information he has given me in personal communications.

[16] *Vivarta-vilāsa* of Ākiñcana-dāsa, p. 171. The rāsa dance was one in which Kṛṣṇa, by his magic power, appeared in the center of a ring of Gopīs and at the same time between each two of them.

gymnastics that came of it. But for the moment it is enough to note that although the extramarital activity of the Gopīs caused a certain consternation among the orthodox theologians, it was completely accepted by poets orthodox and Sahajiyā both as illustrative of true love. The Gopīs were risking home, family, reputation, everything, for their love of Kṛṣṇa. As we have seen the Countess of Champagne conclude independently, this is true love, which does not exist in marriage.

It is to be carefully noted at this point that to the orthodox Vaiṣṇavas, as to most Christian poets, the image of love in separation and of its extension, extramarital love, was no more than an image of the relationship of the soul to God: true love and longing are what the "saved" soul feels. Union is present only as an undertone. The orthodox Vaiṣṇava view of how these things are reflected in human life and worship is just like that of Christianity.

	Vaiṣṇava Poetry	*Vaiṣṇava Doctrine*
Sacred	love in separation	sacramental (i.e., marital) union
Profane	sacramental (i.e., marital) union	love in separation

And here is the first significant difference between orthodox and Sahajiyā Vaiṣṇavas, for the latter feel that love in separation is true in both poetry and in fact.

	Sahajiyā Poetry	*Sahajiyā Doctrine*
Sacred	love in separation	love in separation (or non-marital union)
Profane	marital union	marital union

DOCTRINE. An expression of the yearning of the soul for God implies a dualism between man and God either imaginary (as with the Sahajiyā Vaiṣṇavas) or actual and permanent (as with the orthodox Christians and the orthodox Vaiṣṇavas). To the orthodox Vaiṣṇava view it is natural for the soul to be attracted to Kṛṣṇa as the divine, because man by his very nature seeks that which is most beautiful and satisfying. But although there is communion between the soul and Kṛṣṇa, there is no union of essence, and there can be none. To the orthodox Vaiṣṇavas, as to the troubadours, it is the very longing, the intense desire itself, that is the end; the longing is an act of worship, pleasurable in itself, and giving pleasure to Kṛṣṇa. There is no question of actual union. As the worthy Bengali poet Rāmprasād Sen, though not himself a Vaiṣṇava, wrote, "I like the taste of sugar, but I have no desire to become sugar."

But the sexual image is double-edged. It may also be read as suggesting that the ultimate experience of the divine is not in longing for union, but in union itself, that this ultimate experience is the pleasure, raised to the *n*th degree, of human sexual union. If we knew nothing else of the doctrine of St. Bernard, we might well assume that he is telling us something of the sort. And if we knew nothing else of the doctrine of the Vaiṣṇavas, we might assume that the large number of their poems which deal with the pleasure of Rādhā and Kṛṣṇa in union are telling us something of the sort. But, if one happens to hold a doctrine which says that there is no qualitative difference between the human and the divine, spiritual union of the two is possible, and fleshly union between the two is also not only poetically but actually possible. The search and longing for this union are now the *means* to the ultimate experience, an actual union of flesh and spirit, of human and divine. The distinctions between spiritual and carnal love and between poetic and doctrinal expression are wiped away. Accordingly, the Sahajiyās adopted the poetic paraphernalia of the orthodox Vaiṣṇavas and read the basic image the other way.

To the Sahajiyās, the end of man is the perpetual experience of divine joy. Man is divine, and so has within himself the potential for this experience. But man is also deluded, and his true divine nature and thus his potential are hidden from him by his ignorance. His first task is to realize his divinity.

According to some texts, man and woman have in them both the divine Kṛṣṇa and Rādhā: a woman is female because she has in her a preponderance of Rādhā; a man is man because he is mostly Kṛṣṇa. Love between man and woman thus reduplicates in microcosm the love of Rādhā and Kṛṣṇa, a love that had both phases, separation and union. Thus, when one realizes himself as divine, one experiences in union not the insignificant joys of human love, but the perpetual divine joys of the love of Rādhā and Kṛṣṇa. The cosmic embrace is embodied in the human. But the pleasure of the actual embrace is only the penultimate experience. For as man is microcosm, he contains both male and female elements of the divine couple. Thus ultimately one can pass even beyond the pleasure of actual union—this pleasure being incomplete because the feelings of one partner cannot be completely experienced by the other—and know the divine joy entirely within one's self. The ultimate experience is to know, interiorly, silently, and perpetually, the doubled joy of two in one.

True love is prema, the love that Rādhā and the Gopīs had for Kṛṣṇa, the love that the true worshiper emulates, which, when he has realized himself as Kṛṣṇa and his partner as Rādhā, he could not help emulating. In his attitude and in his worship there can be no trace of kāma, of carnal desire, of desire for the satisfaction of the self; kāma, unless it is transformed into true love, prema, leads not to joy, but to misery and hell. Yet, kāma must be present in the beginning; the woman who knows herself as Rādhā is beautiful, as Rādhā was beautiful, and attracts the worshiper with her beauty:

> She who holds the sahaja is fresh and young, and able to wound with the arrows of her sharp glances. She possesses all the marks of beauty, and the clothes and jewels on her body are brightly colored. Her lips are full of nectar, and her body such that a golden creeper cannot compare with it. . . . This type of *nāyikā* is a *sahaja-nāyikā:* serve such a one, and know her excellence and greatness.[17]

And, like Rādhā and the other Gopīs, she is parakīyā, she is married to another.

The terms parakīyā and svakīyā are not original with either the orthodox or the Sahajiyā Vaiṣṇavas. As the poetic classifications of the emotions of love were adapted by Vaiṣṇavas of all types to their theological system, so were the classifications of women: svakīyā and parakīyā are types of

[17] *Nigūrḍhārtha-prakāśāvalī,* p. 16; text given in Manindramohan Bose, *Post-Caitanya Sahajiyā Cult of Bengal,* p. 60.

women who can appear in drama. The great Vaiṣṇava theologian Rūpa Gosvāmin defines the terms in this way:

> A parakīyā woman is she who, having no dependence on ordinary dharma, belonging to another, is attracted to a man and causes him to be attracted to her, but who does not enter into marriage with him.
>
> A svakīyā woman is she who has been taken in marriage according to the accepted rites, who is obedient to the wishes of her husband, and who does not depart from the dharma of her wifely vows.[18]

Separation of lovers and the longing involved in it are called *viraha* in both Sahajiyā and orthodox traditions, and to both, *viraha* is the way of salvation. For the more intense is *viraha*, the greater is prema. And *viraha* is more intense in a relationship with a parakīyā woman than a svakīyā one. For in a parakīyā relationship, nothing at all is certain; any separation might be the final one. Futhermore, there are degrees of validity of the parakīyā relationship. Parakīyā women can be of two kinds: *paroḍhā*, married women, and *kanyakā*, those who are unmarried. Of these, *kanyakā* women are the lower variety; *paroḍhā* women have more to lose in giving themselves to a man other than their husbands and thus better illustrate the principle of prema.

Rādhā and the Gopīs were *paroḍhā parakīyā* women. To orthodox Vaiṣṇavas, their prema for Kṛṣṇa illustrates the proper love the worshiper should have for God. To the Sahajiyās, the *paroḍhā parakīyā* woman is Rādhā, and it is with

[18] Rūpa Gosvāmin, *Ujjvala-nīlamaṇi, Kṛṣṇavallabhā* 6, Murshidabad edition, 1935, pp. 70, 65 respectively.

her that one can find salvation. This is not poetic, but metaphysical truth.

POETRY AND DOCTRINE, A SECOND APPROACH. The tenth book of the *Bhāgavata-purāṇa* is full of stories about the Gopīs' love for Kṛṣṇa, stories which, from the time of Jayadeva (twelfth century) on, take the form of Rādhā's love for him. Even while he was still a young boy Kṛṣṇa was loved by the Gopīs, both girls and women:

> Sitting in the courtyard of his house, the blue
> jewel Kṛṣṇa plays,
> and the boys of Vraja come to join him.
> The young girls also gather there
> and entreat his mother, saying
> "We have never seen a dance like that your Kānu does;
> make him dance again, that we may fill our eyes."
> His mother said, "Hear me, girls of Vraja:
> now he will dance, according to your wish.
> Take milk and butter and give it to Gopāl,
> and he will dance before you all."
> So she left her housework and had Gopāl dance.
> At her feet Yadunātha sings.[19]

As Kṛṣṇa played with his brother Balarāma, says *Bhāgavata* 10: 8:21, the women of Vṛndāvana "forgot their household duties, and watched them and laughed and were delighted." And as he grew in strength and adept at demon-destroying, as his attractiveness and erotic playfulness increased, the relations of the women to him grew proportionately more complex. Once, for example, when the Gopīs were bathing in the river, Kṛṣṇa came and stole their clothes. He climbed

[19] Text in Harekṛṣṇa Mukhopādhyāya (ed.), *Vaiṣṇava padāvalī*, p. 202.

a tree and made the girls come and stand before him naked before he would return the clothes. The text tells us that this humiliation was in atonement for the sin of bathing naked:

The maidens of Vraja considered that their bathing with their bodies naked was a flaw in the observation of their vows. Being therefore desirous of atoning for their fault, they bowed down to him who is the merit of all auspicious deeds. . . . Beholding them standing in that bent-down posture, as required by him, the almighty son of Devakī was taken with pity and propitiated, and returned their clothes to them.[20]

He had other tricks that were varied and equally imaginative, such as demanding a fee from the Gopīs before he would let them pass on their way to market. Despite, or more likely because of, all this, the Gopīs' love for him increased so much that, charmed beyond caring by the sound of his flute, they left their homes and husbands and families and went to Kṛṣṇa in the forest. And when he went away to Mathurā, they grieved for him deeply.

Such stories of the *Bhāgavata* are ingenuous and charming and, from the lengths to which the exegeticists went to extricate Kṛṣṇa from the implications of them, most troublesome. One of the solutions found—one which has also relieved Christian exegeticists of some of their worries about the Song of Songs—is suggested in the *Bhāgavata* itself, as can be judged from the passage above, that the Gopīs' actions and attitudes are symbolic of the proper actions and attitudes of the worshiper toward God. Such an interpretation was also used to protect the Vaiṣṇava poems of Jayadeva and later poets from the charge of sensuality.

[20] Sanyal (trans.), *Bhāgavata* IV, 97.

For although in Bengali as in other languages songs were written about all phases of Kṛṣṇa's life, most Bengali Vaiṣṇava lyrics are concerned with the love-relationship of Kṛṣṇa and the Gopīs and, among the Gopīs, especially Rādhā. Though Rādhā was a symbol, the poets found in her a real woman also, and their poetry about her love is warm and personal. On the basis of the simple stories of the *Bhāgavata,* the poets built the story of a complicated affair, with all the jealousies and pain, the pique and joy, the angers and satisfactions of human love.

The Vaiṣṇava lyrics can be personal and sensual in the extreme. One reason for this is the warm humanness of Rādhā. Another is connected with the fact that the poets themselves partake in a most immediate way of the emotions and situations with which they are dealing. This is the meaning of the term *bhāva,* which involves a concept vital to the understanding of Vaiṣṇava, and therefore Vaiṣṇava-sahajiyā, poetry and thought.

In the definition of the relationship of man to God, the Vaiṣṇava thinkers drew much from the theories of Sanskrit poetics, and in particular from the so-called rasa theory originated by the rhetorician Bhārata. This debt is recognized by the Sahajiyās, and they consider Bhārata one of the original teachers of their doctrine, an *ādi-guru.*[21] Bhārata's theory was based upon the drama.

A drama, and by extension poetry, arouses in the listener a mental state such as love, grief, anger, or fear. Such states reflect the fundamental mood of the work of art, conveyed by the dramatist or poet by his plot, his characters, his poetic

[21] *Ānanda-bhairava,* p. 147.

language, and in general by all the features of his art taken together. No single element must be allowed to mar or disturb this basic mood. All must be harmony.

The emotional state into which the audience is thus put is called *sthāyi-bhāva,* "permanent" *bhāva.* There are elements in the work of art which enhance this state, and these elements are known as *vibhāva, anubhāva,* and *vyābhicāri-bhāva.* S. K. De in his *Sanskrit Poetics* describes the functions of these in the following way:

> Devoid of technicalities, a *vibhāva* may be taken as that which makes the permanent mood (*sthāyi-bhava*) capable of being sensed: an *anubhāva* is that which makes it actually sensed; while a *vyābhicāri-bhāva* is that which acts as an auxiliary or gives a fresh impetus to it. In the case of love as a permanent mood, the stock examples given of *vibhāva* are women and the seasons, of *anubhāva* glance and embrace, of *vyābhicārin,* the transient subordinate feelings of joy and anxiety.[22]

Thus the reader, unfamiliar with the conventions, finds in Vaiṣṇava poetry what seems like an overabundance of *cakora* birds and peacocks and dark clouds. But he does well to remember that the roles of these are formal; the peacock, with his neck the color of Kṛṣṇa and his uncontrollable urge to dance in the rainy season, which is the time for lovers, both defines and enhances for the reader or listener the poem's mood.

In any case, the proper mixture of these various elements elevates the basic mood, the *sthāyi-bhāva,* to a condition of pure appreciation which is called rasa. When one looks upon

[22] II, 22. *See also* Daniel H. H. Ingalls (ed.), *An Anthology of Sanskrit Court Poetry,* pp. 14 ff.

or listens to a supreme work of art, one's senses become so completely absorbed in that work that they utterly exclude all else. To the Vaiṣṇavas of Bengal, religious devotion, bhakti, is such a state of rasa: the senses and the mind of the worshiper are absorbed in Kṛṣṇa, that personification of rasa, in the most intense experience possible for man.

In the stories of the *Bhāgavata* there are many different types of people who relate and react to Kṛṣṇa in ways appropriate to their sex, birth, and taste. There are Kṛṣṇa's foster parents, Yaśodā and Nanda, who have for him parental affection. There is his brother Balarāma, who considers Kṛṣṇa with both fraternal love and with the loyalty and affection of a comrade. And, most important, there are the Gopīs, to whom Kṛṣṇa is a desirable object of love. The bhakta devoted to Kṛṣṇa takes on himself one or another of these attitudes according to his inclination and capacity, and becomes, by a mental-training process that we will note later, one or another of the people in the *Bhāgavata* stories in his relation to the Lord.

This appropriate condition of relationship to Kṛṣṇa is the *sthāyi-bhāva* of the religious state, which is raised by the subsidiary *bhāvas* to the state of rasa, which is pure bhakti toward Kṛṣṇa. The *sthāyi-bhāvas* that the worshiper can experience are five in number, as are the resultant rasas which correspond to them.

1. *Śānta:* a state in which the worshiper considers Kṛṣṇa the supreme God and himself as lowly and insignificant. This is the "peaceful" condition. As it is not really an emotional relationship, some writers do not consider it a *bhāva* at all. The stimuli to this state are such activities as listening

to the reading of the *Upaniṣads*, dwelling apart from men, and discussing philosophy.

2. *Dāsya:* a state in which the worshiper considers Kṛṣṇa the master and himself a servant. Stimuli are such things as the sound of the conch shell and the sight of a blue cloud or lotus.

3. *Sākhya:* a state in which the worshiper considers Kṛṣṇa his friend, as did the cowherds of Vṛndāvana. Stimuli are such sensations as the sound of a flute and the sight of a handsome youth.

4. *Vātsālya:* a state in which the worshiper considers Kṛṣṇa a child and himself the parent, as did Kṛṣṇa's foster parents in Vṛndāvana. Stimuli are such happenings as the thought of Kṛṣṇa as a child, the sight of a beautiful boy, and so on.

5. *Mādhurya* or *śṛṅgāra:* a state in which the worshiper considers Kṛṣṇa a lover, as did Rādhā and the Gopīs. Stimuli are such things as the thought of Kṛṣṇa's youthful beauty and grace. This *bhāva* and the rasa to which it leads are the most important in the poetry and the thought of the Vaiṣṇavas and the Vaiṣṇava-sahajiyās of Bengal.

Such a rigid analysis, and one which derives so clearly from the seemingly unrelated field of poetics, might at first glance seem artificial. But the transformation of the worshiper from an ordinary earthbound creature to a lover of the Lord is a very real and immediate thing. It is an extreme case of the phenomenon on which Milton Singer comments in speaking of the Vaiṣṇavas in Madras:[23] that a ritual ges-

[23] "Radha-Krishna *Bhajans* of Madras City," *History of Religions* (Winter, 1963), p. 216.

ture, if repeated often enough, may bring about an actual change in attitude. That the Vaiṣṇavas felt this transformation to be real is indicated by the signature lines of their lyric poems; the writer participates in the poem itself. To quote two random examples, from innumerable possible ones:

> I shall not see Śyāma again beneath the *kadamba* tree.
>
> . . . .
>
> Jñāna-dāsa says, My heart has broken.[24]

> And at the last, my life alone remains;
> that too is nearly gone,
> says Jagadānanda-dāsa.[25]

In both of these, the writer speaks as Rādhā, and more than that, he has realized himself as Rādhā.

The *mādhurya* is the most important *sthāyi-bhāva* in both literature and religion. The category is further subdivided according to its various possibilities: (1) *vipralambha*, the lovers in separation or disagreement, and (2) *sambhoga*, the lovers' enjoyment in union.

Vipralambha is further broken down:

a. Purvarāga: when by sight, by listening to descriptions of one another, desire is aroused in the minds of the lovers.

b. Māna: when the lover has attracted the girl and then willfully causes another to be attracted to him, the pang that his beloved feels.

c. Premavaicittya: the pain that is aroused in the heart of one who truly loves even when close to the beloved, at the realization that even in union is potential separation.

[24] Mukhopādhyāya (ed.), *Vaiṣṇava padāvalī*, p. 446.
[25] *Ibid.*, p. 877.

d. Pravāsa: the pain of separation caused by the beloved's departure into another country.

These are of course descriptive of the various conditions of Rādhā. They are conditions of the bhakta in his love for the Lord.

There is another type of analysis, also borrowed from the poetics, that cuts across the one outlined above. It represents another view of the permanent or momentary states of a woman in love—or of a bhakta. One category we have already noticed, parakīyā. The parakīyā woman finds herself in any number of emotional and physical states, such as (*a*) *abhisārikā,* going to meet her lover by assignation; (*b*) *vāsarasajjā,* dressed and ornamented in expectation of her lover; (*c*) *utkaṇṭhitā,* disappointed when her lover does not appear at the place of assignation; (*d*) *vipralabdhā,* deceived by her lover; (*e*) *khaṇḍitā,* outraged at the signs of unfaithfulness on her lover: (*f*) *kalahāntaritā,* separated from her lover by a quarrel: (*g*) *proṣitabhartṛkā,* longing for her lover, who has gone away: and (*h*) *svādhīnabhartṛkā,* having her lover under complete control.

All of these types will appear in our story, sometimes as poetic symbols, sometimes as worshipers in their many-sided love for Kṛṣṇa, and most often in situations in which it is difficult to discern a difference between the two.

2. SOME HISTORICAL CONSIDERATIONS

THE REASONS for the intense and unprecedented revival of the Vaiṣṇava faith in Bengal under the leadership and inspiration of Caitanya (A.D. 1486–1533) are at best uncertain.

That Caitanya was a religious leader of no ordinary power is quite clear. The revival he inspired encompassed the greater part of the populations of those areas now known as Bengal (both East Pakistan and West Bengal), Orissa, Assam, and Bihar. But the greatest and most inspiring of leaders is perhaps doomed to failure in a climate hostile or indifferent to his ideas and qualities. The time in which Caitanya lived was ripe.

The ripeness of the time has been attributed by various scholars to various things, some of them perhaps significant only in retrospect: the decay and subsequent "corruption" of Buddhism, the prevalence of extreme Tāntric schools with their potential licentiousness, the aridness and dogmatic rigidity of Brahmanism in both social and religious spheres, and the impact of Islam, especially Sufi Islam with its emotionalism.[26] Whether or not it was a combination of some or all of these, or some thread of spiritual or social unrest not yet isolated from the fabric of the time, which made for this revival, is not clear. It is perhaps significant that not only in Bengal but all across northern India in the fourteenth and fifteenth centuries there burst forth a "romantic" enthusiasm, the character of which is in some ways best described by juxtaposing it to the classical tradition.

This enthusiastic movement had three discrete characteristics: its expression was through the vernacular languages, not through Sanskrit; it rejected the role of the Brahman as ritual intermediary between man and God, in some ways and

[26] For a discussion of the social environment in Bengal in which the movement developed, see Phulrenu Datta, *La societé Bengalie au XVIe siècle.*

times going further and rejecting caste entirely; and it propagated enthusiastic religion, with singing and dancing as a part of the search for immediate and ecstatic communion with the divine.

Sanskrit in the high classical period of Indian history was not only the religious language, it was the language of culture, the language of men of high learning and sophistication. As time went on, however, the ritual specialists, mostly Brahmans, more and more assumed the language as their own, as Latin became the property of the medieval churchmen. In the period of which we are speaking there was a reaction to this.

There is an ancient saying in Bengal: "Whoever listens to the eighteen *purāṇas*, or to the Rāmāyana recited in the *bhāṣā* [i.e., the vernacular] will surely be cast into hell."[27] In contrast to this, in the fifteenth century the Hindi poet Kabīr was writing:

> Pandits talk in Sanskrit alone, and call those who use the *bhāṣā* ignorant fools . . . but bhakti [devotion] through the *bhāṣā* gives strength, and leads one to salvation. Sanskrit is as the water of a well, but the *bhāṣā* like a running brook.[28]

And against the Brahman curators of Sanskrit who prided themselves on caste, the poets of this time spoke out:

> A Brahman wears a sacred thread that he himself has made. If you are a Brahman, born of a Brahman mother, why haven't

[27] Proverb quoted by D. C. Sen, *History of Bengali Language and Literature*, 2d ed., 1954, p. 7.

[28] *One Hundred Poems of Kabir*, trans. Rabindranath Tagore and Evelyn Underhill. These translations, however, are not made from the Hindi text, but from a Bengali version of it, and are sometimes inaccurate; see F. E. Keay, *Kabir and His Followers*, p. 61.

you entered the world in some special way? And if you are a Turk, born of a Turk, why weren't you circumcised in the womb of your mother? If you milk a black cow and a white one, can you distinguish between the milks that they give?[29]

The Bāuls, modern inheritors of this tradition, sing of the falsity of all notions of caste and sect, and indeed of all that stands between man and God:

Some say that praying to Hari instead of Kālī is an error. Some say that praying to Kālī instead of Hari is an error. I have thought constantly on these things, and have gone mad . . . I used to make a show, bathing three times a day in the Ganges, reciting many mantras; I used to do my yogic exercises all the time, and all I got was out of breath; I used to fast day after day, and all I got was a pain in my belly.[30]

All these cloaks of falsehood can be dispelled by bhakti, by pure devotion. Not by meditation, or fasting, or good works, or knowledge, but by devotion alone can God's true form be known:

The unqualified Brahman is revealed by the way of knowledge, his indwelling form by the yoga-path. . . . But without bhakti no method will yield results, and bhakti alone yields all results.[31]

This does not imply that the way of bhakti or the attitudes toward society which it involved appeared for the first time in India in the fourteenth and fifteenth centuries. The classical statement of the way of bhakti is in the ancient *Bhagavadgītā.* And to be strict about it, even the emotionalism and enthusiasm that attended the bhakti of the Middle

[29] Keay, *op. cit.*, p. 76.
[30] From a song of the Bāul Āli Khān Munsi of Noakhali district, published in the journal *Prabāsi,* XV (1917).
[31] *Caitanya-caritāmṛta,* Madhya-līlā 25:60 ff.

Ages, such as that generated by Caitanya and his followers, was familiar to the *Bhāgavata-purāṇa* or at least, as Thomas Hopkins points out, to its commentator Śrīdharasvāmin.[32] Nor was the bhakti movement's skeptical attitude toward caste entirely unique. The great and ancient Tāntric tradition, as we shall see, was never strong on caste; and Buddhist texts like the *Dhammapada* are never loath to criticize pride based on birth and social position. And the *Bhāgavata* itself, while accepting Brahmans who are devotees as indeed the best of men, scorns those who do not fulfill their Brahmanhood by accepting bhakti.[33]

In several senses, then, the bhakti movement was not new. It is proverbial that nothing in Indian tradition is ever lost; attitudes and thoughts are sometimes lightly buried, to be revealed again by a stirring of the air in the right time and place. And the freshness of what has long been buried is often somewhat surprising.

SOME FACETS OF THE BHAKTI MOVEMENT IN BENGAL. Each part of India is in some sense a microcosm of the whole subcontinent; each part is also in some sense a unique and individual culture. In certain ways, the bhakti movement in Bengal has qualities of form and spirit that distinguish it from those movements in other parts of India. Its peculiarities of spirit were due mostly to the greatness of Caitanya; those of form to the primacy of Kṛṣṇa and the interpretations of the legends of Rādhā and the Gopīs.

[32] Thomas Hopkins, in a personal communication to the author. See Hopkins, "The Social Teachings of the Bhāgavata Purāṇa," in *Krishna: Myths, Rites, and Attitudes*, ed. Milton Singer.

[33] Hopkins, *Vaiṣṇava Bhakti Movement*, pp. 22–24, 133.

Viśvambhara—he took the name Kṛṣṇa-Caitanya after his initiation into an ascetic order—was born in the month of Phālgun (February–March), on the auspicious night of an eclipse of the moon in 1486. The place was Navadvip, a city at that time famous throughout India as a center of learning generally and in particular of the Navya-nyāya school of philosophy. Viśvambhara's family was a pious and respected one, of Vaiṣṇava faith, and there is every indication that they were lavish in their affection toward the boy—the more lavish, perhaps, because their elder son, Viśvarūpa, had broken his mother's heart by leaving home to become an ascetic. Very little can be learned of Caitanya's early childhood from the writings of the time; stories about him are so interwoven with those of Kṛṣṇa's childhood that it is impossible to separate fact from fancy. It does seem that his education was primarily in grammar, which would not have been unusual for a Brahman boy of the time. It is claimed by his biographers that he was a brilliant scholar. Whether or not this is pious exaggeration will probably never be known, for he has left us no writings except for eight short devotional verses in Sanskrit.

In any case, Viśvambhara married young, but his wife died, probably of snakebite,[34] while he was on a trip to his father's village in East Bengal. Soon after his return to Navadvip, he married a second time. He seemed destined for the somewhat uneventful life of a master of a small Sanskrit school. Then, when he was twenty-two, he made a trip to Gayā, to perform in that holy place his father's

[34] The *CC Ādi* 16:21 says obliquely that "the serpent of the pain of separation bit Lakṣmī, and she went to the other place."

funeral rites. What happened in Gayā is a mystery. All that is known is that while there he accepted as guru (teacher) Iśvara Pūrī, an "emotional ascetic" (De). He returned to Navadvip God-maddened and within a short time became the center of frenzied devotional activity in that city. For a year he lived amid wild religious enthusiasm, with nightly singing of devotional songs and ecstatic dancing. Then, as abruptly as it had begun, this phase of his life ended. He entered an ascetic order, taking his initiation at the hands of Keśava Bhāratī and with it the religious name Kṛṣṇa-Caitanya.[35]

His mother, having lost her second son, was inconsolable. Her tears made Caitanya give up his intention of going to live at Vṛndāvana, the place where his beloved Kṛṣṇa had dwelt, and to go instead to Puri in Orissa, a place not so far from Navadvip. He stayed for the rest of his life in Puri, except for an occasional pilgrimage. Here his friends and disciples from Bengal visited him annually at the time of the Car Festival of Jagannāth. He died in 1533. The manner of his death is not known. Some say that he was absorbed into the great image of Jagannāth, others that he walked into the sea. The least orthodox biography, and probably the most factual one, says that he injured his foot during his frenzied dancing and died from an infection.[36]

This is about all that is definitely known of him. Yet, one

[35] There is some question as to the order into which he went. S. K. De in *Vaiṣṇava Faith and Movement*, p. 12, says that "indications are strong that [Caitanya] formally belonged to the Dasanāmi order of Śaṁkara saṁnyāsins, even though the ultimate form which he gave to Vaiṣṇava bhakti has nothing to do with Śaṁkara's extreme Advaitavāda [i.e., monism]."

[36] The *Caitanya-maṅgala* of Jayānanda, B.S.P. edition, p. 152.

of his biographies, the *Caitanya-caritāmṛta,* fills thirty thousand lines. *Caritāmṛta* means "immortal acts." In a sense, what Caitanya was and did is less important than what people thought he was and did; his acts themselves are less important than their quality of immortality.

For even while Caitanya lived, people considered him divine. Some thought he was an *avatāra,* an incarnation, of Kṣṛṇa; some thought he was Kṛṣṇa himself. "Kṛṣṇa, source of *avatāras,* has come to earth in the form of Caitanya."[37] And, most important for us, some saw him as Rādhā and Kṛṣṇa, the divine lovers, in the most intimate possible union —in one body. "Rādhā and Kṛṣṇa were one soul in two bodies . . . then even the two bodies became one, in Caitanya."[38] He was Kṛṣṇa internally, Rādhā externally: his golden color was that of Rādhā; his deep love and longing for Kṛṣṇa were those of Rādhā; and yet, within, he had the full divinity of Kṛṣṇa. When Rādhā and Kṛṣṇa were two, neither could experience love to the full. Kṛṣṇa, giving and receiving love, could not experience fully Rādhā's joy in giving and receiving, and so also with Rādhā. When they became one, in Caitanya, their joy was doubled. The reader will have begun to suspect the significance of this interpretation for the Sahajiyās.

How Rādhā comes to play a major role in the Vaiṣṇavism of Bengal is a major problem. Her name is never mentioned in the basic text, the *Bhāgavata-purāṇa.* However, in the tenth book of the *Bhāgavata* there is mentioned a special Gopī, one who held a special attraction for Kṛṣṇa and whom

[37] *Caitanya-caritāmṛta,* Ādi 2:91.
[38] *Ibid.,* 4:49–50.

"he took to a lonely place." The name Rādhā (although its masculine counterpart, Rādha, occurs in Avestan, according to Sukumar Sen) is very possibly derived from the term used in connection with this special Gopī—*ārādhitā:* "worshipped" or "desired."[39] Although the story of the love of Rādhā and Kṛṣṇa is told in such texts as the *Nārada-pañcarātra* and the *Brāhmavaivarta-purāṇa,* these texts are at best of uncertain date and are not accepted as canonical by the Bengal Vaiṣṇavas themselves.

Until recently, most scholars considered that the first full and datable evidence of the legend of the love of Rādhā and Kṛṣṇa in Bengal was in the *Gīta-govinda,* that series of sensuous Sanskrit lyrics by Jayadeva, court poet to Lakṣmaṇa Sena, who ruled in the late twelfth century.[40] But there are indications that at least the names of Rādhā and Kṛṣṇa were linked in Bengal before A.D. 1130, well before the time of Jayadeva. In the Sanskrit anthology *Subhāṣitaratnakoṣa,* the Bengali poet Ḍimboka writes: "The city folk are waked at

[39] *Bhāgavata-purāṇa* 10:30:28 (10:30:24 of the Murshidabad edition); see Sukumār Sen, *Balarāmadāser padāvalī, bhumikā,* p. 11; *History of Bengali Literature,* p. 17; and *Indian Linguistics,* VIII, No. 1, p. 38. The commentary of Viśvanātha on the *Bhāgavata* passage suggests Rādhā. See also Bhaṭṭācārya, *The Philosophy of the Śrīmad-Bhāgavata,* I, 117. Some traditionalists contend that the name Rādhā occurs in such texts as *Ṛg-Veda* 8:45:24, *Atharva-veda* 19:7:3, and in other places in the Vedas and Brāhmanas, but the meaning of the term in such passages is questioned by more modern critical scholarship. For an account of such traditions and the controversy surrounding them, see Harekṛṣṇa Mukhopādhyāya, *Kavijayadeva o śrīgītagovinda,* pp. 106 ff.

[40] It is interesting to note in this connection that the Vaiṣṇava-sahajiyās were anxious to claim Jayadeva as a follower of their own doctrine. Whatever the facts of Jayadeva's own religious tendencies, it is clear that by his time the concept of Rādhā had been fully developed, at least literarily; this is further borne out by Jayadeva's later contemporary Śrīdharadāsa, whose work *Saduktikarṇāmṛta* S. B. Dasgupta (*Śrīrādhār-kramabikāśa,* p. 1) places in the early thirteenth century.

dawn by pilgrims in the street. With patchwork cloaks sewn of a hundred rags they ward off the winter cold. Their voices are pure and clear as they sing of the holy love of Kṛṣṇa and Rādhā."[41] Sukumār Sen finds a prototype of Jayadeva's songs in the work of the Kashmiri poet Kṣemendra, who lived in the eleventh century.[42] And, to carry speculation even further, there is at least a good possibility that one of the sculptures found on an early Pāla period building at Paharpur represents the joint figure of Rādhā and Kṛṣṇa.[43]

Speculation about Rādhā's ancestry is one of the favorite amusements of scholars who concern themselves with the religious history of Bengal. And indeed, at present, speculation is all that is possible. Perhaps the best we can do is postulate a Q-source for the legend: the story of Rādhā and Kṛṣṇa might well have been current in folk literature and belief since the time of the *Bhāgavata* itself. If popular religious belief had dictated the development of a consort for

[41] See Daniel H. H. Ingalls, "A Sanskrit Poetry of Village and Field: Yogeśvara and his fellow poets," *Journal of the American Oriental Society*, No. 3 (1954). The anthology is one that favors Bengali poets. Ingalls writes: "All these [poets] were Bengalis in the sense I have indicated . . . most of the dialect words used seem to indicate Bengal proper" (p. 120). There are also some of Ḍimboka's verses in the *Saduktikarṇāmṛta*, another anthology compiled in Bengal.

[42] *History of Bengali Literature*, p. 17.

[43] See K. N. Dikshit, *Excavations at Paharpur, Bengal*, (Memoirs of the Archaeological Survey of India, No. 55). The figure in question, on a lower frieze of the building and now buried because of the topographic conditions, dates, according to David McCutchion of Jadavpur University, who has done extensive work on Bengal stone and terra-cotta temples, perhaps as early as the late seventh century. It shows a male and a female form, arms interlinked, the male with one leg bent in a pose typical of Kṛṣṇa found on other Bengal temples. The panel is in the midst of other panels of the frieze showing scenes of Kṛṣṇa's life. The hair style of the male figure is reminiscent of that of the late Gupta period, as for example on the temple of Deogarh.

Kṛṣṇa, the special Gopī of the *Bhāgavata* story would have been a natural choice.

Wherever she came from, Rādhā is crucial to the development of the Vaiṣṇavism of Bengal. To the poets, she is a warm, touchingly trusting woman in love. To all Vaiṣṇavas, she is the symbol of true love, of prema. To the Sahajiyā Vaiṣṇavas in particular, her presence on earth, in women and all human beings, gives men a way to the experience of the divine. And, historically, it was primarily in Rādhā that the streams of the Sahajiyā and of Vaiṣṇavism met and blended.

Some fundamental characteristics. The term sahaja literally means "easy" or "natural," and in this meaning the term is applied to a system of worship and belief in which the natural qualities of the senses should be used, not denied or suppressed. The historical development of such a belief is shrouded in mystery, for the cult, as we shall see, is one which requires mystery and silence. Maurice Winternitz feels that its origin can be traced to a woman named Lakṣmīmkarā, who belonged to the royal family of Orissa and who lived in the eighth century.[44] In Bengal too the belief may be traced perhaps to the eighth or ninth centuries: the Buddhist texts called *caryā-padas* may be that early, and these texts are clearly Sahajiyā in doctrine. In any case, it can be said with certainty that Sahajiyā sects were flourishing long before Caitanya's Vaiṣṇava revival in Bengal.

The roots of these Sahajiyā sects lie well within the ancient tradition of the Tantras. Both Tāntrics and Sahajiyās

[44] Maurice Winternitz, *History of Indian Literature*, II, 393.

believe that man is a microcosm, a miniature universe; both believe in unity as the guiding principle of this universe, that all duality, even that of the sexes, is falsehood and delusion and that cosmic unity is regained, or represented, by man and woman in sexual union. Both believe in certain types of mental and physical control as the means by which man can know his true nature and relate the human and the divine within himself; both believe that there should be no caste division among worshipers; both are humanistic, and begin with the analysis of the nature of man, and see as the end of man the gaining of the "natural state," the sahaja, the state of ultimate and blissful unity.

This is the tradition that met and blended with that of the Vaiṣṇavas. Nor, despite the fact that the Sahajiyā is humanistic and the Vaiṣṇava theistic, that the Sahajiyās are monistic and the Vaiṣṇavas dualistic, is this particularly strange. As we have already noticed in the discussion of poetry and doctrine, there were many features of Vaiṣṇavism, such as the use of sexual symbolism in poetry, that were most congenial to the Sahajiyā point of view. Caitanya, who was considered even by the orthodox to contain Rādhā and Kṛṣṇa within his own body, was a perfect illustration of the Sahajiyā principle of unity in seeming duality (there is of course some question as to whether or not this interpretation was one originally suggested by the Sahajiyā point of view). In general, the whole mechanism of the Rādhā-Kṛṣṇa legend and the theology constructed around it were taken up and put upon a Sahajiyā foundation. It must be remembered, however, that as the Sahajiyās gave doctrinal value to what the Vaiṣṇavas meant symbolically, so in the area of theology the Sahajiyās to a certain extent took symbolically what the Vaiṣṇavas meant doctrinally.[45] The reasoning went like this: Kṛṣṇa the supreme God of the Vaiṣṇavas is indwelling in man as the divine principle. The nature of Kṛṣṇa is love and the giving of joy; therefore the true nature of man is also love and the giving of joy; it is this in man's nature that is to be realized and experienced.

Exactly how and when the Vaiṣṇava-sahajiyā blending took place is a matter of considerable puzzlement to me and, it seems, to a number of scholars. Some, like Shashibhusan Dasgupta, would trace the Vaiṣṇava-sahajiyā directly to the Tantras and to the Buddhist Sahajiyā, ignoring to a large extent such doctrinal requisites as the notion of the necessity of prema for transformation, which is present in the Vaiṣṇava-sahajiyā because of its Vaiṣṇava inheritance and not in the mechanistic Tantras. Others, like Manindramohan Basu, attempt to find its roots in post-Caitanya Bengal, evidently choosing to ignore its obvious debt to the very old Tāntric tradition. The question is more than an academic one; to the contrary, it is sufficiently heated by a number of non-academic considerations. The Vaiṣṇava-sahajiyā is generally considered something less than wholly respectable, for reasons that will by now be clear. M. M. Basu states what is probably the average attitude toward the cult: "Some say that taking women as part of the *sādhanā* [i.e., method of attainment] is [the sect's] only distinct characteristic, and that the Sahajiyās are wicked people, and that there are

[45] See *ORC*, Introduction, p. xxxiv.

among them no educated or intelligent men, and that they follow this *sādhanā* out of desire for immoral women."[46] He himself was too good a scholar to subscribe to this, however, and he goes on to say that "there is in all these systems much that can attract wise and religious minds." Given this attitude, I think it will be clear that such suggestions as the one made above, that thought about the nature of Caitanya may have been influenced by the Sahajiyā view, would be most distasteful to orthodox Vaiṣṇava believers, who consider Caitanya and his followers as aspects of the godhead. It would be in the interest of such orthodoxy to show that the Sahajiyā point of view did not prevail until after Caitanya's time. It is of course true that there is no Vaiṣṇava-sahajiyā writing before the time of Caitanya. Most of the texts which are datable come from the eighteenth century. With the exception of the padas of Narahari, whose doctrinal affiliations are questionable, and those signed "Vṛndāvana-dāsa," whose signatures are questionable, the first definably Vaiṣṇava-sahajiyā works seem to be those of the pupils of Narahari, Raghunandana, and Mukunda of the Śrīkhaṇḍa school, Locana-dāsa, and others. Basu, in his *PCSC* dates some of the main Sahajiyā works as follows: *Āgama*, A.D. 1688, which is the date (B.S. 1075) given in Calcutta University MS 1144 of the work; *Ānanda-bhairava*, A.D. 1832; *Rasatattva-sāra* of Rasika-dāsa, the first quarter of the seventeenth century; and the *Vivarta-vilāsa* of Ākiñcana-dāsa, the middle of the seventeenth century. All such arguments are of course inconclusive, for they merely indicate the plain fact that the Sahaji-

[46] *Sahajiyā sāhitya, bhumikā*, p. 1.

yās did not adopt the Vaiṣṇava theology until after it had been developed by the Gosvāmins of Vṛndāvana under the inspiration of Caitanya. The possibility remains of pre-Caitanya Sahajiyā doctrine influencing both the thought of the Gosvāmins and Bengali thought about Caitanya himself.

On the other hand, if one happened to be a Sahajiyā one would be constrained to show, as Sahajiyā texts like the *Vivarta-vilāsa* try to show, not only that thinking about Caitanya was influenced by the Sahajiyā point of view, but that Caitanya was himself a Sahajiyā. Unfortunately, most Sahajiyas do not want their faith discussed, even in a scholarly fashion. Theirs is an esoteric cult, and its life is based on secrecy and exclusiveness, on the single line of transmission from guru to disciple.[47]

Those who have no particular religious ax to grind can hold to a theory of mutual influence: that some of the ideas and concepts, like that of the dual incarnation of Caitanya, were probably shaped by the already long-existing Sahajiyā and re-adopted by the later Vaiṣṇava-sahajiyās after their implications had been worked out by the orthodox theologians; and that, on the other hand, Vaiṣṇavism lent to the Sahajiyā the whole of its theological structure, which was

[47] My own limited experience, confirmed however by the considerably more extensive one of Dr. Suniti Kumar Chatterji, is that members of esoteric cults such as the Sahajiyās, and to a lesser extent the Bāuls, are reluctant to give even their songs to the uninitiated, even though the chances are great that the songs will not be entirely understood. M. M. Basu, however, in the introduction to his *PCSC* (p. vii), thanks various "Sahajiyā gurus," who "evinced keen interest" in his work and "helped him with their valuable suggestions."

reinterpreted by the Sahajiyās according to the peculiarities of their own view. In no sense did the two traditions merge into a single stream: their aims are essentially different, their means radically opposed. The distinctions are clear; and we shall spend the next few pages examining them.

2

Further Historical Observations

1. CAITANYA AND THE SAHAJIYĀ CULT

THAT THE SAHAJIYĀ CULT existed in Bengal long before Caitanya does not, I think, need proving. Shashibhusan Dasgupta, in his *Obscure Religious Cults*, has discussed the early history of the cult in some detail, and that discussion needs no elaboration here. Furthermore, there is little doubt that the Buddhist *caryā* songs, which although they were discovered by Haraprasād Śāstrī in a manuscript in Nepal are Bengali, date from the Pāla period (eighth to the twelfth centuries) and are Sahajiyā in doctrine.[1] There are many

[1] The manuscript was published by the Baṅgīya-sāhitya-pariṣad in 1918 under the title *Bauddha-gān o dohā*. Sukumār Sen has also edited and introduced the songs in his *Caryāgīti padāvalī*. S. K. Chatterji (*Origin and Development of the Bengali Language*, I, 120 ff.) writes that Kānhu-pāda, one of the *caryā* poets, can definitely be assigned to the twelfth century.

doctrinal peculiarities of the songs that make this clear. The term sahaja is first used in these songs to mean what it means in the later Sahajiyā texts: a state of equilibrium between the self and the world. The means of gaining this state is the same in the *caryās* and in the later Sahajiyā texts: recognition that the individual is the microcosm. All differences between the human and the divine, such as time and space, are falsehoods and misconceptions. "Time enters only the unsteady mind," says a *caryā* writer: the mind that is fixed and stable and easy knows that time vanishes when one realizes one's divinity.[2] And again, describing the infinitely calm state of sahaja: "They are three, they are three. But they are really one, and [in that one] Kānhu says, existence passes away. That which comes also goes—and by this going and coming the mind of Kānhu is perplexed."[3]

Nor should it be necessary to prove that the Sahajiyā stream flowed down to and through Caitanya's time. Kṛṣṇānanda Āgamavāgīśa, the author of the *Bṛhat-tantrasāra* and the "champion of obscure Tāntric rites" (De), was not only

---

S. B. Dasgupta (Obscure *Religious Cults*, pp. 5 f.) is not convinced by Chatterji's arguments on this particular point, but feels that he can place another of the poets, Lui-pā, as early as the tenth century. B. Bhattacarya (*An Introduction to Buddhist Esoterism*, p. 72) dates Lui-pā in A.D. 669, but I think most other scholars agree that this is considerably too early. For a discussion of the whole question, see *ORC*, pp. 1–37, and Haraprasād Śāstrī's introduction to the *Bauddha-gān o dohā*.

[2] *Caryā* no. 1, of Lui-pā. For a discussion of the doctrine of the *caryās*, see Sukumār Sen's or Haraprasād Śāstrī's introductions to their respective editions of the texts, or, in English, *ORC*, pp. 39–57.

[3] *Caryā* no. 7, of Kānhu-pā. The interpretation of the *caryās* is difficult; the language is intentionally obscure, as we shall see. Reasonable suggestions here are that the "three" are past, present, and future, or masculine and feminine, and the union of the two. The state of sahaja is one of utter harmony, in which there is no motion, no passion, and no differentiation.

Caitanya's contemporary but is said to be from Navadvip, where Caitanya was born and flourished. There is in fact a tradition that Kṛṣṇānanda and Caitanya were fellow-students at the grammar school of one Gaṅgā-dāsa.[4] The story goes that at a later time, when both men had become leaders of large groups of people, they met for the sake of debate. Caitanya was so infuriated by the arguments of Kṛṣṇānanda that he attacked him with a stick and drove him away (which might seem a little precipitous considering the Vaiṣṇava ideal that Caitanya himself expressed, that a Vaiṣṇava should be "patient and forbearing as a tree").[5] The works of the great and irreproachable pillars of Vaiṣṇava orthodoxy, the Gosvāmins of Vṛndāvana, are full of allusions to and quotations from the Tantras and Āgamas.[6] In short, there is ample evidence of contact between the Tāntric and Vaiṣṇava schools before and during the time of Caitanya.

Caitanya himself, for reasons already indicated, is the

[4] See *CC Ādi* 15:5. The tradition is fairly old, for it was mentioned, as Daniel H. H. Ingalls has pointed out to me, in Colebrooke's *Two Treatises on the Hindu Law of Inheritance*, p. xii, in 1810. The tradition Colebrooke records makes both men out to be students of Vāsudeva Sārvabhauma.

[5] For biographical information about Kṛṣṇānanda, see Satīścandra Mukhopādhyāya's introduction to the *Bṛhat-tantrasāra* (Basumati edition). The story of Caitanya and Kṛṣṇānanda is recorded by S. K. Ghose in his English biography of Caitanya called *Lord Gauranga*, II, 82. In *CC Ādi* 17:248 ff., Caitanya takes a stick to a student whose remarks were in poor taste, but there is no suggestion that the student was Kṛṣṇānanda.

[6] See especially Sanātana Gosvāmin's *Bṛhat-bhāgavatāmṛta* and Gopāla Bhaṭṭa's *Haribhakti-vilāsa*. Lists of references in these and other works of the Gosvāmins to Tāntric and Āgamic works can be found in De, *VFM*, pp. 193, 367, and 395 ff. The Āgamas are esoteric works that are specifically Hindu; Tantras can be either Hindu or Buddhist. It should be stressed at this point that not all Tantras deal with sexual ritual and such things; the term is used in a general sense to indicate a non-Vedic ritual system.

crucial figure to both orthodox Vaiṣṇava and Sahajiyā Vaiṣṇava schools; the question resolves itself into this: what was the attitude of Caitanya himself toward the Sahajiyā belief?

There is a curious passage in the *Vivarta-vilāsa*, a relatively late seventeenth-century text, which reads as follows: "Blessed be the girl Ṣaṭhī throughout the world, with whom Mahāprabhu [i.e., Caitanya] performed his secret *sādhana*. . . . Let there be eternal obeisance to the lotus-feet of the mother of Ṣaṭhī, whose mind and body were devoted to Caitanya."[7] The passage then goes on to tell us that not only Caitanya but the Gosvāmins and other leading Vaiṣṇavas were dedicated to the Sahajiyā *sādhana*, to list the names of the ritual partners of all of them, and then to direct us to look for proof of the above in the great biography of Caitanya, the *Caitanya-caritāmṛta*. In that text we find the following enigmatic remark: "At Sārvabhauma's house, while preparing Prabhu's [i.e., Caitanya's] meal, the mother of Ṣaṭhī said to him: Let Ṣaṭhī be a widow."[8] The suggestion of the *Vivarta-vilāsa* is that this puzzling verse means that her mother is cursing Ṣaṭhī for participating in the Sahajiya worship. Another possibility, coming out to approximately the same thing, is that the term which I have translated "widow" also means "whore," as it does in modern Hindi and Bengali. In any case, the verse is curious; the more so, because there seems to be no other mention of

[7] Pp. 107–8 of the Tārācānd Dās edition of the work. Sukumār Sen (*Bānāglā sāhityer itihās*, I, 646) says that Ākiñcana-dāsa, the author of the VV, was a pupil of Rāmacandra and lived about the middle of the seventeenth century in the Sahajiyā center of Śrīkhaṇḍa. We shall have later occasion to refer to this passage and what it represents.

[8] CC *Madhya* 1:128, quoted in VV, p. 106.

Ṣaṭhī in the whole CC. The commentary on the verse by Rādhāgovinda Nāth does not help at all: "Caitanya and his devotees were coming from Bengal, and stopped to eat at the house of Vāsudeva Sārvabhauma. . . . The wife of Sārvabhauma often prepared Caitanya's food. One day her son-in-law reproached Caitanya, and Ṣaṭhī's mother said the above, in shame—that she wished her son-in-law were dead."

We shall give these various strange suggestions more attention shortly. The point at the moment is that actually Caitanya's attitude seems to be overtly hostile to a basic Sahajiyā doctrine: a reverential attitude toward women, stemming from the belief in the presence of divinity in women and in attainment of the ultimate state by methods of ritual union. He saw women as at least distracting, at most deluding, and not at all as personifications of Rādhā. In short, it seems as if his attitudes as they are represented to us were all that could be wished of a Vaiṣṇava and an ascetic: "Prabhu said—I can never again look upon the face of an ascetic who has had anything to do with a woman. The senses are weak, and are attracted toward worldly things; even a wooden image of a woman can steal the mind of a sage. . . . Those false ascetics are contemptible. Conversation with women deludes the fickle senses."[9] Caitanya's attitude is clear in the following: "The abandonment of all wicked companions: this is the action of a true Vaiṣṇava. One who consorts with women is immoral, and is opposed to Kṛṣṇa-bhakti."[10]

This attitude, however, does not rule out the possibility

[9] CC *Antya* 2:116–18.
[10] CC *Madyha* 22:49.

that Caitanya was influenced by Sahajiyā belief or tradition, at least on some subconscious level. Sukumār Sen, in the introduction to his edition of the *caryā* songs, which we have seen to be Sahajiyā in doctrine, makes this interesting observation:

> The form of Vaiṣṇava songs is not very different from that of the *caryās*. The styles are similar. . . . In [the same fashion as that in which Vaiṣṇavas worship, sitting in a circle and singing], the Tāntric or Yogic worshipers performed *heruka-sādhana* [Tāntric worship] or *maṇḍala-upāsana* [circle worship], singing their *caryā* songs. Perhaps Caitanya was unconsciously following the older custom of these . . . worshipers.[11]

Caitanya's companions. In any case, there are at least two of Caitanya's early companions whose "orthodoxy" in regard to the Sahajiyā we can question with a good deal more vigor. The first of these is Nityānanda, who was closest to Caitanya both in the early days at Navadvip and later on in Puri. He was so close to Caitanya, in fact, that he was considered by some an *avatāra* of Kṛṣṇa's brother Balarāma, as Caitanya himself was considered an *avatāra* of Kṛṣṇa. The CC states emphatically: "Of one true form, the two were divided in body only. . . . Kṛṣṇa was born in Navadvip as Śrīcaitanya-candra, and with him Balarāma, as Nityānanda.[12]

[11] *Caryāgīti padāvalī*, p. 37. Sen therefore feels that the origin of the *kīrtana*, the Vaiṣṇava form of group worship with singing, lies in this early practice. This is a question that exercises many scholars considerably and one that is essentially still unsettled.

[12] *CC Ādi* 5:5. The notion that Nityānanda was the *avatāra* of Balarāma seems to follow on the disappearance of Caitanya's blood brother Viśvarūpa. It was thought that after Viśvarūpa left home to take *saṃnyāsa* and was never heard from again, Balarāma appeared for a second time, this time in the form of Nityānanda. *CBh Ādi* 6:81 states: "Viśvarūpa . . . was born in a different form, as Nityānanda."

The case that can be made about Nityānanda is of some substance and is strengthened by the fact that owing to his high place in the hierarchy the early writers tend to gloss over any misbehavior on Nityānanda's part.

That Nityānanda was an Avadhūta is unquestionable; he is called so in many places throughout the biographical literature.[13] The Avadhūtas (the "pure ones"), says Bagchi, were a branch growing from the trunk of Mahāyāna Buddhism, others being the Nātha, Sahajiyā, and Bāul sects.[14] Being an Avadhūta is anything but reprehensible, even to the most strict of orthodox Vaiṣṇavas. The *Mahānirvāṇa-tantra* describes the ideals of one class of Avadhūtas (the *haṁsa* Avadhūtas) in this way:

> Let them not seek the company of women, nor to acquire property; let them keep themselves apart from desire, and from prohibitive rules and injunctions; let them abandon the signs, symbols, and requirements of their castes and those of the householder; let them seek the fourth stage of the spirit [*turīya*—the state of the pure impersonal Brahman], having no desire for the things of the world.[15]

The impression of the extreme purity and asceticism of the Avadhūtas is heightened by the expansion of this passage by Rādhāgovinda Nāth in his commentary. He says that there are four types of Avadhūtas: Brāhmāvadhūta, Śaivāva-

[13] See, for example, *CC Ādi* 5:139, *Madhya* 12:186; *Bhaktiratnākara* 7:171 ff., *CBh Ādi* 2:134, etc.

[14] See P. C. Bagchi's chapter on the religions of Bengal in the Dacca University *History of Bengal,* I, chap. xiii, 423 ff.); Charlotte Vaudeville in a personal communication has pointed out that the Nāthas are often called Avadhūta.

[15] *Mahānirvāṇa-tantra* 8:283, quoted in the commentary on *CC Madhya* 3:84.

dhūta, Bhaktāvadhūta, and Haṁsāvadhūta. Nityānanda was a member of the fourth group, the best:

They do not perform *sādhana* with women, nor honor any prohibitive rules, nor hold symbols of their own castes; they are at peace with the world, indifferent to pain and sorrow, satisfied with their lot, without permanent home, perservering . . . and not holding to the caste-structure of society [*varṇāśraya-dharma*]. Many of the others are wanton, but [the *haṁsāvadhūtas*] spend their time studying philosophy.[16]

But important for the argument, as we shall see, is that the Avadhūtas, like some other ascetics, were prepared to dispense with the system of caste for themselves and perhaps for others.

That Nityānanda was still an Avadhūta at the time he was close to Caitanya may be questioned. He is in many places in the texts called "Svarūpa," which, according to Sen, was a name given to a man who had taken Tāntric orders and then renounced them to return to the householder (*gṛhastha*) stage of life.[17] As an indication of this, we are told that Nityānanda broke Caitanya's staff, the symbol of asceticism (at which Caitanya became extremely angry, threatening to leave Nityānanda and continue his journey alone).[18] And, if there remains a doubt that he had renounced his ascetic vows, it is recorded that Nityānanda married, at a fairly advanced stage of life, the two daughters

[16] Rādhāgovinda Nāth in his commentary *Gaurā-kṛpa-taraṅginī* on *CC Madhya* 12:185–86 and *CC Madhya* 3:82–84.

[17] Personal communication with Sukumār Sen. See *BRK* 8:170 ff. Svarūpa is also a Vaiṣṇava-sahajiyā technical term meaning the true divine essence of a person, as opposed to his rūpa or physical form. According to Charlotte Vaudeville, the name is also one applied to a Nātha *yogin*.

[18] The story is told in *CC Madhya* 5:141 ff.

of Sūrya-dāsa, a Brahman paṇḍit, thus making Caitanya again furiously angry.[19]

Whether or not he had renounced his orders is not really the crucial matter, for clearly his attitude toward women was not that usually described as "ascetic." And there is a curious story that may indicate that in any case his order had been of the "left-handed" Tāntric variety, the variety of Tāntric ritual which employs the famous "five M's" (*madya, māṁsa, matsya, mudrā,* and *maithuna*—wine, flesh, fish, parched grain, and sexual intercourse). The story also indicates the differences in attitude between Nityānanda and Caitanya. The incident took place in the village of Lalitpur, near the home of Sūrya-dāsa; the *saṃnyāsī* concerned is obviously a Tāntric of the "left-hand" school; he must have recognized Nityānanda as a member of the same school, for the offering of wine is hardly a part of ordinary hospitality in India. It is also interesting that the term used for wine is *ānanda* (supreme divine bliss).

The *saṃnyāsī* of the left-hand path drank wine. He said to Nityānanda with a wink, "Shall I bring *ānanda?*" . . . Nityānanda knew. . . . "Shall I bring *ānanda?*" the *saṃnyāsī* said again and again, and Nityānanda said, "That is not for us." When she saw the beauty of the two men, the wife of the

[19] *BRK* 12. Sūrya-dāsa was the brother of Gaurī-dāsa paṇḍit, a prominent Vaiṣṇava; the two girls were named Vasudhā and Jāhnavā and both have crucial roles to play in future developments. We shall return to them. That Caitanya was angry about all this seems clear; see the *Prema-vilāsa of* Nityānanda-dāsa, p. 45. It was possibly because of this marriage that Caitanya sent Nityānanda away from him; Nityānanda returned to Bengal and caused quite a stir by his activities there. This separation occurred about six years before Caitanya's death. The *CBh* is the only source to claim that Caitanya and Nityānanda met again, and since Vṛndāvana-dāsa is Nityānanda's partisan, perhaps his testimony in this case can be discounted.

saṃnyāsī fixed her eyes intently upon them. . . . Caitanya said, "What is this *ānanda* of which the *saṃnyāsī* speaks?" Nityānanda replied, "Wine." "Viṣṇu, Viṣṇu!" cried Caitanya, and rinsed his mouth and went quickly away.[20]

Whether because he had affiliation with left-hand Tāntric or Sahajiyā schools or for some other reason, Nityānanda was looked upon a little askance by his companions and contemporaries in Caitanya's movement. Despite his prominent place beside Caitanya, he is not mentioned in the theological works of the Gosvāmins of Vṛndāvana, except in an occasional formal salutation.[21] This, although we are told in the CC that one of the great orthodox theologians of the sect, Rūpa Gosvāmin, had known Nityānanda in Puri and had liked him.[22] But of most significance are the remarks of Vṛndāvana-dāsa, the author of the *Caitanya-bhāgavata*. Vṛndāvana-dāsa was a partisan of Nityānanda and mentions charges against him in order to present a defence. For example, we are told:

There was a Brahman in Navadvip, who had previously studied with Caitanya. He saw the actions of Nityānanda-svarūpa, and suspicion was born in his mind. [This Brahman] had profound bhakti for Caitanya, but did not recognize the power of Nityānanda. He went to Puri and said to Caitanya: "My mind and body are dedicated to you; I am your slave. Therefore explain to me why Nityānanda-avadhūta has gone to Navadvip.

20 The incident is recounted in *CBh Madhya* 19:44–100. The immediately relevant verses are 85 ff.

21 Sanātana Gosvamin mentions Nityānanda in the beginning of his *Vaiṣṇava-toṣanī*. See De, *VFM*, p. 80, n.3.

22 *CC Madhya* 1:173 ff. *Narottama-vilāsa*, p. 10. Nityānanda was not universally popular, even in Bengal. We are told by the *CBh* (*Madhya* 3: 169) that some people, when they hear the name of Nityānanda, "get up and run away."

I do not understand his actions. He has left the ascetic life. . . . He is concerned with material things, and this is not a proper way for a *saṃnyāsī*. He wears gold and silver and pearls on his body. He has put aside his russet-colored cloth, and wears the finest silk. . . . and he always stays with Śūdras.[23]

The last remark is most interesting, not because it is an unnecessary additional indication of Nityānanda's affiliation with the Avadhūtas, who have never had much use for the accepted caste structure of society, but because it may indicate a reason for the peculiarly ambiguous treatment that Nityānanda is accorded in the orthodox texts and because it is an indication that Nityānanda may have been responsible for whatever egalitarian tendencies the Vaiṣṇava movement shows.

It is usual of course to think that Sahajiyā and other "degraded" points of view are inseparable from low-caste and non-caste people. Thus it is perhaps natural that with his concern for the low-caste and casteless, Nityānanda is credited by tradition with the creation of the Vaiṣṇava-sahajiyā school. The act of creation, we are told by the Bengali literary historian Dinesh Chandra Sen, was the admission of a group of "fallen" Buddhists into the Vaiṣṇava fold:

In Khardah and Santipur, however, Nityānanda and Advaita initiated a great movement for organizing the Vaishnava community on a new basis. The place is still pointed out near Kardah, were 1200 *neḍas* or shaven men and 1300 *neḍis* or

[23] *CBh Antya* 6:8 ff. We shall see a good bit more of Nityānanda's desire to associate with lower social groups and shall examine in some detail the reasons for it.

shaven women—the Buddhist *bhikshus* and *bhikshunis*—came to . . . Nityānanda, and he took them into his new order.[24]

How much this tradition is worth in any historical sense is at least open to question. The earliest textual evidence I have been able to find for it is the early eighteenth-century Sahajiyā text *Ānanda-bhairava* of Prema-dāsa.[25] This is so late that the textual reference may well be to a legend. In any case, as I have tried to show and shall try to show further, there is reasonable evidence even apart from this story that Nityānanda was crucial in the joining of the Vaiṣṇava and Sahajiyā streams; this, however, because he was probably a Tāntric and certainly a powerful leader, not only because he opened the floodgates to the lower social orders.

There is one final way in which Nityānanda will emerge as crucial in this matter: one of his wives, Jāhnavā (or Jāhnavī), was a Tāntric and a Sahajiyā leader of considerable power in her own right.[26]

Another of Caitanya's followers who, it seems, must be considered a Sahajiyā is Rāmānanda Rāya. Rāmānanda was a scholarly, poetic, and devout man, who seems also to have

24 *History of Bengali Language and Literature*, p. 483. The story is repeated by Melville Kennedy, *The Caitanya Movement*, p. 70; Kennedy, however, attributes the action to Nityānanda's son Vīrabhadra. The latter is in keeping with the textual evidence.

25 Sen (*BSI*, I, 644 f.) gives 1720 as a date for Prema-dāsa. If this is the Prema-dāsa who wrote the *Ānanda-bhairava*, he lived a good hundred years after Nityānanda, who must have died sometime about the middle or toward the end of the sixteenth century: ample time for a legend to grow. The *Ānanda-bhairava* text can be found in M. M. Basu's *Sahajiyā sāhitya*, pp. 126–54. The relevant passage is on p. 148 and reads: "Vīrabhadra Gosvāmi . . . gave initiation to twelve hundred *neḍas* and thirteen hundred *neḍīs*."

26 This will be treated in detail in chap. 3. See Sukumār Sen, *Balarāma-dāser padāvalī, bhūmikā*, p. 17. Jāhnavā seems to have become a Sahajiyā through her adopted son Rāmacandra.

been a high official in the court of the Rājā Pratāparudra of Orissa. Caitanya first met him while on a pilgrimage to the south of India and was captivated by the depth of his devotion. Rāmānanda is called a Sahajiyā by Kavikarṇapura, an early Vaiṣṇava writer, and we shall see good reasons why.

In the first place, it seems that Rāmānanda practiced an interesting technique of chastity, one which is characteristic of the Sahajiyā school and important in the training of a Sahajiyā worshipper. If it seems paradoxical that chastity is essential in a religious system of which a crucial element is sexual intercourse, one should remember that it is necessary to transform desire into true love, or prema, before ritual union can be effective. And the Sahajiyās consider that chastity, especially under extreme temptation, has the power to transform desire into love. Self-enforced separation, when union is easy, purifies desire by intensifying it. The old homeopathic principle is one of like curing like. This view of desire purifying desire is again not unique to the Sahajiyās, but is in fact nicely expressed by the troubadour Arnaut Daniel: "By excess of desire, I think I shall remove her from me, if nothing is to be lost by dint of loving well."[27] The particular technique that Rāmānanda used, according to the CC, was to keep two girls "of surpassing beauty," who were skilled in dance and song, whom he would treat in a somewhat intimate fashion, bathing and dressing them, rubbing their bodies with oil, etc. But, the text says, he abstained from sexual intercourse with them:

Rāmānanda had two *devakanyās* [i.e., *devadāsīs*, temple girls], of surpassing beauty, youthful, skilled in music and the dance.

[27] See *Love in the Western World*, pp. 151, 117.

Rāya used to take them both into a lonely garden, where they would sing to him. . . . With his hands he would rub their bodies with oil and bathe their bodies and limbs and clothe and decorate them; but still the mind of Rāmānanda remained unaffected. His passion was the same at the touch of a piece of wood or a stone as it was at the touch of a young woman: such was the nature of Rāmānanda Rāya. He played the role of servant to them.[28]

The passage has two interesting aspects. The first, of course, is Rāmānanda's remarkable continence. The second is contained in the last line. As we shall see, part of the discipline of the Sahajiyā worshiper is to "serve" the woman as Rādhā, both literally and in the ways in which a worshiper serves a deity.

That Rāmānanda was a Sahajiyā seems reasonably clear. That he had a profound effect on the development of the Vaiṣṇava-sahajiyā sect is worth considering. It has already been suggested that the concept of the dual incarnation of Caitanya—that he was Rādhā and Kṛṣṇa in one body—is central to the doctrine of the Sahajiyā Vaiṣṇavas. S. K. De suggests an origin of this concept. He says that the dual incarnation perhaps had its origin with the writers of the lyric poems called padas, but that in these poems "the idea is only poetically suggested; its theological implications never appear to have been fully worked out until Kṛṣṇadāsa Kavirāja set it forth much later as the view of Rāmānanda Rāya in his Bengali *Caitanya-caritāmṛta*."[29] Although, as De has suggested earlier in his work (p. 70, n.1), Kṛṣṇadāsa may well be attributing to Rāmānanda Rāya a view that is his

[28] *CC Antya* 5:11 ff.
[29] *VFM*, p. 325.

own, it is interesting that he chooses to put it into the mouth of one who was a Sahajiyā. There is at least a possibility that this basic doctrine, which fits so neatly the Sahajiyā concept of the essential unity of things, is of Sahajiyā origin and may even have originated with Rāmānanda Rāya.

So Caitanya may well have had immediate contact with the Sahajiyā schools through the two men who were among his most intimate and beloved friends and followers. There were, of course, other occasions for exposure to the schools.

TEXTS AND "CAṆḌĪDĀSA." It is recorded in the texts at various places that among the books which Caitanya knew and loved were the lyrics of Jayadeva, whom we have already briefly met, and the two Bengali poets Caṇḍīdāsa and Vidyāpati: "Vidyāpati, Caṇḍīdāsa, and the *Śrīgītagovinda*—these three gave Prabhu great joy."[30] Furthermore, he knew the text called *Brahma-saṃhitā*, a manuscript of which he brought back with him from a pilgrimage to the south: "The *Brahma-saṃhitā* and the *Karṇāmṛta*—he obtained these two manuscripts, and brought them with him to the north."[31]

It is clear that the fifth book, at least, of the *Brahma-saṃhitā*, is a Vaiṣṇava-sahajiyā text. For example: "The lotus of a thousand petals is named Gokula, the dwelling-place of the Lord."[32] The "lotus of a thousand petals" is Tāntric and Sahajiyā terminology for the seat of bliss, which in microcosmic physiology is the brain. That it is

[30] CC *Madhya* 10:113.
[31] *Ibid.*, 1:111.
[32] *Brahmā-saṃhitā* 5:2.

also called Gokula (a dwelling-place of Kṛṣṇa) is held by later Bengali Vaiṣṇava-sahajiyās. Although the rest of the chapter is free of references that might be called specifically Vaiṣṇava, it is full of references which are Tāntric. For example, verses 3–10 treat the Tāntric *yantra* (magical diagram), and speak of Śiva as *liṅgam* (male generative organ) and Śakti, Śiva's female counterpart or consort, as *yoni* (female generative organ). This concept of the metaphysical character of sexual union is basic to the Sahajiyās, and to all sects oriented toward the "left-hand" Tantra.

Much more vexing, complicated, and interesting problems are those of Jayadeva on the one hand and Caṇḍīdāsa on the other. Most of the critical difficulties connected with Vidyāpati are the same as those in connection with Caṇḍīdāsa and need not be treated in separate detail.

The traditional view is that Jayadeva and Caṇḍīdāsa were practicers of a Sahajiyā type of *sādhana*. The late scholar Haraprasād Śāstrī, who did so much for studies of religion and literature in Bengal, held and stated this view: "From those works of Jayadeva which we have, we can understand that he was a Vaiṣṇava-sahajiyā. He worshipped a joint image of Rādhā and Kṛṣṇa. . . . There are other indications of Sahajiyā feeling in his poetry."[33] Unfortunately, Haraprasād Śāstrī does not lucidate this, nor does he elucidate his remark that "Vanamāli-dāsa, who wrote [Jaya-

[33] In the article "Caṇḍīdāsa," in *Haraprasād-racanāvalī*, I, 286. For a discussion of the textual evidence for these traditions, which seem to be relatively late, see Sukumār Sen, "Śrīkhaṇḍer sampradāy o caṇḍīdāsa," in *Bicitra sāhitya*, pp. 127 ff. We have seen from the evidence of the *Subhāṣita-ratnakoṣa* that at least the names of Rādhā and Kṛṣṇa were linked by the twelfth century.

deva's] biography, leaves no doubt that he was a pure Sahajiyā." Apart from the traditions (which may, however, have solid foundations), there seems to be no more actual evidence that Jayadeva was a practicing Sahajiyā than that the writer of the Song of Songs was a member of a mystery cult.

About Caṇḍīdāsa, however, a good bit more can be said. This time the traditional view is represented by Shashibhusan Dasgupta.

> Judging from the heaps of tradition centering around the figure of the poet Caṇḍīdāsa, and also from the number of Sahajiyā poems ascribed to him, it will not be far off the mark to hold that there might be some truth in the tradition of Caṇḍīdāsa himself being a Sahajiyā *sādhaka* and that his practical culture of the divinisation of human love had supplied him with the deep inspiration that made him the immortal poet of the Rādhā-Kṛṣṇa songs.[34]

The question is, which Caṇḍīdāsa are we talking about?

In the course of the past seventy years or so, a great many songs with the signature "Caṇḍīdāsa" have turned up.[35] This has made a number of scholars wonder why, in the earliest collection of Vaiṣṇava lyrics, the anthology called *Kṣanada-gīta-cintāmaṇi*, which was compiled by Viśvanātha Cakravartī in 1704, no lyrics with this signature occur at all. These same scholars also noted that in the various anthologies the number songs with the signature "Caṇḍīdāsa" seems to increase in proportion to the lateness of the com-

[34] *ORC*, p. 132.

[35] It was a practice in medieval India for a poet to insert his name into the closing lines of his poem. We have seen, for example, " 'Vidyāpati' says: How will you pass this night without your lord?".

pilation. For example, in the *Padāmṛta-samudra* (first quarter of the eighteenth century) and the *Padakalpataru* (about twenty years later), there are nine and 118 Caṇḍīdāsa poems respectively.[36] In the period immediately preceding the twentieth century, Ramaṇimohana Mallik published a book called *Caṇḍīdāsa,* the first edition of which contained 301 poems with the signature "Caṇḍīdāsa" and the second edition 340, all "collected from earlier compilations." This was quickly followed by a collection by Nīlaratna Mukhopādhyāya, also called *Caṇḍīdāsa,* which contained 500 previously unpublished songs, compiled from manuscripts "previously unknown." At the turn of the century came the Baṅgīya-sāhitya-pariṣad edition of *Caṇḍīdāsa,* which contained 847 songs, many previously unpublished. This edition remained the standard one for about fifteen years. Then Caṇḍīdāsa songs began to turn up everywhere. In 1916 a text called "Śrīkṛṣṇa-janmalīlā" was published in the *Sāhitya-pariṣad-patrikā,* in which there were 63 new songs. In 1918 the unique and now-famous manuscript called by its editor *Śrīkṛṣṇa-kīrtan* was published by the Baṅgīya-sāhitya-pariṣad; the text included 415 songs, all previously unknown. In 1928–29 Manindramohan Basu published in the *Sāhitya-pariṣad-patrikā* 110 new songs of Caṇḍīdāsa, which he had found in two manuscripts at Calcutta University (Nos. 2389 and 294). There were various other instances.

It struck many people as somewhat extraordinary that

[36] Sukumār Sen (*History of Brajabuli Literature,* pp. 4–6) writes that the *Padāmṛta-samudra* was compiled "sometime toward the end of the first quarter of the eighteenth century" by Rādhāmohana Ṭhākur, a great-great-grandson of Śrīnivāsa Ācārya. The *Padakalpataru* was compiled by Vaiṣṇavadāsa "about two decades after his guru Rādhā-mohana's compilation."

one man, however prolific, could have been responsible for all these songs; it was also noted that the signatures differed slightly. Some were signed "Baḍu-caṇḍīdāsa," some "Dvija-caṇḍīdāsa," "Ādi-caṇḍīdāsa," or "Kavi-caṇḍīdāsa;" some simply had "Caṇḍīdāsa says . . ." Speculation arose whether the different signatures indicated that the songs were written by different poets.[37] This led to an examination of the contents of the songs.

That "Caṇḍīdāsa" was a Sahajiyā poet was the generally accepted if generally unvoiced view. The reasons for this are more than clear: consider these bits of songs that occur with the signature "Caṇḍīdāsa":

> Worship the sahaja. Perform the sacrifice, and omit nothing. Abandon the repetition [of mantras—magical formulas] in your mind, and abandon asceticism. Gain union in your mind.[38]

> Caṇḍīdāsa says . . . only he who has gained the mercy of Śrīrūpa [perhaps Kṛṣṇa, perhaps the self] can grasp the sahaja.[39]

> Always worship by means of the *bāṇas;* this is the culture of the sahaja. Never go to the right; if you do, you will be lost in error.[40]

The last verse is especially interesting and significant. And for a full appreciation of it, one or two facts ought to be noted. First, the *bāṇas* are the five flower arrows of Kāma,

[37] For a detailed summary of the early phases of the controversy, see M. M. Basu's introduction to his *Dīna-caṇḍīdāsa* (*bhūmikā*, pp. 2–5).

[38] *Caṇḍīdāsa-padāvalī* (Basumati edition), p. 149.

[39] *Ibid.*, p. 154.

[40] *Ibid.*, p. 149. According to *Rasabhakti-candrikā* of Caitanya-dāsa (*VSP*, II, 1658 f.), the five *bāṇas* or arrows are: *madana* (delight in love), *mādana* (intoxication, assumedly in love), *śoṣana* (absorption in love), *stambhana* (suspension of all sensation but that of love), and *mohana* (complete stupefaction or bliss).

the god of love, who has a special meaning for the Vaiṣṇava-sahajiyās. Secondly, the terms "right" (*dakṣiṇa*) and "left" (*vāma*), as previously suggested, have a technical meaning. M. M. Basu says this about it:

In the sphere of practical culture, the Sahajiyās say that the worshiper should not follow the Dakṣiṇa course, but should stick to the Vāma mode. In the Tantras it is also said that the Vāma is better than the Dakṣiṇa, for the latter is practically based on Vedic principles, and hence falls within the sphere of Vaidhi [i.e., external ritual] culture, which is also denounced by the Sahajiyās, because they prefer the Rāgānuga mode [i.e., the way of immediate realization].[41]

It is said in one of the Sahajiyā texts that the "femaleness" of the individual is located in the left side of the body and the "maleness" in the right. The individual must know both in union within himself to experience the ultimate pleasure.[42] It is perfectly clear that some of the poems of "Caṇḍīdāsa" are Sahajiyā poems.

The problem of sorting out these "Caṇḍīdāsas" was greatly simplified by the discovery and publication, in 1917, of the manuscript called by its editor Vasanta-rañjan Rāy, *Śrīkṛṣṇa-kīrtan*.[43] It is an old manuscript of a work that is even older. The language of the text, according to S. K. Chatterji, is no later than the first part of the fifteenth century.[44] Some scholars date the manuscript itself as early as the fifteenth century, suggesting that the work may be

41 *Post-Caitanya Sahajiyā Cult*, p. 132.

42 See the *Sahaja-tattva* of Rādhāvallabha-dāsa, *VSP*, II,1655 ff., and Basu, *PCSC*, pp. 41–42.

43 First published by the Baṅgīya sāhitya pariṣad in 1917.

44 *Bāṅgla-bhāṣātattver-bhūmikā*, pp. 18–19.

considerably older.[45] Sukumār Sen, a very careful scholar and conservative in these matters, feels that the manuscript was written by three different hands at three different times and, on the basis of comparison with a manuscript of the *Gītagovinda* which contains the date 1544 (A.D. 1622–23), dates the earliest of the three sections of the *Śrīkṛṣṇa-kīrtan* manuscript as no earlier than A.D. 1600.[46] Excluding the possibility, however, that there were several Caṇḍīdāsas equally early, this relatively late date still indicates that the author of the *Śrīkṛṣṇa-kīrtan* was the same Caṇḍīdāsa Caitanya "read with pleasure."

The question then becomes this: Was the writer of the *Skk* a Sahajiyā poet? Some indications are that he was not. There are no Sahajiyā poems of the type quoted above, the so-called *rāgātmika-padas*, in the *Skk* text. There is in that text no mention of Rāmī, the washerwoman, with whom, according to legend and some texts, Caṇḍīdāsa performed his Sahajiyā *sādhana*.[47] Finally, the language of the *Skk*, which because it is relatively early has become the measure against which all Caṇḍīdāsa songs are placed for dating, is substantially earlier than that of any of the presently known Sahajiyā or *rāgmātmika-padas*.[48] On the basis of these facts, Vasanta-rañjan Rāy, the editor of the *Skk*, states categorically: "[Baḍu] Caṇḍīdāsa was not a Sahajiyā. In his poetry, there is not a hint of the Sahajiyā *sādhana*. He was not even

[45] Sen (*BSI*, I, 165) notes that Rādhāgovinda Basak dates it between A.D. 1450 and 1500.

[46] *Ibid.*

[47] See Vasanta-rañjan Rāy's introduction to the *Skk*, pp. 5–7; Haraprasād Śāstrī's essay "Caṇḍīdāsa," in *Haraprasād-racanāvalī*, pp. 284 ff.; and Sukumār Sen's "Śrīkhaṇḍer sampradāy," in *Bicitra sāhitya*, pp. 110 ff.

[48] V. R. Ray, *Skk*, *bhūmikā*, p. 12.

a follower of the Gauḍiya-vaiṣṇava movement [i.e., the Caitanya movement], but was a devotee of Caṇḍī."[49] That the poet was, or had been, a devotee of Caṇḍī is obvious from his name, "Servant of Caṇḍī"; it is one of those points so often overlooked in concern with subtlety. The author of the *Skk* signs himself "Baḍu-caṇḍīdāsa" or simply "Caṇḍīdāsa."[50]

Both M. M. Basu, in the introduction to his *Dīna-caṇḍīdāsa,* and Sukumār Sen, in his article "Śrīkhaṇḍa sampradāy o caṇḍīdāsa," have shown conclusively that there were at least two Caṇḍīdāsas.[51] One of them, the author of the *Skk* and probably a non-Sahajiyā, lived at or before the time of Caitanya. The other or others, truly Sahajiyā, probably lived after Caitanya's time. Basu writes:

> There are no padas in the *Śrīkṛṣṇa-kīrtan* in which Baḍu-caṇḍīdāsa reveals a relationship to the Sahajiyā; on the other hand, padas signed Dvija-caṇḍīdāsa or Dīna-caṇḍīdāsa have many examples of the *sahaja-dharma-tattva* [i.e., the religious and philosophical point of view of the Sahajiyās]. Dīna-caṇḍīdāsa appeared after the time of Caitanya.[52]

Basu has reached what is probably the right conclusion in regard to Dīna-caṇḍīdāsa's date, although the basis of his argument—that Caitanya originated the thinking in which prema was the focal point and that therefore the Sahajiyā, to which prema is also focal, must have begun at some time after Caitanya—is faulty. We have already seen that the concept of prema is present in the *Bhāgavata-purāṇa.*

[49] *Ibid.*, p. 9.
[50] For example: "So sings Baṛu-caṇḍīdāsa, the devotee of Vāsulī" (*Skk*, p. 1.); "So sings Caṇḍīdāsa, bound to the head of Vāsulī" (*Skk*, p. 7).
[51] *Bicitra-sāhitya,* pp. 110 ff.
[52] *Dīna-caṇḍīdāsa, bhūmikā,* p. 51.

A more convincing argument, which leads to the same conclusions, is offered by Sen. He shows that many of the *rāgātmika-padas* are signed in some compilations "Caṇḍīdāsa" and in others by some other name. For example, the famous pada "Pīritī baliyā" occurs in the Baṅgīya-sāhitya-pariṣad edition of Caṇḍīdāsa with the signature "Caṇḍīdāsa" (No. 335). In many other manuscripts the same pada is signed "Narahari [Sarkār]."[53] It is possible and perhaps even likely that the name "Caṇḍīdāsa" became attached to songs written by other poets. Caṇḍīdāsa was early recognized as a good poet; even if he had not been, the fact that his songs were "read with pleasure" by Caitanya would have been enough to give his name great prestige. This would be reason enough to attach it to the songs of others, and some of these others may well have been Sahajiyās. In fact, in the same article, Sen shows that various songs of the known Sahajiyā Taruṇīrāmaṇa have appeared with the signature "Caṇḍīdāsa."

Why this should have taken place is clear enough. Scribes of Sahajiyā tendencies may simply have put the names of famous poets to the poems written by people of their own sect and persuasion. Or, for the advancement of their own point of view, lesser poets might actually have signed the names of greater ones to their own work. Or, perhaps most likely, later poets might have adopted the names of earlier ones as titles. The desire for individuality and recognition was not as strong in medieval Bengal as it is in the modern West. Basu suggests, for example, that "Caṇḍīdāsa" was in actuality a title of the Sahajiyā poet Taruṇīrāmaṇa.[54] Sen

[53] *Bicitra-sāhitya,* p. 117.
[54] *Basumati* for *Āsāḍh,* B.S. 1344 (A.D. 1929).

identifies a poem in the Sahajiyā text *Rasasāra* that is signed "Vidyāpati" as being a poem of the Sahajiyā poet Kavirañjana of Śrīkhaṇḍa and feels that "Vidyāpati" was the title which Kaviranjana assumed.[55] There is an interesting legend that described a meeting between Vidyāpati and Caṇḍīdāsa" If there is any historical basis to it at all, it is probable, as V. R. Rāy suggests, that a meeting took place between this later "Vidyāpati" and this later "Caṇḍīdāsa."[56]

It seems then to be fairly well substantiated that there were at least two Caṇḍīdāsas, now known as Baḍu-caṇḍīdāsa and Dīna-caṇḍīdāsa. According to the theory, at least, the former was the author of the *Skk* and the poet who was read with such delight by Caitanya; the latter was a Sahajiyā poet, who lived after Caitanya and therefore could not possibly have influenced his thinking. There are, however, several difficulties with the theory, as the reader may have noticed. The two main ones are anticipated by Haraprasād Śāstrī in his article "Caṇḍīdāsa."

There is in the *Skk* a song that is found in various other manuscripts in more modern language. Haraprasād Śāstrī therefore suggests the argument that although the language of the *rāgātmika-pada*s is more modern than that of the padas found in the *Skk*, it does not necessarily follow that the *rāgātmika-padas* themselves are. It may be that we just do not have the *rāgātmika* songs in their earlier form. This in turn suggests that although there is little *Skk* which is of a Sahajiyā nature, it does not necessarily follow that Baḍu-caṇḍīdāsa was not a Sahajiyā, for he may have written

[55] *Bicitra sāhitya,* p. 124.
[56] *Skk, bhūmikā,* p. 14.

the *Skk* without revealing his own doctrinal bias, and he may have written other things.

The second main argument carries more weight. It is, in essence, that there is every likelihood that Baḍu-caṇḍīdāsa was himself a Tāntric; if this is true, it is very possible that, whatever the evidence of the *Skk*, Baḍu-caṇḍīdāsa is actually responsible also for some of the *rāgātmika-pada*s attributed to him. If, as a worshipper of the goddess (as his name tells us he was), Baḍu-caṇḍīdāsa could write a Vaiṣṇava text, he could certainly also write Sahajiyā songs, which would in any case be closer to his own doctrinal position. Haraprasād Śāstrī bases his argument that Baḍu-caṇḍīdāsa was a Tāntric on two facts. First, he points out, in almost all of the poems of the *Skk* the poet signs himself as "a devotee of Vāsulī," or says that he is writing the poem "by the grace of Vāsulī." Vāsulī is a name by which the goddess Caṇḍī is called in the Birbhum district of West Bengal. And in that district in the worship of the goddess the Śākta (Tāntric) ritual is used. Secondly, he says that Birbhum district is an area in which the Tāntric tradition is ancient and all-pervasive. Caṇḍīdāsa came from Kenduli village in Birbhum. Thus, he says, it is most probable that Caṇḍīdāsa was a Tāntric.

To follow his argument through, Haraprasād Śāstrī feels that there were two Caṇḍīdāsas, but not the same two as those described above. One of Śāstrī's Caṇḍīdāsas was a Vaiṣṇava-sahajiyā, the one who wrote the *Skk*, the other a "pure" Sahajiyā or Tāntric. He comes to this conclusion in an interesting if somewhat tenuous manner. He mentions a manuscript he found in the library of the Baṅgīya-sāhitya-pariṣad that tells the story of the death of a Caṇḍīdāsa at the hands of a certain jealous king of Bengal sometime in the late fourteenth century. From this manuscript, he pieces together evidence to show that no such king as the one described was reigning in Bengal at that time. Therefore, the Caṇḍīdāsa who was executed by the king was not the author of the *Skk*, which he feels was written in 1385. He concludes that there were two Caṇḍīdāsas who lived before Caitanya, either of whom could have been the one whom Caitanya read:

The first Caṇḍīdāsa, who wrote the *Śrīkṛṣṇakīrtana*, was a Vaiṣṇava of the type of Jayadeva [i.e., a Vaiṣṇava-sahajiyā]; the other was not a Vaiṣṇava at all. Sometimes he wrote pure Sahajiyā songs, and sometimes Sahajiyā songs dealing with Rādhā and Kṛṣṇa. Probably it was he who met his death in the house of the ruler of Bengal.[57]

A third argument is similar to this, namely, that there is a poem in *Skk* which displays a fair acquaintanceship with Tāntric technical terminology and philosophy, of a sort which also appears in Sahajiyā texts. The references are to techniques of Tāntric yogic practice, and the terms *iḍā*, *piṅgalā*, and *suṣumnā* refer to the three channels which, according to Tāntric physiology, are located along the backbone, and through which the "power," urged on by ritual practice, rises to the brain, thereby causing the experience of bliss. The offending poem reads in part:

Day and night I spend in yogic meditation,
I remain in the firmament, the air of my mind.
I drank nectar from the lotus-root,
and now I have gained the knowledge of Brahma.

[57] *Op. cit.*, p. 293.

O lovely Rādhā, you go far,
and seek to gain your Kṛṣṇa—this is in vain.
I have captured the wind of my mind
in the joining of *iḍā, piṅgalā,* and *suṣumnā.*
I have closed the tenth door,
and now ascend along that yoga-path.
I have cut the arrow of Kāma with the arrow of knowledge.

. . . .

I have seen that all the world is meaningless . . .
So sings Baḍu-caṇḍīdāsa, a follower of Vāsulī.[58]

The poem is obviously Tāntric, and the poet's suggestion to Rādhā that she need not look afar, that Kṛṣṇa, Truth, is within herself, is the suggestion of a Sahajiyā. It is true that the poem is unique in the collection, thus allowing the possibility of interpolation. It is also possible that Caṇḍīdāsa could have written this poem even though he himself was not a subscriber to its doctrines. To the first argument there is no answer. To the second, it must be allowed that the poem has a ring of Sahajiyā truth to it, and that the poet, whoever he was, was most familiar with obscure and secret phraseology.

All the arguments on the question are inconclusive. There are simply too many variables. What is clear is that historical circumstances were right for Caitanya to have been influenced by the Sahajiyā movement, though he himself was not a Sahajiyā. Secondly and more important, two of his companions were Sahajiyās, and were in a position to bring together, both socially and doctrinally, the Sahajiyā stream with that of Caitanya's Vaiṣṇavism. To those special characteristics of the Vaiṣṇava-sahajiyā we shall now turn.

[58] *Skk,* p. 141.

3

Caste, Women, and the Sahajiyā Movement

1. ATTITUDES TOWARD CASTE

THE GOSVĀMINS OF VṚNDĀVANA. Scholars have strongly suggested, as we have seen, that it is at the feet of Nityānanda that the wreath must be laid for introducing "immoral elements" into Bengal Vaiṣṇavism. Melville Kennedy, a keen observer of Bengali society though an ardent Christian apologist, lays this out for us while contrasting the attitudes and tradition of Nityānanda with those of Nityānanda's chief rival, the orthodox Brahman Advaita Ācārya:

The Santipur Gosvamins [i.e., the descendants of Advaita] are more conservative and orthodox from the viewpoint of Hindu society than the Nityananda Gosvamins, and they have refused to minister to, or admit into the sect, the lower castes and immoral elements of the population, who have traditionally found help at the hands of Nityananda's descendants.[1]

Mr. Kennedy has echoed the not uncommon opinion that low social status and immorality go hand in hand. The point, however, is that in Nityānanda, Avadhūta training and concern for the more depressed social groups were combined with a strong devotion to Caitanya and strong Vaiṣṇava beliefs.

That Nityānanda was concerned for the lower echelons of society is well attested. He stayed, as we have already heard from the tattletale Brahman from Navadvip, "with Śūdras."[2] We are told by the pada-writer Locana-dāsa that he was not averse to going to visit the houses of the untouchable Caṇḍālas.[3] And he is described in one place as the apostle to the not-so-low-caste, but still non-Brahman, Bāṇias.[4]

It is not clear what Nityānanda's own original caste was. Nor is it particularly significant, for as an Avadhūta he not only renounced his own caste but renounced the caste structure of society. The caste structure of society has never been viewed with particular favor in the Tāntric tradition, especially in ritual matters. In discussing the divisions in society from the point of view of ritual, Sir John Woodroffe says:

The Tantra-shāstra [i.e., the sacred teaching according to the Tantras] makes no caste distinction as regards worship, in the

[1] *The Chaitanya Movement*, p. 151.

[2] "Śūdra" is a general classification referring to castes in the lowest of the four main subdivisions of society. In Bengal the term is often used in reference to all non-Brahmans.

[3] See the *Caitanya-maṅgal* of Locana-dāsa, Amrta-bājār Patrikā edition, p. 255. See also the article "*Bolāna-gān*" by Amalendu Mitra in *SPP*, No. 2 (B.S. 1362 [A.D. 1956]).

[4] *BRK* 8:174.

> sense that though it may not challenge the exclusive rights of the twice-born [i.e., the upper castes] to the Vaidik rites, it provides other and similar rites for the Shūdra. Thus there is both a Vaidik and Tāntrik Gāyatrī [i.e., most sacred ritual formula] and Sandhyā [morning, noon, and evening devotions] and rites available for worshippers of all castes. . . . All castes, even the lowest Chandāla, may, if otherwise fit, receive the Tāntrik initiation and be a member of a Chakra [i.e., the Tāntric congregation for ritual circular worship].[5]

And, perhaps more important, in discussing the *Yoginītantra,* Woodroffe says that "the Shāstra is for all castes, and for women as well as men."[6]

That the Vaiṣṇava-sahajiyā had this same indifference to caste and to the Vedic tradition is clear enough. Caste is not a matter of birth, but a matter of attitude. The *Pāṣaṇḍa-dalana,* a text less definable as Sahajiyā on the basis of its content than on the basis of its authorship, puts forward an attitude that is also that of the *Bhāgavata-purāṇa:* "He who worships Kṛṣṇa is not a Śūdra; rather, he is a holy man among men. [But] he of any caste who does not worship Kṛṣṇa is a Śūdra. This all the *śāstras* attest."[7] And, according to a pada attributed to Nityānanda-dāsa, there are several things that impede a proper devotional attitude, among them consciousness of caste: "[Where] caste, or intellectualism, or fear, exist, bhakti cannot exist; in these things there

[5] *Shakti and Shākta* ("Essays and Addresses on the Shākta Tantrashāstra"), p. 504.

[6] *Ibid.*, p. 532.

[7] *Vaiṣṇava-granthāvalī,* p. 206. The *Pāṣaṇḍa-dalana* is sometimes attributed to Narottama-dāsa (as in the *Vaiṣṇava-granthāvalī* anthology), but Sukumār Sen cites the evidence of Prema-dāsa's Vaṃśi-śikṣā that its author was Rāmacandra Gosvāmi, a known Sahajiyā (*BSI*, p. 645).

is evil."[8] In keeping with its Tāntric heritage, the teachings of the Vaiṣṇava-sahajiyā are clear on the matter. Unfortunately, not as much can be said for orthodox Vaiṣṇavism.

Even during Caitanya's lifetime, various well-defined sectarian divisions among his followers could be seen. S. K. De describes the situation thus:

> An important difference arose early in the sect which had enduring consequences. It was aggravated by the fact that there was no real coordination between the different groups which had sprung up spontaneously and independently around Caitanya or around some of his immediate associates. We hear of the adorers of Caitanya . . . followers of Advaita, admirers of Gadādhara, devotees as well as detractors of Nityānanda. Each of Caitanya's associates and devotees appears to have developed a considerable community of disciples of his own, and taught the cult of bhakti according to the light which each had received in his own way from the Master.[9]

In some ways this mitosis was along caste lines. The primary subdivision was that between the scholars and theologians of Vṛndāvana on the one hand and the devotees of Bengal on the other.

Caitanya himself, like many another great religious leader, was neither an organizer nor a theologian. His interest was in the realization of the immediate presence of God. As a result, the physical shape that his sect took was almost entirely due to accidents of social circumstance and to the attitudes of later and in most ways lesser men. The theological shape the movement took, however, was less accidental.

[8] *Sahajiyā-sāhitya*, pada 12.
[9] *VFM*, p. 82.

It was impossible for Caitanya, as it is impossible for any educated man in India today, to escape the influence of the great Sanskrit theological and philosophical tradition; he did not attempt any exception to the rule that one must connect one's thought or system to that of the Vedic and Upaniṣadic tradition in order to have it accepted as authoritative. Though Caitanya himself was probably no theologian, he recognized the importance of this connection and sent some among his followers who were scholars and theologians to Vṛndāvana, the holy place of Kṛṣṇa, to establish there a center for Vaiṣṇavas and to shape the doctrines of the new sect.[10] These six "Gosvāmins," as they are called, were Rūpa, Sanātana, Jīva, Gopāla Bhaṭṭa, Raghunātha Bhaṭṭa, and Raghunātha Dāsa. It is relevant at this point to look briefly at the histories of these six important men.

Rūpa, Sanātana, and Jīva were members of a single family. Rūpa and Sanātana were brothers, brilliant men who before their conversion by Caitanya had held high positions at the court of Husein Shah (1494–1525), the Muslim ruler of Bengal at the time. Not only were they brilliant thinkers, as the careful and complex system they worked out amply shows, but they were "learned in the *śāstras*," texts of law, theology, and every other conceivable category of learning.[11] The *Caitanya-caritāmṛta* tells us that Caitanya "sent Rūpa and Sanātana to Vṛndāvana; upon the order of Prabhu the two brothers came there. They preached bhakti and . . . propagated the worship of Govinda-madana-gopāla [i.e.,

[10] The story of how Vṛndāvana was rescued from obscurity and reestablished as a religious center and place of pilgrimage is told in *CC Madhya* 4.

[11] See for example *BRK* 1:589–94.

Kṛṣṇa]. They brought many books of the *śastras*, and wrote works on bhakti, thus becoming the cause of salvation to all deluded people."[12] Jīva was their nephew, the son of a third brother called Anupama or Vallabha, who had died. "Sanātana, Rūpa, and Vallabha the lord of bhaktas; the eldest of the three was Sanātana; younger than he was Rūpa; and the youngest of all was Vallabha, full of prema. Jīva Gosvāmin was his son."[13] Jīva was perhaps an even greater scholar than his illustrious uncles and has some twenty major works to his credit on such varied subjects as grammar, poetry and poetics, ritual, theology, and philosophy. His *Bhāgavata-saṃdarbha* or *Ṣaṭ-saṃdarbha* is the first full and systematic treatment of the theology and philosophy of the Bengal school. Jīva seems to have been considerably younger than his uncles; so young that the chances are slim that he actually ever met Caitanya.

But what is of interest to us at present is that Rūpa and Sanātana had worked for the Muslims and had lived with them. It is fairly certain, on the testimony of Rūpa, Sanātana, and Jīva themselves, that their family was Brahman and had migrated to Bengal from the Carnatic area of South India. Sanātana, in his commentary on the third *śloka* of his own *Bṛhad-bhāgavatāmṛta*, describes his family in these terms: "famous in the Karṇāṭa country" (*karṇāṭadeśavikhyāta*), "Brahman family" (*viprakula*), and "settled in Bengal" (*gauḍadeśi*).[14] The same story is told in Rūpa's *Sanātāṣṭaka* and in Jīva's *Vaiṣṇava-toṣaṇī*; the three are of course

[12] *CC Madhya* 1:25 ff.
[13] *BRK* 1:579.
[14] See B. B. Majumdār, *Caitanya-cariter upādān*, p. 124.

followed in the story by later and dependent texts such as the *Bhaktiratnākara, Prema-vilāsa,* and by the *Caitanya-caritāmṛta,* whose author was their pupil. Whether or not they had been converted to Islam, as some scholars feel, is open to question.[15] But it is certain that they had lost caste by their association with Muslims. According to the testimony of the CC, they were considered by at least some Vaiṣṇava devotees as untouchable, and they considered themselves so. There is an interesting story in the CC in which we are told that Sanātana and Anupama were visiting Caitanya. A certain Brahman named Vallabha Bhaṭṭa heard that Caitanya had come to the village and went to pay his respects:

> The two then sat and talked of Kṛṣṇa, and in the talk great prema rose up in Caitanya's heart. . . . Then Caitanya introduced the two brothers to him; the two brothers bowed to the ground, remaining at a distance—with great humility they greeted Bhaṭṭa. Bhaṭṭa went forward to meet them, and the two fled. "We are untouchable—do not touch us!" Bhaṭṭa was greatly surprised, and Caitanya pleased. He said: "Do not touch them; they are of very low caste [*jāti ati hīn*]. And you are a Vedic priest, and a learned Kulīn Brahman."[16]

The point of the story is that Caitanya goes on to say that this makes no difference, the two brothers are worshippers of Kṛṣṇa. But it is significant that Kṛṣṇadāsa constantly puts

[15] Majumdār (p. 123) feels that there is some evidence that it was their father who had been converted and quotes an article in *Bhāratvarṣa* (B.S. 1341 [A.D. 1935]) that suggests that this conversion took place at the hands of one Pirali Khān in the Yaśohar (Jessore) district shortly after the birth of Rūpa and Sanātana.

[16] *CC Madhya* 19:56–65. A Kulīn Brahman is a member of the very top stratum of the Brahman caste cluster.

such protestations of castelessness, which are more powerful than the usual formal Vaiṣṇava expressions of humility, into Sanātana's mouth. In *CC Madhya* 1:179 he says, "I am of low caste, have kept low companions, and have done low work." In CC *Madhya* 1:186 he says "my birth was in a low family. I have served Muslims and have done Muslim work. I have associated with the murderers of Brahmans and cows;"[17] and in *CC Antya* 6:27 f., "Sanātana said, 'My birth was in a low family. The dharma of my family was opposed to the true dharma.' "[18] The last statement is curious and perhaps lends weight to the argument that the father of Rūpa and Sanātana had become converted to Islam. In any case, it is clear that Rūpa and Sanātana, and probably by association Jīva, were not considered Brahmans and possibly not even caste Hindus at the time of their association with Caitanya and his sect.

There was another of the Gosvāmins who was clearly not a Brahman. Raghunātha Dāsa was a member of the second-ranked caste cluster called Kāyastha.[19] He was the son of a wealthy landowner of a place called Saptagrāma, and from their first meeting Caitanya was attracted to him, not in this case because of his intellectual abilities, but because of his great devotion to Kṛṣṇa. "Inwardly, he was an ascetic, but in daily life he performed all the duties appropriate [to his

[17] The term I have translated "Muslim" is *mleccha*, "foreigner," which has also come to mean "barbarian" or "savage." In texts of this period the term was usually applied to Muslims.

[18] The term dharma is difficult to translate, since it indicates the whole complex of actions and attitudes toward what is right and to be done. Here the "true" dharma is bhakti.

[19] *CC Antya* 6:22 says that he was "within the Kāyastha estate." The *Haribhakti-vilāsa* of Gopāla Bhaṭṭa also describes him as Kāyastha.

caste and station], and the minds of his mother and father were put at ease."[20] But he did become an ascetic. He went to stay with Caitanya in Puri, and after Caitanya's death departed for Vṛndāvana (*CC Antya* 6). Interestingly, we are told that Nityānanda stimulated Raghunātha Dāsa greatly, that it was "Svarūpa" (perhaps Svarūpa Dāmodara) who was instrumental in Raghunātha's acceptance into the circle of bhaktas, and that it was "Svarūpa" to whom his religious instruction was entrusted when he joined Caitanya in Puri.[21] Raghunātha is also singled out by the Sahajiyā text *Vivarta-vilāsa* as being important in the transmission of the true (i.e., the Sahajiyā) meaning of Caitanyā teaching. Caitanya taught Svarūpa, and Svarūpa "taught Raghunātha; from him [Kṛṣṇadāsa] Kavirāja learned of the *pāñca-guṇa* [Sahajiyā doctrines?], and . . . taught Mukunda."[22] And so on.

The other two Gosvāmins were Brahmans. Caitanya had once stayed at the house of Gopāla Bhaṭṭa's family for four months and was deeply impressed by the devotion of the young Gopāla. "Caitanya made the heart of Gopāla steadfast in bhakti and . . . gave him instruction. Again Gopāla said, 'Soon I shall go to Vṛndāvana, where I shall join the precious jewels Rūpa and Sanātana.' "[23] This ambition was soon fulfilled. Whether or not he was specifically deputed by Caitanya is open to question. It should be noted here that the story, and especially its chronology, about which the

[20] *CC Antya* 6:14.

[21] *Ibid.*, 6:200 f. Svarūpa may have been Nityānanda, although it is more likely that the reference is to Svarūpa Dāmodara, an early follower of Caitanya.

[22] VV, p. 40. This is based on a text in *CC Ādi* 4:137, with which we shall deal further.

[23] *BRK* 1:120 f.

early writers had something of a cavalier attitude, is a bit confused. When Gopāla says that he is off to join Rūpa and Sanātana, Caitanya had not met those two Gosvāmins, much less sent them to Vṛndāvana.

The sixth was Raghunātha Bhaṭṭa, of the family of Tapana Miśra, with whom Caitanya stayed in Benares.[24] Raghunātha Bhaṭṭa also joined Caitanya in Puri, remained there for eight months, returned to Benares for four years, and again went back to Puri, where, we are told, "Prabhu instructed him: 'My command, Raghunātha, is that you go to Vṛndāvana. Remain there with Rūpa and Sanātana. Read the *Bhāgavata* constantly, and repeat the name of Kṛṣṇa; soon the Lord Kṛṣṇa will shed his grace on you.' "[25]

There were others sent by Caitanya to Vṛndāvana, for example, Lokanātha, the son of Padmanābha Cakravartī and Sītā, from the village of Tālakhāirā. "Abandoning everything, Lokanātha came to Navadvip, to the side of Prabhu. Prahbu was most gracious toward him, and instructed him to go to Vṛndāvana."[26] But these, though their pupils were in some cases prominent in the spread of the movement, had little part in shaping its doctrine.

The six Gosvāmins among them produced over 219 different works in Sanskrit—it is most significant that they wrote in Sanskrit—tying every teaching of the Bengal school into the orthodox traditions of Indian religion. They created a great corpus of canonical works. And in creating a theology in the great and sacred but learned language of tra-

[24] *Kṛṣṇacaitanya caritāmṛtam* 4:1:15.
[25] *CC Antya* 13:119.
[26] *BRK* 1:299 f. Lokanātha was the guru of the great Vaiṣṇava Narottama; see *Narottama-vilāsa*, pp. 1–7.

dition, they cut themselves off with surprising effectiveness from the vital and enthusiastic religion, inspired by the living figure of Caitanya himself, that continued to develop in Bengal. In the refined and intricate systems of the Gosvāmins, Caitanya found no place. Their thought was centered not on the Kṛṣṇa who lived among them, but on the Kṛṣṇa of tradition, the Kṛṣṇa of the *Bhāgavata-purāṇa.*

Caitanya himself, by taking no real position, at least in the social sense, on the matter of caste, had left it open. Unlike Nityānanda, it is extremely doubtful that Caitanya considered the matter of caste from the social point of view at all. He was a religious leader, not a social reformer; it is a mistake to assume that one implied the other, as it so often does in the modern West. His position on caste was what Milton Singer has called "ritual," not "individual"; in other words, he acted and considered the actions of others in one way when the "scene," to use a Burkean term, was religious, and in another way when it was not. His religious position followed the *Bhāgavata:* social superiority was not a matter of birth but a matter of right-mindedness (which meant devotion to Kṛṣṇa). Kṛṣṇadāsa has him take the strongly antitraditional position that anyone of any caste can be a guru, if he is sufficiently devoted: "Prabhu said, 'Whether he be Brahman or *saṃnyāsī* or Śūdra, he who is versed in the knowledge of Kṛṣṇa is a guru.' "[27] For Kṛṣṇa distributes his grace to all without distinction of caste:

> Kṛṣṇa is the non-dependent deity, the storehouse of profound prema; nor does he make distinction as to whom he grants it.[28]

27 CC *Madhya* 8:100.
28 CC *Ādi* 8:18.

Hearing this, Sārvabhauma asked Prabhu, "Why did Purī Gosvāmi serve Śūdras?" And Prabhu answered, ". . . the grace of God does not depend upon the Vedas, nor does it respect caste or family. For Kṛṣṇa himself took food at the home of an outcaste."[29]

And Caitanya's actions were in certain contexts suited to his words. In Benares, he stayed at the home of one Candra-śekhara, a Śūdra.[30] And there is the wonderful story of Caitanya's meeting with Rāmānanda Rāya:

"Prabhu asked, 'Are you Rāmānanda Rāya?' Rāmānanda replied, 'I am he, your servant and a lowly Śūdra.' Then Caitanya held him in a firm embrace. . . . When they saw this, the Brahmans said to one another, 'How can he weep and embrace a Śūdra?' "[31]

When the scene was that of individual conscience, however, it seems that Caitanya was more a product of his orthodox Brahman heritage. Although in one place Caitanya argues against Sārvabhauma that Kṛṣṇa himself broke the rules and ate at the home of a casteless person, when he himself was staying with Candra-śekhara in Benares it seems as if he ate at the home of Tapana Miśra, a Brahman.[32] And when Haridāsa, an ardent devotee who had been converted from Islam, refused to eat with other bhaktas because of an awareness of his power to defile, Caitanya tacitly agreed:

" 'Haridāsa!' Caitanya called repeatedly. But Haridāsa remained at a distance and replied, 'Prabhu, please eat with your bhaktas. I am unclean and cannot sit with them. Govinda will bring

[29] CC *Madhya* 10:133 f. "Purī Gosvāmi" probably refers to Īśvara Purī, who was Caitanya's *dīkṣā-guru*. See also CC *Madhya* 20:98.
[30] CC *Ādi* 7:43.
[31] CC *Madhya* 8:18 f.
[32] CC *Ādi* 7:44.

me food afterwards, outside the door.' Knowing his mind, Caitanya said no more to him."[33]

We have seen Sanātana in a similar situation.

Thus, without Caitanya's consistent model to follow in the matter and being constrained to take some position as time went by and enthusiastic anarchy developed rules and regulations, various members of the various branches of the Bengal school adopted various positions. Kṛṣṇadāsa, a product of Vṛndāvana and probably reflecting the opinion of the three great Gosvāmins in the matter, enthusiastically has Caitanya take the anticaste religious position mentioned above. And in other places he says that the reason for Kṛṣṇa's incarnation as Caitanya is to save the lowly and the fallen.[34] Furthermore, as we have seen, some of the Gosvāmins were non-Brahmans and in one or two cases perhaps even non-caste Hindus, and they took non-Brahmans as pupils. Narottama, a pupil of Lokanātha, was probably a Kāyastha, as his surname was Datta.[35] Yadunandana-dāsa, a pupil of Jīva, describes himself in his *Karṇānanda* as a Vaidya.[36] The

[33] *CC Madhya* 11:157 ff. The food in question is *prasāda*, food that has been blessed by being offered to the deity. The word that I have translated "unclean" is *chāra* meaning "vile."

[34] *Ibid.*, 1:176 f. and in other places throughout his text.

[35] *Narottama-vilāsa* of Narahari-dāsa, p. 9. His father was Puruṣottama, who is described as the elder brother of Kṛṣṇānanda Datta. Narottama was accused of being a Śūdra, although it is not clear exactly what the accusation means. The *Narottama-vilāsa* (pp. 146–47) records the story of a Brahman *paṇḍit* who, "in his pride," called Narottama a Śūdra before a group of students. The Brahman was immediately stricken with leprosy and was cleansed only by his confession and subsequent embrace by Narottama. The moral, according to the text, is, "Do not call Narottama a Śūdra."

[36] P. 28 of the Murshidabad edition reads: "His name is Dīna-Yadunandana, a Vaidya, whose home is in Malahāṭi-grām. He is devoid of prema

great Kṛṣṇadāsa was probably also a Vaidya.[37] And not only did the Gosvāmins have non-Brahmans as pupils, but the non-Brahman pupils broke the cardinal rule and took Brahmans as their pupils. Because of this Narottama raised the eyebrows of the Brahman Gopāla Bhaṭṭa, who says that Brahmans "were greatly angered because Narottama-ṭhākur makes Brahmans his pupils, and reported it to the king."[38] But even Gopāla, a staunch Brahman who states in no uncertain terms in his *Haribhakti-vilāsa* that a man of lower caste cannot give initiation to a man of a higher one,[39] was, as S. K. De says, "liberal enough to permit persons other than Brahmins to act as preceptors to men of their own or lower castes."[40]

All of this might seem somewhat surprising to those who are used to equating social and religious orthodoxy. The causes of the Gosvāmins' attitudes toward caste are, I suspect, two. First and foremost, the Gosvāmins were the inheritors, perhaps more than were certain branches of the Bengal school, of the *Bhāgavata* and its traditions, which included, as Thomas Hopkins has shown, a skepticism toward the usual types of social distinctions based on birth.[41] Secondly, and possibly related to this, the Gosvāmins to some extent at least inherited the social and (right-handed) ritual position of the Tantra. Proof of this is ample.

---

and as low as ashes." The author's use of the third person and his self-abnegation are formal Vaiṣṇava expressions of humility.

37 *VFM*, p. 41, n.1.

38 *Narottama-vilāsa*, p. 157.

39 Gopāla's *Haribhakti-vilāsa* 1:36. Gopāla quotes the *Nārada-pañcarātra* as his authority and then goes on to make his own statement on the matter.

40 *VFM*, p. 343.

41 Thomas Hopkins, *The Vaiṣṇava Bhakti Movement in the Bhāgavata Purāṇa*, pp. 126–37.

In the section of his *Ujjvala-nīlamaṇi* that is devoted to Rādhā, Rūpa Gosvāmin described her as *tantre pratiṣṭhitā*, "established in the Tantras" as the *hlādinī-śakti* or bliss-giving power of Kṛṣṇa: "The *hlādinī*, the *mahāśakti*, is the greatest of all the śaktis; [Rādhā] is that—thus it is established in the Tantras."[42] In his *Saṃkṣepa-bhāgavatāmṛta*, Rūpa cites seven Tāntric or Āgamic works. Gopāla Bhaṭṭa, on whose *Haribhakti-vilāsa* the influence of Tāntrism is very extensive, says in the first *vilāsa* of that work that the man whom one chooses as guru must be "versed in Tāntric lore."[43] In this work Gopāla cites a large number of Tantras and Āgamas as authorities.[44] According to Gopāla, the Vaiṣṇava guru must have a knowledge of the Tantras and their mantras or ritual formulas; Tāntric mantras and *maṇḍalas* or diagrams for ritual or magical purposes are to be used in initiations; and the *kāma-bīja*, a mantra of particular significance to the Sahajiyās also, is to be used.[45] The *Satkrīyāsāra-dīpikā*, also ascribed to Gopāla, is a book of ritual that depends to a large extent upon the Tantras. S. D. De sums it up:

Like the orthodox Smṛti, again, of Bengal, which absorbed very largely Tāntric ideas, rites, and formulas since the time of Raghunandana, most of the ritual and ceremonial of this Vaiṣṇava Smṛti appears to have been profoundly influenced by the

[42] *Śloka* 4 of the section entitled *Atha rādhāprakaranaṃ* (p. 102 of the Murshidabad edition).

[43] *Vilāsa* 1:8 (p. 43 of the Murshidabad edition).

[44] For a list of them, see *VFM*, p. 397.

[45] *Haribhakti-vilāsa*, pp. 56–58 of the Murshidabad edition. Gopāla cites as his authority (p. 58) the *Gautamīya-tantra*. The *kāma-bīja* is, as we shall see, also a mantra of importance to the orthodox Vaiṣṇavas.

tenets and practices of Tantra, which must have been widely and deeply spread in Bengal at this time.[46]

There is very little doubt that the Gosvāmins were deeply influenced by the Tantras, and that this influence was passed on by them to their pupil Kṛṣṇadāsa. This the Sahajiyās seized upon with a great deal of enthusiasm; although the Tāntrism that affected the Gosvāmins was of the right-hand variety, its doctrinal and social position had something in common with the left-hand Tantra that the Sahajiyā embodies. The Sahajiyās, able to cite the Gosvāmins as authorities for their own position, thereby felt justified. They went somewhat further than the truth seems to have warranted, and said that the Gosvāmins taught in a secret and esoteric fashion the way of sahaja, suggestively putting Raghunāthadāsa in the middle of the line through which the "deep and hidden meaning of the līlā of Caitanya" was passed, eventually taking shape in the Vaiṣṇava-sahajiyā theology.[47] The VV, somewhat superciliously, asks: "The *vivarta-dharma* [i.e., the Sahajiyā] is witnessed by the Tantras; if there is no meaning in this witness, why did the Gosvāmins accept it?"[48]

Feeling proprietary toward the Gosvāmins, the Sahajiyās translated a great many of their Sanskrit works into Bengali. These translations included not only many of the great works, but many of the lesser-known ones. Among these, according to Sen (*BSI*, I, 402–3) are the *Uddhava-saṃdeśa* or *Uddhava-dūta* of Rūpa, translated variously by Dvija Na-

[46] *VFM*, p. 341.
[47] In many texts, e.g., VV, p. 40, *Amṛtarasāvalī*, p. 157.
[48] VV, p. 156.

rasiṃha, Kiśora-dāsa, and others; the *Vilāpakusamāñjali* of Raghunātha-dāsa, translated by Rādhāvallabha-dāsa, the pupil of Śrīnivāsa Ācārya, and again by Kṛṣṇacandra-dāsa of Śrīkhaṇḍa; the *Muktā-caritra* of Raghunātha-dāsa, translated by Nārānyaṇa-dāsa, the grandson of Śrīnivāsa and the pupil of Jagadānanda; the *Svaniyama-daśaka* of Raghunātha-dāsa; and Rūpa's *Cāṭupuṣpāñjalī*, both translated anonymously. The prominence given to the works of Raghunātha-dāsa is pointed.

The Gosvāmins, writing as they did in Sanskrit, seemed to have no trouble hiding the true meaning of the Caitanya-līlā from the unworthy, who, assumedly, had no access to that noble language. A charming story is told by Ākiñcana-dāsa of how Jīva, being considerably put out by the fact that Kṛṣṇadāsa had written in Bengali rather than Sanskrit, took the manuscript of the *Caitanya-caritāmṛta* and hurled it into the river. The book, however, being holy, floated back to the bank unharmed; the sign was so obvious that even Jīva had to allow that the book was worthy of respect.[49] The reasons for Jīva's objections to Kṛṣṇadāsa's revelation of the truth in Bengali, says Ākiñcana-dāsa, were two. First, that he was afraid that the work would become more important than the Sanskrit works of the Gosvāmins. And, secondly, that he saw no reason why the common people should be given access to the new dispensation. The legend aside, Ākiñcana-dāsa's observations suggest that the old Brahmanical notion that the only appropriate language for truth is Sanskrit was again at work.

It must be admitted that apart from the Tāntrism he had

[49] *Ibid.*, pp. 22 f.

inherited from his gurus, Kṛṣṇadāsa himself left his book open for appropriation by the Sahajiyās. Sprinkled through it are such passages as the following: "This theory of rasa is very mysterious and profound. Svarūpa Gosvāmin alone knew its meaning."[50] "All this is impossible to explain . . . only the *rasika-bhakta* [i.e., the bhakta steeped in the love-philosophy] will understand it, and not see it as hidden."[51] According to the Sahajiyās, Kṛṣṇadāsa's real intention was to write a book revealing the true, or Sahajiyā, meaning of the Caitanya-līlā. Since he did not choose to hide his meaning in the natural obscurities of Sanskrit, he had to hide it in oblique statements of multiple meaning.

Caitanya granted his grace to Kavirāja Gosvāmi, and said to him [in a dream], "describe these things in a book." Kṛṣṇadāsa said, "It is not in my power to write a book." But Nityānanda said, "Take hope; Caitanya will enter into you and write. . . ." While he was writing, an idea came to him, which he greatly desired to make known . . . about the sahaja . . . but Prabhu snatched away his pen. Thus he could only hint at the sahaja in his *Caitanya-caritāmṛta*. In fear of people, Gosvāmi concealed what he meant about the sahaja lest it become known to ordinary men.[52]

Kṛṣṇadāsa was the link between the Tantra-influenced Gosvāmins and the Vaiṣṇavas of Bengal.

THE DEVOTEES OF BENGAL. While the theology and ritual of the Bengal school was being developed at Vṛndāvana, the enthusiasm and devotion inspired by the person and subse-

[50] *CC Ādi* 4:137–38.
[51] *Ibid.*, 4:188.
[52] *Amṛtarasāvalī*, pp. 156–57.

quently the memory of Caitanya was going on to the east, in Bengal and Orissa. The devotees of Bengal and Orissa were people less concerned with theology than with the conviction of salvation that stemmed from the realization that Kṛṣṇa himself had lived among them. They expressed this powerful religious emotion and conviction in lyrics called padas. The passion of these songs is inescapable, though their form and imagery might seem strange:

> Come, let us go to see the Fair One, in all his beauty;
> Come, let us go to Navadvip, to see his wondrous form.
> His body glows like melted gold,
> and waves of tears swell in the oceans of his eyes.
> Let us look upon the golden columns of his arms,
> reaching to his knees, and on the cloth
> colored like the dawn, around his waist.
> Let us look upon the jasmin garland
> swinging to his feet.
> Vāsu says: Come! Let us worship the living God.[53]

It is not difficult to appreciate the fact that these devotees in the early period, during Caitanya's life and just after his death, took but little interest in what was going on in Vṛndāvana, and there is little mention of the Gosvāmins in the writings that came out of Bengal.[54] (It should be re-

[53] *Padakalpataru*, no. 793. The poem is by Vāsudeva Ghoṣ; see my "The Place of Gaurandrikā in Bengali Vaiṣṇava Lyrics," in *JAOS*, LXXVIII (1958), No. 3.

[54] The writing of the Gosvāmins did not become widely circulated in Bengal until the very late sixteenth and early seventeenth centuries, long after Caitanya's death. The story of their dissemination, itself a matter worthy of study, is described in detail in such texts as the *Bhakti-ratnākara*, *Narottama-vilāsa*, *Prema-vilāsa*, and *Karṇānanda*. The three great Vaiṣṇavas, Śrīnivāsa Ācārya, Narottama Datta, and Śyāmānanda, were sent by the Gosvāmins to carry manuscripts of various works to Bengal from Vṛndāvana. It is an interesting sidelight that while on their way, the

iterated that there is little mention of the leaders of the Bengal branch, and even of the divinity of Caitanya, in the writings of the Gosvāmins.) It was enough for them that Kṛṣṇa had entered, through Caitanya, directly into their lives. Nor will it be difficult to appreciate the significance of the fact that the writings of the Bengal school, of which the most representative extended work is usually taken to be Vṛndāvana-dāsa's *Caitanya-bhāgavata,* were in Bengali, not in Sanskrit.

Despite the power of Caitanya's personality, even while he lived divisions and conflicts of loyalty arose among his followers; many more arose after his death. We have noticed S. K. De's description:

> We hear of the adorers of Caitanya's *Nāgara-bhāva* [i.e., incarnation of Kṛṣṇa, the lover], followers of Advaita, admirers of Gadādhara, devotees as well as detractors of Nityānanda. Each of Caitanya's associates and devotees appears to have developed a considerable community of disciples of his own, and taught the cult of bhakti according to the light which each had received in his own way from the Master.[55]

---

three were robbed of their manuscripts by some men in the employ of the Rājā Vīrahamvīra of Viṣṇupur. The story is that the apostles, in search of their manuscripts, went to the Mahārājā and, in the process of persuading him to restore their treasures, converted him to Vaiṣṇavism. Sukumār Sen (*BSI,* I,396) feels that the dissemination of the writings of the Gosvāmins had much to do with damming up the great stream of creative Vaiṣṇava literature which was at its flood during the sixteenth century. The definitive words had been said. Sen writes: "From the end of the 16th century . . . the Gosvāmins of Vṛndāvana were linked by lines of communication with Bengal and with the north-western part of India. This meant . . . the deterioration of Bengali literature. The sources of Vaiṣṇava literature in Bengal were dried up by attempts to imitate the Gosvāmins."

[55] *VFM,* p. 82.

This is strikingly seen in the *Vivarta-vilāsa* (pp. 6–8), the *Caitanya-caritāmṛta* (*Ādi* 11, 12), as well as in the *Bhaktiratnākara* and other later texts, where long lists of names of the followers of Nityānanda, Advaita, Gadādhara, and others are given. Part of the reason that such divisions took place while Caitanya still lived is that, after whipping Navadvip into a religious froth, he suddenly went to live in Puri. People went from Navadvip to Puri every year on the occasion of the Car Festival of Jagannāth to see Caitanya, but this did not seem to be enough.[56] Vṛndāvana-dāsa tells us that Caitanya recognized the need of his devotees in Navadvip (and at the same time supplied Nityānanda with unquestionable authority for his concern with the lower social strata): "Hear, O Nityānanda. Go quickly to Navadvip. It is my promise, made with my own mouth, that ignorant and low-caste and humble people will float upon the sea of prema . . . you can set them free by bhakti."[57] But it seems that not even Nityānanda had the strength to hold the Navadvip devotees together. In fact, if we can judge from the remarks of the jealous Brahman who reported back to Caitanya in Puri, his social attitudes split them even further apart.

After Caitanya's death, the situation became worse. It seems that the splinters polarized themselves around Caitanya's two primary followers, Nityānanda and Advaita Ācārya. There was little love between these two men, and at least part of the reason seems to have been the matter of caste. Their words together as reported in various texts seem

[56] *CC Madhya* 13:25 ff.; *Ādi* 10:126.
[57] *CBh Antya* 5:222 f.

a little strong, although the biographers are, naturally enough, concerned to pass them off as joking. For example, in several places Advaita calls Nityānanda a "fallen Avadhūta" (*bhraṣṭa avadhūta*), which does not sound very much like a jest. For example: " 'You are a fallen Avadhūta, filling your belly. You have taken *saṃnyāsa* in order to punish Brahmans . . .' Nityānanda, . . . took a mouthful of rice in his hand and threw it down in front of him, as if in a rage."[58] It is also clear that Advaita, the scion of an eminent Brahman family of Śāntipur, was concerned about his status or his fate as a Brahman who did not follow the rules: "Advaita and Nityānanda were sitting together in a certain place, and they began a mock quarrel. Advaita said, '[Here I am], at table in the company of an Avadhūta. If I eat with you, who knows what my fate will be?' "[59]

Judging from his name, Advaita had been a teacher of the *advaita* or non-dualistic system of philosophy before his devotion to Caitanya, and there is an interesting though possibly apocryphal story in the *Prema-vilāsa* of Nityānanda-dāsa that after Caitanya had gone to live in Puri, people came to him with the news that Advaita had defected and returned to the monistic philosophy: "Some say that Advaita Gosvāmi has abandoned the way of bhakti, and that he has taken *mukti* [liberation, the goal of the monistic systems] as his primary object."[60] And we are told that among Advaita's followers there were people who did not honor Cai-

[58] *CC Madhya* 3:82–84. It is quite obvious that Nityānanda was to say the least a controversial figure. See also *CBh Antya* 5:5 f., 6:137, and *BRK* 12:1740 f.

[59] *CC Madhya* 12:185–86.

[60] *Prema-vilāsa,* p. 2.

tanya at all, perhaps suggesting that they gave Advaita primacy over him.[61]

This division of the Bengal branch of the school remains to the present day, since beginning with Advaita and Nityānanda, its double leadership became hereditary. And it is not particularly surprising that in Bengal the house of Advaita heads the division which is considered orthodox:

The leading Gosvāmi families are descendants of the two leaders of the sect, Caitanya's right-hand men, Nityānanda and Advaita. . . . The descendants of Nityānanda have maintained the primacy in the sect gained by him down to the present day. Three distinct lines claim descent from Nityānanda: those living at Kardaha . . . the place where Nityānanda and his famous son resided, . . . those of Soishipur in Maldah district; and those of Lata, in Burdwan. . . . The Nityānanda and Advaita Gosvāmins are looked upon with more reverence than is accorded any other Gosvāmi family. . . . The descendants of Advaita have always been held as next in importance among the gurus of the sect. . . . Śantipur, in Nadia district, where Advaita lived, is still their center.

Kennedy goes on:

True to the characteristics that distinguished the two leaders, their descendants have continued to exhibit sharp differences. The Śāntipur Gosvāmins are more conservative and orthodox from the view-point of Hindu society.[62]

Fairly obviously, within the Bengal branch of the school it is the line and tradition established by Nityānanda that is the more significant for our present inquiry. In regard to

[61] *CC Ādi* 12:65–67.
[62] Melville Kennedy, *CM*, pp. 150–51.

attitudes toward caste, one cannot draw the primary line between the Vṛndāvana and Bengal groups, as might be expected; it must be drawn between the Nityānanda and Advaita factions of the Bengal group itself. Thus, at least in this regard, the Nityānanda faction of Bengal and the Gosvāmins of Vṛndāvana are both on the Tāntric side of the line, and the Advaita Ācārya tradition of Bengal on the orthodox.

If attitude toward caste or caste status is an index of affiliation to the Sahajiyā belief, we might expect to find a large number of non-Brahmans among Nityānanda's followers. Unfortunately, the lists given in the *Vivarta-vilāsa, Caitanya-caritāmṛta,* and *Bhaktiratnākara* give specific information about only one: a certain Raghunātha is called a Vaidya. In several other cases surnames are given that are non-Brahman (e.g., Sen, Datta, Gupta, Basu), but more than that we cannot tell. The whole difficulty, of course, is that religious names were usually taken, usually names with the suffix *-dāsa,* "servant," upon initiation into Vaiṣṇavism, which give no indication of family or origin.

But, for a change, we need not be so roundabout. There is considerable evidence of the Sahajiyā leanings of many of Nityānanda's followers. A list of those followers is given in the *Vivarta-vilāsa.* It might be argued that since the *Vivarta-vilāsa* is an avowedly Sahajiyā text, it selects Sahajiyā followers of Nityānanda for mention while omitting others. But the list is substantially the same as that given in the *Bhaktiratnākara* (10:372 ff.) and that of the *Caitanya-caritāmṛta* (*Ādi* 11), neither of which can realistically be called Sahajiyā in doctrine. The followers of Nityānanda who can be at all identified are:

Vīrabhadra: Nityānanda's son, who did not have much to do with the development of the Vaiṣṇava-sahajiyā school.

Rāmadāsa: There were many Rāmadāsas; this one is perhaps "Tilakarāmadāsa," whom Sukumār Sen calls "a follower of Nityānanda." Only one short work, the *Vaiṣṇava-kathā*, has come down with this signature. There is also a possibility that this is Balarāma-dāsa, a "pupil of Jāhnavā," who might have been the author of a large number of Sahajiyā works, including *Gurubhaktikalpa-candrikā, Gurusāra-tattva-kathā,* and *Vaiṣṇava-vidhāna.*[63]

Gaṅgādhara-dāsa: Probably the author of the Śākta poem to Caṇḍī called *Kirīṭī-maṅgala.*[64]

Purandara: Probably the author of a late work called *Śrīcaitanya-carita.*[65]

Kṛṣṇadāsa: There were a great many Kṛṣṇadāsas, many of them Sahajiyās.[66]

Caitanya-dāsa: Quite possibly the author of the Sahajiyā work *Rasabhakti-candrikā* (or *Āśraya-nirṇaya*), to which we shall have frequent occasion to refer.[67]

Jīva Paṇḍit: Possibly the writer who signs himself "Jīva Gosvāmī" in such Sahajiyā works as *Campaka-kalikā* and *Sadhyabhāvāmṛta.*[68]

Paramānanda Gupta: A famous and easily identifiable

[63] See Sukumār Sen, *BSI*, pp. 421, and *Balarāmadāser padāvalī, bhūmikā,* p. 17.

[64] *BSI*, p. 705.

[65] *Ibid.*, p. 649.

[66] *Ibid.*, p. 417.

[67] The text is given in Dineścandra Sen, *VSP*, II; see also *BSI*, p. 642.

[68] *BSI*, pp. 206–7, 293–94.

man, and the writer of many padas. There is, however, no indication that his work was of a Sahajiyā nature.[69]

Manohara: Many Sahajiyā texts have come down with the signature "Manohara-dāsa," such as the *Āśrayakalpalatikā* and *Bhaktirasojjvala-cūḍāmaṇi*.[70] He should not be confused, however, with the author of the standard *Anurāgavalli*, which was written in Vṛndāvana in A.D. 1753; the VV itself was probably written before that time.

Puruṣottama: Again easily identifiable, but there is no indication that his leanings were Sahajiyā.[71]

Yadunātha: Probably Yadunandana-dāsa, the author of a large number of Vaiṣṇava and Vaiṣṇava-sahajiyā works, including the *Karṇānanda;* he was a follower of Śrīnivāsa Ācārya, who was a pupil of Jīva Gosvāmin.

Kānu-ṭhākura: Possibly the son of Puruṣottama, but equally possibly the son of Raghunandana of Śrīkhaṇḍa, who had a close connection with the Sahajiyā school of that place.

Mukunda: A great many writers, including several Sahajiyās, used this name.

Rāmānanda Basu: A pada-writer, some of whose songs have been confused with those of the Sahajiyā Jñāna-dāsa, a pupil of the Sahajiyā guru Jāhnavā-devī, the younger wife of Nityānanda.

Mukundarāma: Very likely the resident of Śrīkhaṇḍa and the author of a number of Sahajiyā texts such as the *Amṛtaratnāvalī, Ānanda-laharī, Rasasamudra,* and *Rāgaratnāvalī*

69 *Ibid.*, p. 421.
70 *Ibid.*, pp. 412–16.
71 *Ibid.*, p. 303.

(which occur with the signatures "Mukunda-dāsa," "Mukunda-deva," and "Mukunda-rāma-dāsa"). He is possibly the Mukunda who is referred to in the VV as a pupil of Kṛṣṇadāsa the author of the CC, although Sen feels otherwise.[72]

Jñana-dāsa: A great pada-writer, a Brahman, and the author of a number of Sahajiyā texts, including the *Āgama* and *Bhāgavatatattvalīlā.*[73] He also lived at Śrīkhaṇḍa.

Avadhūta Paramānanda: His name speaks for itself.

Sulocana: Almost without question Locana-dāsa, a pupil of Narahari Sarkār at Śrīkhaṇḍa, the author of the *Caitanya-maṅgala,* large numbers of Vaiṣṇava and Sahajiyā padas, and of the middle-ground Vaiṣṇava-sahajiyā work *Durlabhasāra.*[74]

Govinda: Again, a very common name; but there are many Sahajiyā works signed "Govinda" or "Govinda-dāsa," including the *Nigama-grantha, Rasatattva-sāra,* and *Rasa-bhakti-candrikā.*[75]

Vṛndāvana: Without doubt Vṛndāvana-dāsa, the author of the *Caitanya-bhāgavata* and the most famous of Nityānanda's followers. He has many Sahajiyā padas attributed to him.[76]

[72] *Ibid.,* p. 419.
[73] *Ibid.,* p. 421.
[74] *Ibid.,* p. 248 f.
[75] *Ibid.,* p. 421.
[76] *Ibid.,* p. 419. Among the names in the list (all of which are not given here) can be found many of the men known in the literature of the sect as the *dvādaśa gopāla,* the "twelve apostles," the missionaries who carried the movement into all corners of Bengal. The *dvadaśa gopāla* are mentioned in many of the texts. In Kavikarṇapūra's *Gauragaṇoddeśa-dīpikā* (Murshidabad edition, pp. 127–37) they are listed in the following way: Abhirāma (or Rāmadāsa Abhirāma), Uddhāraṇa Datta, Kamalākara Piplāi, Kālakṛṣṇa-dāsa, Gaurīdāsa-Paṇḍita, Parameśvarī-dasa, Dhanañjaya-paṇḍita, Puruṣottama Datta (or Nāgara-puruṣottama), Puruṣottama-dāsa,

Although such tentative identifications can be given only twenty of the total of sixty-seven in the VV list, this is a large enough number either probably or certainly connected with the Vaiṣṇava-sahajiyā school to bolster the suggestion that the strength of the Vaiṣṇava-sahajiyā lies within Nityānanda's tradition.

It will have been noticed that several of the names above can be connected with the town of Śrīkhaṇḍa in western West Bengal. The town was unquestionably one of the major centers of Vaiṣṇava-sahajiyā activity, as well as a literary center and the home of a number of people who were prominent in the court at the Muslim capital at Gaur.[77] Sukumār Sen, in his *Bāṅgālā sāhityer itihāsa,* tells us this about the history of the place:

> In the beginning of the 16th century, with the blessings of Caitanya and Nityānanda, Mukunda-dāsa, Narahari, and Raghunandana made Śrīkhaṇḍa a center of Gauḍiya-vaiṣṇava [i.e., Vaiṣṇavism of the Bengal school] activity. From the first, the ideas of the school of Śrīkhaṇḍa were independent. . . . Narahari-dāsa, the younger brother of the court physician Mukunda-dāsa, established images of Caitanya and Nityānanda at Śrīkhaṇḍa, and . . . initiated Gaurāṅga-pūjā [i.e., worship of Caitanya]. At one time, the area around Śrīkhaṇḍa had been a center of Śākta Tāntrism. . . . I do not think that there were elements of it in the worship of Narahari and Raghunandana, but some elements of it can be found in that of their followers. Many of the books and padas of the Śrīkhaṇḍa school are of Vaiṣṇava-sahajiyā character.[78]

Maheśa-paṇḍita, Śrīdhara, and Sundarānanda-ṭhākura. In other sources a thirteenth—Halāyudha-ṭhākura—is added. See *Gauḍiya-vaiṣṇava-abhidhāna,* I.

[77] See Nalinikānta Bhaṭṭaśāli, "Gopāladāser rasakalpāvalī," in *SPP,* XXXVIII (B.S. 1338 [A.D. 1953]), No. 3, pp. 151 ff.

[78] *BSI,* p. 289. See also "Śrīkhaṇḍa sampradāya o caṇḍīdāsa," pp. 110 ff.

The other main center of the Vaiṣṇava-sahajiyā was at Kuliyā near Navadvip, and was begun by Vaṁśi-vadana and his father Chakari-caṭṭa, who was such an intimate friend of Caitanya that it was to him that Caitanya entrusted the care of his mother Śacī and his wife Viṣṇupriyā when he became a *saṃnyāsī*.[79] About this school Sen writes:

Vaṃśi-vadana's father Chakari-caṭṭa was one of the several initiators of the *rasa-rāja* [i.e., Vaiṣṇava-sahajiyā] *sādhana*, another of them being Narahari Sarkār of Śrīkhaṇḍa . . . and Vaṃśi-vadana disseminated this type of *sādhana*. . . . At almost the same time, Narahari at Śrīkhaṇḍa and Chakari and Vaṁśi-vadana at Kuliyā began the Vaiṣṇava-Tāntric *sādhana* and writing padas dealing with this *sādhana*. These writings became current through their pupils.[80]

A primary spokesman for the Kuliyā school was Prema-dāsa, who lived in the late seventeenth and early eighteenth centuries and wrote various works dealing with the Vaiṣṇava-sahajiyā thought and ritual, including the *Vaṁsi-śikṣā*[81] and the *Caitanya-candrodaya-kaumudī*.[82] Not the least interesting part of these texts is their reverential acknowledgment of Nityānanda's wife Jāhnavā-devī (or Jāhnavī-devī).

2. WOMEN IN THE VAIṢṆAVA-SAHAJIYĀ MOVEMENT

WE HAVE ALREADY NOTICED that late in life Nityānanda abandoned his asceticism and married the two daughters of the Brahman *paṇḍit* Sūrya-dāsa. By Vasudhā he had one

79 *BRK* 4:24.
80 *BSI*, pp. 645–56.
81 *Ibid.*, p. 645.
82 Calcutta University MS 2145.

son, Vīracandra or Vīrabhadra, and, except for the legend that it was he who initiated the Buddhist monks and nuns into the Vaiṣṇava fold, there is no indication that he was anything but orthodox. It is Nityānanda's other wife, Jāhnavā-devī, and her adopted son Rāmacandra who are of more immediate interest to us here.

As the story is told in the *Nityānanda-vaṁśāvalī*, the natural father of Rāmacandra was Caitanya-dāsa. Caitanya-dāsa was childless and prayed to Jāhnavā that his wife bear him sons. Jāhnavā told him that he would have two sons if he promised to give the first-born to her: "When your two sons have become grown, you will present the elder to me." The two sons were duly born, the elder being named Rāmāi (Rāmacandra) and the younger Śacīnandana. When the time came, Caitanya-dāsa "took Rāmāi-ṭhākura and presented him to Jāhnavā. Jāhnavā said, 'Come, Rāmāi, . . . let us go to our own home.' "[83] In his notes to the *Padakalpataru*, Satīścandra Rāy gives us the added information that Rāmacandra was the grandson of Vaṃśī-vadana, that he was born in 1533 and died in his fiftieth year.[84]

There is every indication that Rāmacandra was a Sahajiyā. Among his writings are the Sahajiyā texts *Kaḍacā, Ānanda-mañjarī-sampuṭikā*, and the middle-ground *Pāṣaṇḍa-dalana*. He was the grandson of Vaṃśi-vadana, the founder of the Sahajiyā school of Kuliyā. Among his pupils were various

[83] The story is told in *Nityānanda-vaṃśāvalī*, p. 149, which quotes the *Muralī-vilāsa*. See also Sen, in the introduction to *Balarāmadāser padāvalī*, p. 17. It is perhaps relevant that in the *Prema-vilāsa* we are told that Caitanya predicted the birth of Śrīnivāsa to his father, whose name was also Caitanya-dāsa (pp. 9–10 of that text).

[84] *Padakalpataru* (BSP edition), V, 202.

Sahajiyās, including Ākiñcana-dāsa, the author of the *Vivarta-vilāsa,* and one "Śrībaḍu-ṭhākura," whom Sen considers to have been the author of many of the Sahajiyā poems that occur with the signature "Caṇḍīdāsa."[85]

It is said that Rāmacandra persuaded his foster mother to the Sahajiyā position.[86] However she arrived at it, it is certain that at some point she did adopt such a position. In fact, she succeeded her husband as the leader of a considerable Sahajiyā group; the list of Jāhnavā's followers given in *Bhaktiratnākara* 10:372 ff. shows many of the same names given in the lists of Nityānanda's, including known Sahajiyās. It is significant that it was to a woman that the leadership fell.

The permission that a woman become guru is, as far as I know, peculiar to the Tāntric tradition. To quote Woodroffe:

Though according to Vaidik usage, the wife was cooperator (Sahadharminī) in the household rites, now-a-days, so far as I can gather, they are not accounted much in such matters, though it is said that a wife may, with the consent of her husband, take vows, perform Homa, Vrata, and the like. According to the Tantra Shāstra, a woman may not only receive Mantra, but may, as Guru, initiate and give it (see Rudraya-mālā II.ii, and XV). She is worshipped both as wife of Guru and as Guru herself (see ib. I.i. also Mātrika-bheda Tantra [c.vii] Annadakalpa cited in Prāṇatoshini p. 68, and as regards the former, Yoginī Tantra cap. i, *guru patnī maheshani gurur eva.*) The Devī is Herself the Guru of all Shāstras and women, as indeed all females. Her embodiments, are in a peculiar sense Her representatives. For this

[85] *BSI,* p. 646.
[86] *Balarāmadāser padāvalī, bhūmikā,* p. 17.

reason all women are worshipful, and no harm should ever be done to them, nor should any female animal be sacrificed.[87]

In Vaiṣṇava-sahajiyā thought, women of course embody Rādhā, and as such are the means to realization. But because of the primacy of Rādhā in the thought of Bengal and probably also because of the Tāntric tradition, women were highly esteemed among orthodox Vaiṣṇavas as well.

There is ample evidence of this. While they find no place in theology, Śacī and Viṣṇupriyā, the mother and wife of Caitanya, were highly honored and respected. When the great Vaiṣṇava apostle Śrīnivāsa went to see Viṣṇupriya in Navadvip after Caitanya's death, she "in kindness and motherly affection, spoke sweet words to him, and placed her blessed feet upon his head."[88] This is perhaps to be expected, by virtue of her relationship to the Master, and there is no indication that Viṣṇupriyā became a guru or played a particularly active role in the movement either before or after her husband's death. The situation was quite different with certain other ladies, although in most of the following cases it is difficult if not impossible to tell whether we are dealing with the orthodox or the Sahajiyā school: the texts that tell the stories are clearly neither one nor the other.

There are many stories of the part that women played.[89] Among the most interesting is that of two girls named Kṛṣṇapriyā and Visṇupriyā, daughters of Gaṅgā-nārāyaṇa who lived in Vṛndāvana. It was to their care that the Govard-

[87] *Shakti and Shākta,* p. 540. See also pages 160–63 of that work, and the article "Bauddha o śaiba ḍākini o yoginīdiger kathā" by Rameś Basu, in *SPP,* B.S. 1333 (A.D. 1927), pp. 37 ff.

[88] *BRK* 4:42 ff.

[89] See *Karṇānanda,* pp. 27–30; *BRK* 9:282–97; *CC Ādi* 10:22 ff.

hana-śilā, the black stone representative of Viṣṇu that had been given by Caitanya himself to Raghunātha-dāsa, was entrusted. The story is in the *Narottama-vilāsa:*

> Śrīkṛṣṇa-caitanya gave the Govardhanaśilā into the care of Raghunātha-dāsa Gosvāmin, who served it. . . . At the death of Dāsa Gosvāmin, Kṛṣṇadāsa Kavirāja became absorbed in it, and when he died, Mukunda served it with tears of prema. Narottama-ṭhākura was the beloved [pupil] of Lokanātha, and his pupil was Gaṅgā-nārāyaṇa Cakravartin. Gaṅgā-nārāyaṇa had two daughters, Viṣṇupriyā . . . and Kṛṣṇapriyā, who was bhakti personified. . . . He entrusted the stone to Kṛṣṇapriyā-ṭhākurāṇi.[90]

This unusual affair, plus the permissiveness with which these girls were treated, raised eyebrows among the more tradition-oriented dwellers in Vṛndāvana. It seems that Kṛṣṇapriyā used to listen to the reading of the *Bhāgavata,* to which a man named Rūpa Kavirāja objected on much the same grounds as Gopāla Bhaṭṭa objected to Narottama's taking Brahman pupils: it was just not done. There was an exchange about it. It is recorded that Rūpa Kavirāja went away angry; it is not said that Kṛṣṇapriyā did not listen to the reading that day:

> One day, when it was time for the beginning of the reading of the *Bhāgavata,* all the Vaiṣṇavas of the place had come . . . and paid respect to Kṛṣṇapriyā-ṭhākurāṇi. . . . She also came there, great joy in her mind. Everyone except Rūpa Kavirāja made obeisance to her, but this did not disturb the peace of her mind, and she sat down to listen to the reading of the sacred story. Then Rūpa Kavirāja asked her how two types of karma could be

[90] *Narottama-vilāsa,* p. 204.

performed at one time [i.e., presumably, how she could be both saint and woman], . . . and asked her how she could listen to the reading of the *Bhāgavata*. Kṛṣṇapriyā replied, "It is the wagging of tongues that makes listening to the reading difficult, not my presence." And when he heard this, Rūpa was furious.[91]

Actually, Rūpa's feeling for tradition, if not his temper, was as we have seen Caitanya's own. In showing such respect to Kṛṣṇapriyā, the Vaiṣṇavas had come a long way from Caitanya's position that even conversation with a woman is deluding and destructive to true devotion. Tāntric views were at work here, as we have seen Tāntrism affecting the thinking of the Vṛndāvana-dwelling Gosvāmins in other ways. But it is equally likely that the change in attitude among the orthodox was a reflex of the increasingly exalted position of Rādhā in all forms of Bengali Vaiṣṇava thought.

It is considerably easier to see why women were important to the Sahajiyās; they were the embodiments of a theological principle as well as a ritual necessity. And the fact that women can be gurus is a direct legacy from the Tantras. Woodroffe said that the Devī is guru and that all women in some way participate in the qualities of the Devī. The Vaiṣṇava-sahajiyās also state this forthrightly. The *dīkṣā-guru*, the guru who gives the initiatory mantra, is Kṛṣṇa, and the *śikṣā-guru*, the guru who conducts the worshipper in his search for realization, is Rādhā.[92] All women participate in the qualities of Rādhā, therefore all women are in some sense gurus. In a pada attributed to Caṇḍīdāsa, the writer speaks to Rāmī, the washerwoman who is reputed by tradi-

[91] *Ibid.*, pp. 205–6.
[92] VV, p. 41. We shall return to this in our discussions of doctrine.

tion to have been the ritual partner of Caṇḍīdāsa: "The washerwoman of that country is the queen of the blissful state; in her heart is the true form of Rādhā. You, O Rāmī, are my guru in *sādhana*, you are the wishing-tree of bliss, and I am your slave."[93]

Thus women are gurus by their nature. They can also be gurus in the more usual sense of teachers. Jāhnavā-devī, as we have seen, was the leader of a sizable group and was paid great respect in Vṛndāvana as the wife of Nityānanda and in Bengal as both the wife of Nityānanda and his spiritual successor.[94] Not the least of her followers were Vṛndāvana-dāsa and Nityānanda-dāsa, the author of the *Prema-vilāsa*, which he wrote at her request.[95] Hemalatā-devī, a daughter of Śrīnivāsa, was the *dīkṣā-guru* of Yadunandana-dāsa, the author of the *Karṇānanda*, which he wrote at her request: "That hearing it, Śrīmatī's [i.e., Hemalatā's] heart might be filled with joy, I wrote the *Karṇānanda*. At the command of Śrīmatī, in great joy I wrote the book."[96] And Gurucaraṇa-dāsa wrote his *Premāmṛta* at the order of Śrīnivāsa's second wife Gaurāṅgapriyā, who was his guru.[97]

[93] *Caṇḍīdāsa-padāvalī* (p. 152 of the Basumati edition).

[94] The *Narottama-vilāsa* (p. 130) describes one of Jāhnavā's visits to Vṛndāvana: "Gopāla Bhaṭṭa, Bhūgarbha, Lokanātha, Jīva, Kṛṣṇa-paṇḍit, and the rest. . . . When they saw Jāhnavī, were [filled with such joy as] I cannot describe. All the Gosvāmins, at the sight of her, were greatly moved, and could not control their tears. Falling to the earth, they made obeisance to her feet."

[95] P. 22 of the Murshidabad edition. Nityānanda-dāsa was also a dweller at Śrīkhaṇḍa (*BSI*, p. 409).

[96] *Karṇānanda*, p. 122 of the Murshidabad edition.

[97] *BSI*, p. 409.

4) The Ideal Man in Society

S. B. DASGUPTA speaks of the "bitter attacks" of the Tāntrics on "the commonly accepted practices and religious views of the orthodox systems."[1] The Sahajiyās, at least, seem to have been relatively quiet about it. Society being what it is, few Sahajiyās seem to have gone about advertising their manner of worship, which was somewhat unconventional. Women were essential to its progress—and not merely women, but, some indications are, women of the lowest possible castes. The *caryā-padas* speak of Ḍom women in this connection,[2] and we have already noted that according to tradition Caṇḍīdāsa's partner was a washer-

[1] *ORC*, p. 78.

[2] For example, *caryā* no. 10 of Kānhu opens: "Outside the city, O Ḍomnī, you go to your hovel, after touching the shaven Brahman." The Ḍom woman represents a curious complex of symbols and beliefs, some of which are suggested by Eliade in *Yoga, Immortality and Freedom*, p. 261 n.

woman. The extremity of this contrariness is intriguing.

Many societies in one way or another allow for deviation. Hoebel, for example, tells us that among the Cheyenne Indians there is a conventionalized kind of "contrariness," according to which the "contrary" man rejects normal social relations to such an extent that everything he does and even says is the reverse of the accepted pattern.[3] The same allowance is made by the Comanches.[4] A noteworthy characteristic, however, of such contraries as these is their extreme recklessness in battle. The institution, therefore, says Hoebel, "may be seen as providing a customary outlet through which extreme cases of anxiety are turned constructively to the social benefit of a warrior nation."[5] It would seem then that in these cases the contrary man is allowed his contrariness because, in the last analysis, it affirms a basic value of the society.

There is something of the same tolerated deviation in the institution of the Saturnalia, or Holi, or Carnival, or New Year's Eve, or whatever it may be called in various times and places—a periodic, ritual overturning of the social order. Such phenomena Mircea Eliade calls the periodic "retrogression of the cosmos into chaos,"[6] the point of which is less the participation of the individual in chaos (although there is certainly some psychological value in a societally countenanced blowing-off of steam) than it is his participation in the re-creation of order after chaos. For the social

[3] S. Adamson Hoebel, *The Cheyennes*, pp. 95 f.

[4] Ralph Linton in Abram Kardiner (ed.), *The Psychological Frontiers of Society*, p. 62.

[5] Hoebel, *loc. cit.*

[6] Mircea Eliade, *The Sacred and the Profane*, pp. 79 ff.

order is re-created pure, and assumedly the individual resumes his place within it a more contented, if not necessarily a better, man. But such a ritual re-creation of the social order is again an affirmation of the essential validity of that order.

It is tempting to feel that the Sahajiyā and Tāntric anti-traditionalism is a mechanism for deviation and protest provided by the society itself and to see in it a protracted Saturnalia. But in fact an unqualified case would be difficult to make for this. The Tāntric tradition did indeed provide a refuge for antinomians of various types, as well as a tradition and set of rituals for those who, because of caste or sex, could not participate satisfyingly in the Brahmanical system. But in thinking about the Sahajiyā and other left-hand Tāntric systems, certain modifying factors must be considered.

First of all, though the aim of the Sahajiyā and in fact that of all of Tāntrism was conscious deviation from the Veda-derived Brahmanism, this deviation was not welcomed by the dominant Brahmanical society as enthusiastically as contrary men or the Saturnalia have been in their settings; Tāntrism does not affirm the basic social order; it rather provides an alternative to it. Secondly, the Sahajiyā was an esoteric school. Its deviation was not always socially visible. In most social ways, it seems that the Vaiṣṇava-sahajiyās were exemplary citizens, rarely given, like the Pāśupatas and other Indian deviants, to demonstrating their convictions of the meaninglessness of the world by public exhibitions of obscenity and sloth.[7] Whatever demonstrations the Sahajiyās

[7] See Daniel H. H. Ingalls, "Cynics and Pāśupatas: The Seeking of Dishonor," *Harvard Theological Review,* LV (1962), No. 4.

might have made were largely private. Thirdly, the number of the Sahajiyās was rather strictly limited. The transmission of the secret doctrines from guru to disciple effectively stemmed whatever tendency there may have been for crowds of people whose desire was merely for release from sexual or other tensions to demand admission to the mysteries. It has often been suggested that it is a characteristic of a society with rigid sexual mores—the Cheyenne, for example—to provide controlled means of indulgence, for the release of what George Orwell calls "the unofficial self," whose tastes "lie toward safety, soft beds, pots of beer, and women with 'voluptuous' figures."[8] A few people whose major concern was with pots of beer and voluptuous women may have got by the Sahajiyā screening processes. But one's lusts would have had to be very strong indeed, and one's frustrations very great, to carry him through the stringent and arduous, though interesting, training necessary before sexual ritual was undertaken. And though from one point of view a society with rigid sexual mores, Indians have always had sufficiently ambivalent values to allow satisfaction for those whose fancies lay in voluptuous directions, without the necessity of any pretense of religion.

There are innumerable social and psychological reasons why a man may act in a manner contrary to the accepted norm, and innumerable reasons apart from those above why his society may, if not giving its blessing to such adverse behavior, at least tolerate it. Some people, like those called

[8] See Orwell's essay, "The Art of Donald McGill"; the notion is taken up by Tillyard in *Shakespeare's History Plays*, where it is applied to Falstaff and Prince Hal.

Kālāmukhas, seem to feel that power, magical power, is gained by the flouting of moral and social law, and as a result bathe in the ashes of burned corpses, eat from human skulls, and drink wine.[9] Others, such as the Kāpālikas, "attain to emancipation through the meditation on a supreme being residing in the female organ. [The Kāpālika] is adorned with garlands of human bones, takes his food from a skull, drinks wine from the skull of a Brahmin, worships Mahābhairava with human sacrifice, and offers oblations of human flesh to the fire."[10] And others, less dramatically, go naked or make gestures of fornication or insult women, and in various other ways behave like madmen.[11] Indian society has always tolerated such expressions as outward manifestation of personal release from the world and from the laws of society. Within its own system, even Brahmanical society allowed for such behavior: a *saṃnyāsin*, by shaving his head and taking the staff and begging bowl, shucks off caste and family and proclaims the fact that society no longer has any hold over him. It is possible too to imagine that in such a highly structured society as that of India a deviant individual performs the role of scapegoat, taking the frustrations of an admiring society upon himself and relieving them vicariously. The social deviant is a drunken Indra, or a Śiva, who drinks the poison that is about to flood the world.[12]

[9] C. H. Chakravarti, *The Tantras: Studies on their Religion and Literature,* p. 50.

[10] *Ibid.*, p. 52. See also Jitendranāth Banyopādhyāya, *Pañcopāsanā,* pp. 160–62.

[11] Ingalls, "Cynics and Pāśupatas."

[12] Mrs. Wendy O'Flaherty of Harvard pointed this out in a paper called "The Immoral Immortals," presented at a seminar at the American Institute of Indian Studies in Calcutta in 1963.

The Sahajiyās seem to have been little prone to flaunt their convictions openly. But the convictions are there. To the Sahajiyās, society and the whole seeming order of the universe are based on māyā, on falseness. Thus social values have no real meaning, and the actions of a Sahajiyā cannot be judged in terms of such values. The way of truth is entirely different from the accepted way of society; the two ways may occasionally overlap, or they may not.

The crucial point in considering the social attitudes of the Sahajiyās is the doctrine of "equality" or "sameness." To the boy Caitanya, sweets and dirt were the same. So, to a Sahajiyā, a Brahman and an untouchable are the same. So are men and women. So are "pure" and "impure" things to eat and drink. It is a translation into practice of the old Tāntric (and Jungian) belief in the conjunction of opposites: the apparent duality of things must be destroyed before there can be reversion to the true and ultimate unity, the undisturbed and blissful state of sahaja. The state of unity is emulated in the union of male and female, of Brahman and Ḍom, of high and low; in flesh and fish and wine is recognition of the fact that there is neither pure nor impure, that mud and sweets are the same—as indeed are the blessings and curses of mankind.

The question that arises is one of the tension between the necessity of the Sahajiyā to live according to his Sahajiyā belief and deny the world as untrue and that of his continuing to live within society. For while man is the microcosm, himself divinity, and thus the sole repository of truth and standard of proper conduct, he evidently still feels some necessity for interacting with the other microcosms around.

As opposed to the Kāpālikas and others, the standard of this interaction is unexpectedly exemplary. At least, it is as exemplary as that of the orthodox Vaiṣṇavas.

There are two ways of explaining this. The first is that the Sahajiyā is an esoteric cult that needs esoterism to live; it is a flower that blooms only in the darkness and is destroyed by exposure to the light of day. What is unseen is unexposed, and to take on the protective coloring of orthodox Vaiṣṇavism is at least to allow the Sahajiyā to remain unseen.

The second explanation is that in the social, rather than the religious, situation the Vaiṣṇava half of the Vaiṣṇava-sahajiyā personality exerts itself. The Vaiṣṇava self, it might be said, is the official self; this self—excepting certain manifestations of religious conviction, such as the ecstatic expression of devotion, which are looked on by the rest of society as somewhat strange—is a social being. The unofficial self is then the Sahajiyā self, which, while not the same as Orwell's libertine, is not only its own moral arbiter but which because of its elect nature goes against all normal standards. The personality of the Vaiṣṇava-sahajiyā, it would seem, was somewhat schizophrenic. As a Vaiṣṇava, his actions in social situations usually coincided with the standards of the society, though when he was behaving in a socially acceptable way, it was because the ideals of the society and the ideals of his religious belief happened to come together at that point. As a pure Sahajiyā, believing that the ideals of society could never be true, the foundations of society being themselves false, he would have been compelled to act not asocially, but antisocially. The Sahajiyās accepted the poetic imagery of the orthodox Vaiṣṇavas, reserving the right to interpret it differently; therefore, only one familiar with differences in doctrine could identify most poems as either Vaiṣṇava or Sahajiyā. In the same way, the Sahajiyās behaved much like other Vaiṣṇavas who have attained their goal. The goals of the two were different, but the expression of their attainment was the same. How then did the orthodox Vaiṣṇava behave?

THE VIEWS OF ORTHODOX VAIṢṆAVISM. The literature of the orthodox Vaiṣṇavas devotes a fair amount of space to the consideration of what constitutes an ideal man, a true bhakta. The true bhakta is a man of very considerable mettle. He has, for example, no desire for material things or for the gratification of himself. His sole object in life is the worship and service of Kṛṣṇa. He is as indifferent to pleasure and to pain as were the Gopīs, to whom "their own pleasure and pain was not a concern; the happiness of Kṛṣṇa was the sole root of all their desires."[13] He has, in fact, complete indifference. All things are the same to him, as is shown by the story that one day Caitanya's mother brought him some sweets, and said to him:

> "Eat this," and went about her house-work. But the boy hid himself, and began instead to eat a lump of dirt. When Śacī saw this, she came running, and snatching away the dirt, she said, "Why are you eating this?" The child began to weep, and said, "Why are you angry? You gave me dirt to eat; how am I at fault? Sweets are only dirt in changed form. This is earth, that is earth; what is the difference between them?"[14]

[13] *CC Ādi* 4:149.
[14] *Ibid.*, 14:21 ff.

The true bhakta is as humble and unassuming as a blade of grass; he is patient and forbearing and never reproaches or censures anyone for any cause: "[The bhakta] will be humble as grass; he will take the name of Hari incessantly; he will be modest, and will honor others. He will be patient as a tree; though he be beaten and cursed, he will say nothing, as a tree says nothing even when it is cut. A tree does not beg for water, even when it dries and shrivels in the heat of the sun."[15] The true bhakta is merciful and harms no one; he is truthful; he sees all things as equal, pleasure and pain, sweets and dirt; he is pure;[16] he is charitable, gentle, holy, lowly, and humble, friend and benefactor to all, calm; he has Kṛṣṇa as his only refuge; he is free from desire, moderate in taking food and in all things; he honors all things other than himself; he is humble, grave, compassionate, friendly, poetic,[17] skilful, and silent.[18]

It will be generally agreed that these are excellent ideals. But to the analyst, however admiring, their very excellence raises problems. These virtues are social as well as personal. But the Vaiṣṇavas were not always accepted by the society

[15] *Ibid.*, 17:23 ff.

[16] The term used is *nirdoṣa*, "free from fault." The commentary says: "The *doṣas* [faults] can be of various kinds; among them, eighteen are most serious: delusion or folly, sloth, error, coarse passion or passion without benefit of prema, passion which brings pain to others, inconstancy, drunkenness, envy or spite, injury to others, sexual passion [or lassitude: *kheda*], laziness, untruth, anger, bearing a grudge, fear, association with non-Vaiṣṇavas, inequality [i.e., preference of pleasure to pain, etc.], and reliance on others." The commentator Rādhāgovinda Nāth gives no indication of the source of his list.

[17] The term *kavi* means much more in the Indian context than the term "poet" does to us; *kavi* is, to use Krishna Kripalani's word (*Tagore*, p. 2), a "seer," incarnate wisdom.

[18] The list is from *CC Madhya* 22:45 ff.

in which they lived, and they did not always accept it. Vaiṣṇavism itself was slightly socially deviant.

We are told by early Vaiṣṇava writers (though perhaps with pious exaggeration) that sixteenth- and seventeenth-century Bengal was rife with the fairly fundamental blood rites of Śāktism: "The whole world was devoid of Kṛṣṇa-Rāma bhakti . . . the people sang the praises of Caṇḍī far into the night, and made offerings in pūjā to Vāsulī; with wine and flesh they worshipped the Yakṣas. In the uproar . . . no one heard the name of Kṛṣṇa."[19] And in the area of Ketori-grām, the *Narottama-vilāsa* tells us, that "the people of the country are practiced in godless deeds, knowing nothing of true dharma and *karma*, and doing indescribably evil things. At the doors of their houses is the blood of goats and sheep and buffaloes. Some say that they use the severed heads of men. . . . Lascivious women stay with them, and they use flesh and wine in their worship."[20]

The Vaiṣṇavas, to judge from the tone of their texts, had little appreciation of such practices; and the people who practiced these rituals returned the feeling in kind. One day, when *kīrtana*, the Vaiṣṇava worship with the singing of the praises of Kṛṣṇa, was going on in the house of Caitanya's neighbor Śrīvāsa, the unbelievers "gathered outside the house, fuming and burning with rage, and talked about how they might bring sorrow to Śrīvāsa. One day a Brahman named Gopālacapala, the chief among these evil people and a foul-mouthed man, brought all the paraphernalia for the

[19] *CBh Ādi* II: 86 ff. Vāsulī is a local (Bīrbhūm) name for Caṇḍī; the *yakṣas* are demigods.
[20] *Narottama-vilāsa*, p. 89.

worship of [the goddess] Bhavānī, and in the night scattered them and smeared them on the door of the house of Śrīvāsa."[21] The "paraphernalia" included a pot of wine, which was most offensive to a gentle Vaiṣṇava. Nor were the Śāktas the only ones who felt offended by the Vaiṣṇavas. We are told that Haridāsa, a convert from Islam and a Sufi epitome of Vaiṣṇava humility and strength, was betrayed to the Muslim rulers by jealous Brāhmans and whipped because of his apostasy through twenty-two market places, a brutal punishment through which he lived only because of his deep faith.[22] And various other Brahmans tried their best to destroy Caitanya's movement by going to the Muslim rulers and telling them that Caitanya was a drunkard, a trouble-making saboteur of real Hinduism, and in general a man whom both Muslims and Hindus could very well get along without.[23]

The reasons for such antagonism are several. First, Haridāsa was persecuted by the Brahmans because of his exceptional piety and by the Muslims because he had left Islam. Indeed, the magnetism of Caitanya and the warm, internalized religion that he taught, most congenial to Islamic Sufis, may have been responsible for extensive "conversion" and for equally extensive antagonism.[24] Secondly, the Vaiṣ-

[21] *CC Ādi* 17:32 ff. Bhavānī is also a name for the goddess. Śrīvāsa was the elderly neighbor of Caitanya in whose courtyard many of the Vaiṣṇavas' *kīrtan* parties took place.

[22] The story is movingly told in *CC Antya* 3:94 ff.

[23] *CC Ādi* 17:203–11, *CBh Madhya* 23.

[24] The question of the extent to which the Vaiṣṇavas were persecuted by the Muslims is largely open. There actually seems little reason to believe that Husein Shah himself was violently opposed to them, although his annoyance at having two of his chief officers (Rūpa and Sanātana Gosvāmin) defect to follow Caitanya is understandable. It seems, in fact, that except for a few lapses (e.g., the *Caitanya-maṅgal* of Jayānanda, pp. 10, 11, where it is said that it had been reported to Husein Shah that a

ṇavas did not always interpret the social hierarchy in terms of caste, as did the carriers of the Brahmanical tradition. This would have been enough to have made them disliked by believers in the status quo. For Caitanya, whom we have noticed countenancing the caste structure of society in various situations, saw society somewhat differently in the light of religion. He said, in effect, that the accepted ways of society were not wrong, but merely external and therefore incomplete. The Brahmanical tradition had provided an outlet for asocial activity in its institution of *saṃnyāsa.* But *saṃnyāsa* was an institution, to be undertaken by men as a stage in the well-ordered life structured by Brahmanical tradition. The Vaiṣṇavas, coming upon the scene, claimed that the laws of society do not apply to any man who knows in his heart that he is released; thus all social control was potentially eliminated.[25] It is not hard to imagine that this may have been considered subversive.

To the Vaiṣṇavas, the immediacy of God, felt in bhakti, and not the standards set by men, should be the measure of acceptable behavior. If the bhakta, then, is gentle and humble and forbearing, it is because these are religious virtues that also happen to be social ones. This does not mean that society is wholly wrong. Its values are just not profound enough. If a man is a true bhakta, his actions are inevitably good. When such actions coincide with social values, so

---

Hindu insurrection was in the wind and that he took rather drastic measures to prevent it), Husein Shah was exceptionally tolerant and that what persecution there was was carried out by local officials such as Haridāsa's tormentor Rāmacandra Khān (who was perhaps himself a converted Hindu).

[25] This is the interpretation of Professor Nirmal Kumar Bose, whose suggestions have in many ways been of great value to me.

much the better; and such coincidence is far more frequent among the Vaiṣṇavas than among, for instance, the Kāpālikas.

Sometimes the two sets of values did not coincide, however. There is an instructive story of how Caitanya persuaded Vāsudeva Sārvabhauma, the great scholar, to take *prasāda,* food which had been offered to the deity and thus blessed, without first having washed his hands. Caitanya says: "Today all my desires have been fulfilled, for today Sārvabhauma has put his faith in *mahāprasāda* [i.e., the great or true *prasāda,* the grace of Kṛṣṇa, which has nothing to do with convention or ritual]. Today he is freed form delusion, and has taken refuge in Kṛṣṇa. . . . Today, O Sārvabhauma, you have broken the ties with your body, and have lopped off the bonds of falseness."[26] Things are pure because they are sacred to Kṛṣṇa, not because they are thought to be pure by men. If a Vaiṣṇava acts like a madman, singing and dancing, it is Kṛṣṇa in his heart that makes him act so. "I repeated Kṛṣṇa's name incessantly, and my mind became unhinged. I could not be calm—I became mad, and so I laugh and weep and dance and sing. . . . Once, my mind was calm, but in the name of Kṛṣṇa my rationality has disappeared."[27] It seems that others agreed and looked at the bhaktas a little askance.

Not only were the bhaktas recognized by their unashamed "madness," but they recognized their own differences from the rest of society. True to their conviction of salvation, they

[26] *CC Madhya* 6:209 ff. The commentator defines the term *niṣkapaṭa* ("free from delusion or deceit") as "having abandoned Vedic ritualism."
[27] *CC Ādi* 7:74 f.

did not hesitate to proclaim all those who were not bhaktas fools who indulged themselves in sophistry and idle argument and did not understand the truth.[28] Śiva and the other gods, they said, can be worshipped only as aspects of Kṛṣṇa.[29] "Sin" is denial of Kṛṣṇa as the highest god.[30] In general, despite the gentleness and charity of the Vaiṣṇavas, it is not hard to understand why people were on occasion annoyed by them.

The Vaiṣṇavas say that there are essentially two types of people, those who have the capacity for bhakti and those who are naturally beyond the pale. The former group is twofold: those who by their birth and nature are in a state of worship and devotion, and those who are entangled in the web of material nature—in other words, the vast majority of us. Or, borrowing from Tāntric thought, which divides matter into three types, and from the *Bhagavadgītā*, which classifies men accordingly, they say that people can be, like Caitanya, *sāttvika*—calm, pure, refined, wise, free from passion and desire, and so on—or they can be, like most of the rest of us, *tāmasa* (or, sometimes, *paśu*—"beast")—lustful, bound by pity, delusion, fear, shame, hatred, and so on. The middle men, *rājasa*, are not especially significant for these purposes.[31]

[28] *BRK* 6:57.

[29] *Bhakti-saṃdarbha*, see De, VFM, p. 275.

[30] *CC Ādi* 6:72, *Ādi* 3:47; conversely, "taking Kṛṣṇa's name once wipes away all sin" (*CC Ādi* 8:22).

[31] For such divisions among men, see *Shakti and Shākta*, p. 495. The *Bṛhat-tantrasāra* (1:26–28) gives lists of qualities that a man must possess before he can begin his instruction: he must be calm, humble and modest, pure of soul, reverent, intelligent, skilful, of good birth, learned, and of good character.

The views of the Sahajiyās. The Sahajiyās, of course, adopted these classifications.[32] The *sāttvika* man is one who has attained the goal, the *sahaja-mānuṣa*, one who has realized his own true nature. Some men may be born in such a state of realization, but most of us must reach it by arduous training, purified by discipline. The *Rūpānuga-bhajana-darpaṇa* makes the point by an analogy: a mother's love for her child is natural, a state of grace that can be reached by non-mothers only by training. "The mother's love for her son is natural [sahaja] and constant in her heart; the hearts of corrupted people need training. In the same way, the ever-perfect wonderful prema for Kṛṣṇa is not apparent to the creature bound in delusion; he gains the state of sahaja only by cultivating it. But when that state is brought about, his bonds are loosed, and he dances in the joy of Vraja."[33] The state of sahaja is obtainable by all men except those who are naturally beyond the pale and for whom there is no hope whatever.

Of the two major classes of men, the Sahajiyā texts concern themselves with those who are trying to reach the sahaja and how they act once they get there. Metaphysically, once a man reaches the state of sahaja, he is not subject to rebirth; he remains in the eternal place of Kṛṣṇa, in bliss, to eternity: "He who is subject to rebirth in the Brahma-egg [i.e., the world] is a *sāmānya* [ordinary] man; he comes and goes in life and death. The Sahajiyā man remains forever in the eternal place, within Goloka; in him is mani-

32 *SS* pada 29, attributed to Locana-dāsa, recognizes three categories corresponding to the three in the Tāntric texts. Other texts have only two.

33 Pp. 2–3, quoted in *PCSC*, pp. 228–29.

fested the Lord of Vṛndāvana, absorbed in bliss."[34] This is manifested in worldly life in various ways. As he is in possession of the truth, he can dispense with ritual matters. He needs a guru no longer; meditation and repetition of the mantras alone can give him the complete religious experience: "He needs no guru nor direction; his constant refuge is in the *bīja-mantra*."[35]

The rest of the world, meanwhile, wanders about in error: "All the people of the world wander about in error; they do not know the hidden truths. They do not know the prema of the Sahajiyā man."[36] One who knows the sahaja is "dead in life"; he no longer feels the pull of kāma and the delusive, ensnaring qualities of the world on his material nature. "He is dead while yet alive; he is the best of men. A sign of him is that he experiences the ultimate state [*mahābhāva*]: he has reached the farther shore."[37] His condition is one of complete indifference, in which there is no longer any distinction between the human and the divine in him: "His material self [rūpa] has become divine [*svarūpa*]; there is no difference between them."[38] Like Caitanya, who was born a *sahaja-mānuṣa*, he distributes prema throughout the world: "The *sahaja-mānuṣa* is the highest of the gods, who spreads prema throughout the world. . . . He enjoys the bliss of prema."[39] He is calm and steady and moves directly toward the goal; he is not distracted by the wild activity of the

[34] *SS* pada 22, attributed to Caṇḍīdāsa.
[35] *Ibid.*, 50, attributed to Caṇḍīdāsa.
[36] *Ibid.*, 21, attributed to Caṇḍīdāsa.
[37] *Ibid.* There are several variants of the pada, one of them reading "he is the most fortunate of all men, and different from all others."
[38] *Ibid.*, 26, attributed to Narahari.
[39] *Ibid.*, 27, attributed to Locana-dāsa.

world: "He knows the truth about himself and about what is not himself and about the ultimate pleasure; his mind is firmly fixed upon the motionless sahaja."[40] "He who remains steadfast amidst the dance of māyā is accounted a wise man in all three worlds; he alone who is unshaken is called *śānta,* who is at peace; if he is fearless, the world [māyā] does not devour him."[41]

In a manner of speaking, these are ways in which a Sahajiyā knows himself; they are not necessarily characteristics that make him visible in the world at large. There are some ways in which the texts say a *sahaja-mānuṣa* may be discerned. Like other Vaiṣṇavas, he stands out vividly because he is silent about his accomplishments: "He who keeps saying 'I am a *rasika*' is no true *rasika*"[42] In other ways too, he behaves like other Vaiṣṇavas. He is also pure, morally good, and true.[43] He has conquered the attractions of māyā,[44] he is indifferent to the world: poison and nectar are the same to him.[45] He accounts himself as insignificant:

> Being at peace within himself, he does not attempt to take precedence, nor does he know good or evil. He looks upon other men as great, but accounts himself as nothing. He does not say, in conceit and pride, 'I am a servant of Kṛṣṇa.' He thinks of himself as grass or a tree, which says nothing even when it is cut.[46]

[40] *Nigūḍhārtha-prakāśāvalī* (*SS*, p. 180, n. 1).

[41] VV, p. 79. The first part of the passage is quoted from *CC Madhya* 8:160.

[42] VV, p. 91, quoting a pada of Caṇḍīdāsa.

[43] *Ibid.*, p. 74.

[44] See *Ānanda-bhairava*, p. 147, and Basu's note on the passage.

[45] *Durlabhasāra*, p. 141.

[46] Calcutta University MS 564, pp. 6, 7, and 11, quoted in *PCSC*, p. 215. The last lines are almost verbatim from the *CC* passage quoted previously. Both passages, however, are based on one of the eight *ślokas* that

It would have been difficult for a bystander to tell the difference between an orthodox and a Sahajiyā Vaiṣṇava. And it is difficult for the unpracticed Bengali eye even today: the contemptuous term *boiṣṭom* (Vaiṣṇava) is sometimes used colloquially with reference to a group reputed to have questionable sexual practices. No finer distinctions are made.

It seems that the possibilities of such confusion were recognized by the orthodox Vaiṣṇavas even in Caitanya's time. Caitanya's companion Svarūpa Dāmodara was a wise and perceptive man. Once it happened that Caitanya had taken under his wing a young Brahman boy whose mother was a young and beautiful widow. Svarūpa said to Caitanya:

> You are God, absolute and independent. You can do whatever you will, and no one can contest your actions. But you cannot silence the foul-mouthed people of the world. You are learned, and do not consider such things. But why do you have to do with the son of the Brahman widow? Though she is a Brahman, and pious, and ascetic, she has a fault, and that is that she is young and beautiful. You are young and handsome. You are giving people the opportunity to gossip.[47]

As we have noticed, the possibilities of such misinterpretation push even further the natural Vaiṣṇava tendency toward asceticism.

The distinctions were not always visible, even to some who

---

have come down to us with the name of Caitanya attached. See for example, *CC Antya* 20:55 ff. The eight verses are known as the *Śikṣāṣṭaka* and appear in various places in the Vaiṣṇava literature, for example in Rūpa Gosvāmin's *Padāvalī* (Dacca University ed., nos. 22, 31, 32, 71, 93, 94, 324, and 337, with the signature "Śrī-bhagavat"). For a critical discussion of the *Śikṣāṣṭaka* and the question of their authorship, see S. K. De in the *IHQ*, 1934, pp. 310–17.

[47] *CC Antya* 3:13 ff.

can hardly be classed as idle onlookers, among them the Gosvāmins of Vṛndāvana. For it is recorded in several places that Jāhnavā-devī, herself a Sahajiyā, was welcomed by them with great warmth. Even allowing for pious exaggeration, the *Narottama-vilāsa*, which is not noticeably a Sahajiyā text, waxes rather enthusiastic on the subject: "Gopāla Bhaṭṭa, Bhūgarbha, Lokanātha, Jīva, Kṛṣṇa-paṇḍita, and the rest, when they saw Jāhnavā-īśvarī, were indescribably happy. . . . They were greatly moved, and could not control their tears. Falling to the earth, they made obeisance at the feet of Īśvarī."[48] But then perhaps they did not care whether she was a Sahajiyā or not.

As for the orthodox Vaiṣṇava, standards of morality for the Sahajiyā are not set by society or tradition;[49] they are set entirely within the individual himself.[50] The *sahaja-mānuṣa* is thus not at all concerned with what the world calls right and wrong. He knows neither good nor evil, for "in the sahaja all is undifferentiated. The [*sahaja-mānuṣa*] is not a slave to material things. He knows neither right nor wrong. He opposes nothing, but holds God perpetually in his heart."[51]

All of this being so, there were occasions on which Vaiṣ-

[48] NV, p. 130.

[49] *SS* pada 27, attributed to Locana-dāsa, says that "the dharma of the *sahaja-mānuṣa* is not within the society of men."

[50] *Ānanda-bhairava*, p. 127, says that "he who is free from attachment to the world looks within himself." *Nigūḍhārtha-prakāśāvalī* adds that "his actions must be judged good or evil according to his own standard [*svaicchate*]; he must not be judged . . . according to the standards of others" (p. 28).

[51] *Rasaratnasāra*, p. 6 (*PCSC*, p. 215). In *CC Madhya* 8:159, the Sahajiyā Rāmānanda Rāya voices the thought that the true bhakta "knows nothing of good or evil."

ṇava-sahajiyās, like their orthodox counterparts, ran head-on into the rest of society. The society, not making fine distinctions, considered them all mad. But that "even the wise do not understand the speech and actions" of the *sahaja-mānuṣa*[52] did not trouble the Sahajiyās in the least. The uninitiated see only his outward actions; they do not see his inner calm. "In this way, in emotion, he raves, seemingly mad, like a man who has lost all his earthly wealth. But inwardly he is calm, as he inquires about the five."[53]

All Vaiṣṇavas, then, follow the inner light that seems to lead them along the same paths. But the Sahajiyās are singularly outspoken about the necessity for this. The actions of the ordinary men of the world are based on fear, shame, and ignorance. These are the products of a false view of the world.[54] The *sahaja-mānuṣa* knows better than this. "Neither the Vedas nor the dharma of men hold any meaning for him, for the *sahaja-mānuṣa* has abandoned [the duties of] his birth and [accepted] conduct. . . . He has neither shame nor fear, and is not controlled by these, which are the constant companions of all."[55] Ordinary standards are based on falsity, on untruth, on māyā. The *sahaja-mānuṣa* who knows truth must go against them. This is different from the orthodox view, that the bhakta goes against societal standards when they differ from his own. The Sahajiyā, doctrinally at least, stands against society and all its values: "In the abandonment of the Vedas and the giving up of family is the

[52] *VV*, p. 132.
[53] *Amṛtarasāvalī*, p. 179.
[54] *Ibid.*, pp. 162–63.
[55] *SS* pada 35, attributed to Kṛṣṇadāsa.

birth of prema."[56] It cannot be put much more strongly than this: "The actions of the *sahajiyā-mānuṣa* are strongly contrary."[57]

The pure Sahajiyā, the unofficial self, would then be an entirely antisocial being if the official Vaiṣṇava self did not remain in control. But as a different doctrine did not prevent them from adopting Vaiṣṇava poetic imagery, so a basically different attitude toward society did not prevent the Sahajiyās from adopting, overtly at least, Vaiṣṇava behavior. Sahajiyās reserved the logical consequences of the Sahajiyā part of their belief for the privacy of their ritual.

[56] *Ibid.*, 38, attributed to Caitanya-dāsa.
[57] *Ibid.*, 24, signed "Kavi-vidyāpati."

5

Man and Superman: Physical and Metaphysical Bases for the Sahajiyā Sādhana

1. THE NATURE OF THE SUPREME

THE VAIṢṆAVA VIEW. The fact that it is not a system tends to make a systematic presentation of Sahajiyā thought a bit difficult. What can be said about Sahajiyā thought has to be gleaned, a line or a hint or a metaphor here and there from texts that cannot be accused of being clear. The texts are, in fact, deliberately obscure and are written in a kind of code language called *sandhā-bhāṣā* or *sandhyā-bhāṣā*. According to Winternitz, who follows Vidhuśekhara Bhaṭṭācārya in the matter, the term means "intentional speech," i.e., "enigmatical speech in which a secret meaning is intended."[1] There are no texts that advance, in the meticulous

[1] *History of Indian Literature,* II, 392, n. 4. Winternitz quotes Bhaṭṭācārya's article in the *Indian Historical Quarterly,* IV (1928), 287 ff. As Winternitz further points out, there has been a lot of confusion about the

fashion of the orthodox Vaiṣṇavas, refined speculations concerning the nature of God and the relationship of man to Him. There was, in the first place, not much demand for a special Sahajiyā theology; for the Sahajiyās, being above all things practical people, were much more concerned with questions of doing things than with refined ontology. In the second place, their relationship to Vaiṣṇavism was such that the Sahajiyās were supplied with a ready-made theology of the most careful and intricate kind. The Vaiṣṇava theology is all that the fussiest of theologians could ask for, and the Sahajiyās seemed perfectly content with it, reserving the right to make a slight change here and there where it suited them. The shoe fit, so they wore it.

It is thus pertinent at this point to suggest briefly the way in which the Vaiṣṇavas looked at things. A most complete analytic statement is presented to us by Jīva Gosvāmin in his monumental *Ṣaṭ-saṃdarbha*, and a full account of the intricacies of Jīva's arguments and general feats of philosophical craftsmanship can be found in S. K. De's excellent *Vaiṣṇava Faith and Movement*.[2] This account being available in most readable English, it is perhaps not necessary here to do more than touch on those points most relevant to Saha-

meaning of the term. Haraprasād Śāstrī thought that it meant "twilight language" (*sandhyā-bhāṣā*), and for some reason Panchcowrie Banerjee, writing in the *Visvabharati Quarterly* in 1924 (p. 265), called it "the language of the borderland between the ancient Aryavarta and the actual Bengal." There is an instructive article, "Intentional Language in the Tantras," by A. Bharati in *JAOS*, LXXXI (1961), 261–70. See also T. P. Mukherji, *The Old Bengali Language and Text*, pp. 12, 13. In Bengali, *sandhāna* means "searching," seeking information about something which has been lost.

[2] Pp. 254–421, 2d ed.

jiyā teaching, especially as they are outlined by Jīva's student Kṛṣṇadāsa in his *Caitanya-caritāmṛta*.

Jīva tells us that there are three aspects of ultimate reality, three gradations, as it were, in a kind of hierarchy of reality. These are called, in order of ascending importance, Brahman, Paramātman, and the Bhagavat. Brahman is the unqualified, undifferentiated absolute of the philosophers, and as such is least important to the devotion-oriented Vaiṣṇavas. The relevance of Brahman to the highest reality is merely that it provides a bodily luster, a certain splendor, to the Bhagavat. Brahman is thus included in the Bhagavat, but is an incomplete or partial manifestation of the godhead, and those who seek identity with it, as the followers of monistic philosophy tend to do, are foolishly seeking a part when they could know the whole. Thus are Śaṃkara and his followers put in their proper place.[3]

[3] It is characteristic that Vaiṣṇava thought gives a place to the *advaita* system, saying that it is true as far as it goes, but that bhakti supersedes it. The Sahajiyā text *DBhS* (p. 125) says that bhakti gains for the bhakta "the other shore of the Vedānta." Kṛṣṇadāsa has Caitanya arguing against the proponents of the *advaita* school of thought, and of course defeating them; see, for example, *CC Madhya* 6:142. And in *CC Madhya* 12:190, Nityānanda says that "the *advaita* system is an obstacle to the performance of pure bhakti." The reason for this attitude is clear enough: if one were the same as Kṛṣṇa, one could not worship him, thereby tasting his sweetness (*CC Ādi* 6:89). For statements on the superiority of bhakti to *mukti*, see *CC Ādi* 1:51 ff.; 8:16; 5:27; 17:60; *Madhya* 6:236, 241, etc. See also Baladeva's *Prameya-ratnāvali*, *śloka* 60. It is not a concept that is confined to Vaiṣṇava literature, however. Jagaddhara's *Stutikusumañjali* 3:44:58, translated by V. Raghavan in *Prayers, Praises and Psalms*, p. 295, has: "May you have that firm devotion to the moon-crested Śiva, those who know the greatness of which consider as an impediment even that one supreme end of man called liberation." And the famous song of the Bengali Śākta poet Rāmprasād Sen, translated by E. J. Thompson in *Bengali Religious Lyrics, Śākta*, p. 40, has: "Śiva has said that if a man dies at Kāśi he wins salvation. But devotion is the root of everything, and salvation but her handmaiden who follows her. What is the worth of salvation if it

Paramātman, which will turn up more logically later in the discussion, occupies a kind of middle ground between the Bhagavat, the full divinity, and man and intermediates between these two. The Bhagavat is the Lord in full manifestation. Far from being unqualified and undifferentiated, the Bhagavat is infinitely qualified and infinitely differentiated (thus being able to include the qualification "unqualified") by an unlimited number of perfect attributes. And in the Bhagavat are infinite śaktis, the active powers and operative energies of the divinity.

These śaktis are essential to the Bhagavat; they are reflexes, in a manner of speaking, of his nature. The CC puts it this way: "As a beam of light is a part of the sun, or a flame a part of the fire, so his śaktis are of the nature of [the Bhagavat]."[4] They are of course infinite in number, but can be grouped under three main heads, namely, *svarūpa-śakti, jīva-śakti,* and *māyā-śakti.* To carry Kṛṣṇadāsa's image a little further, these three relate to the Bhagavat as the rays of the sun and the reflection of the sun relate to the sun itself. The *svarūpa-śakti* is as the sun itself, in which all sun-like properties are contained. The *svarūpa-śakti* is thus called intrinsic (*antaraṅga*) to the Bhagavat. The rays of the sun are among the sun's properties but are related to the solar disc itself in a somewhat limited way: they emanate from the sun, but are not the sun itself. Such is the *jīva-śakti* in relation to the Bhagavat. But the rays of the sun carry the light of the sun to the mirror; they are the intermediaries between

---

means absorption, the mixing of sugar with water? Sugar I love to eat, but I have no desire to become sugar."

[4] *CC Madhya* 20:102.

the sun and its reflection. *Māyā-śakti* is related to the Bhagavat as its reflection is to the sun. *Māyā-śakti* is a function of the Bhagavat, but it is extrinsic (*bahiraṅga*); it is not directly connected with the essential self of the Bhagavat. *Māyā-śakti* is the cause of the creation of the world, the *śakti* that in the first instance has control of men and material nature. Thus the world is, albeit indirectly, a creation of the Bhagavat, though not a part of the essential nature of the Bhagavat. But *māyā-śakti,* as a function of the Bhagavat, is real, and its creation is therefore also real. The crucial importance of this conclusion to the Sahajiyās can by now be glimpsed: as the body is real, it can be the means of knowing the highest reality.

Jīva-śakti is the domain of the Paramātman aspect of the godhead, and as such intermediates between the individual being, the jīva, and the Bhagavat. Like the rays of the sun, it is neither wholly intrinsic nor wholly extrinsic to the Bhagavat, but is partially both. It is through the office of the Paramātman that the jīva relates to the Bhagavat. Such an intermediary is necessary, for until the jīva is able to transcend it, he is under the control of *māyā-śakti; and māyā-śakti* is extrinsic to the Bhagavat. Thus, until its release from the control of māyā, the jīva can have no direct knowledge of the Bhagavat. But when release comes, by bhakti, the jīva comes under the control of the *svarūpa-śakti* and can then perceive the fullness of the godhead, the Bhagavat itself.

What is the nature of the jīva? The jīva is a part (*aṁśa*), an atomic part (*aṇu*), the smallest indivisible part of the infinitely qualified Bhagavat. As a part, the jīva participates in the qualities of the Bhagavat, but to a limited extent: its qualities are not, like those of the Bhagavat, infinite. The jīva is also a discrete entity, and although part of the Bhagavat, it remains eternally distinct both from the Bhagavat and from other jīvas. The jīva possesses an organic body that brings it under the control of māyā; and because it is under the control of māyā, the jīva is deluded into identifying itself with its body. But in truth the jīva, as part of the Bhagavat, is always essentially pure and essentially unaffected.

Although the jīva is a part of the Bhagavat and participates in the qualities of the Bhagavat, it is at the same time different from the Bhagavat. This is demonstrated by the fact that the jīva has a separate existence, and because it is liable to the control of māyā: māyā, as an extrinsic śakti, can have no effect on the Bhagavat itself. Thus, Jīva Gosvāmin sounds the keynote of Bengali Vaiṣṇava theology: the relation between the jīva and the Bhagavat, as between śakti and *śaktimān* (the possessor of śakti), is *bhedābheda*—the same, yet different. And, adding a mystic note also characteristic of Bengal Vaiṣṇavism, this relationship is also *acintya:* it cannot be comprehended by the human mind.

The point, however, is this: the fact that there are qualities shared by the jīva and the Bhagavat means that it is possible for the jīva to approach the Bhagavat and to remain near the Bhagavat for all eternity. And the fact that there is a difference between the jīva and the Bhagavat means that there can never be unity between the two. To the Vaiṣṇava way of thinking, the ultimate good that men can attain is to spend eternity in worship of the deity. By worship, the deity's pleasure grows, and as it grows it increases the pleasure of the worshiper, and so on to infinity. By tasting the sweetness of the Gopīs, Kṛṣṇa's sweetness increased, thereby increasing the sweetness of the Gopīs. But, as the CC sums it up: "If one were the same as Kṛṣṇa, one could not taste his sweetness. As a bhakta one can taste it."[5]

This is another point at which, needless to say, the Sahajiyās parted company with their orthodox brethren. The Sahajiyās cheerfully accepted the theory of *acintya-bhedābheda,* but only insofar as it met their needs. As they did with the eroticism of the Vaiṣṇava religious poetry, they read the basic image the other way. To the Sahajiyās, the aspect of difference between human and divine, as between male and female, makes union possible. The aspect of identity of human and divine makes union true.

There are two other essential points that must be noticed. The first is based on the assumption that energy, to be meaningful, must have a container, that śakti must have a *śaktimān.* It is postulated that the Bhagavat has a person, that his qualities define him in some sense physically. The Bhagavat then has a form, though this form is in no real sense the gross physical form of the human body. The Vaiṣṇavas, like many other theologians, have had their troubles in dealing with the problem of the form of the Bhagavat. In the last analysis, infinity can only be described as non-finite. But their solution was this: The jīva has a limited form, as it is the product of an extrinsic śakti. The form (called *mūrti* or *vigraha*) of the Bhagavat is a function of the unlimited svarūpa, the true essence, of the godhead that consists of infinite *sat* (pure existence), infinite *cit* (pure consciousness

[5] CC *Ādi* 6:89.

or knowledge), and, the highest and most important of all, infinite *ānanda* (pure bliss). Since there is no distinction of form and essence in the Bhagavat, his form also is made up of these three. Jīva Gosvāmin goes into great detail on this somewhat knotty problem, most of which detail is not relevant to this discussion. But ultimately, since the only proof he accepts is the authority of scripture, Jīva concludes on the basis of the statements of the *Bhagavad-gītā* and the *Bhāgavata-purāṇa* that the true form of the deity is like, though not identical with, the human form. The divine form is, for example, unlike the human form, not subject to change.

Since the Bhagavat is untouched by māyā, when he incarnates himself upon the earth (*avatāra*), the form he assumes, though like a human body, is not subject to the limitations of the human body. The assumption of a form like a human body in no way limits his svarūpa, his eternal existence, nor does it imply any change in his nature. For, Jīva argues, all forms that the Bhagavat may take are real and eternal, all exist in the eternal Bhagavat. The appearance of the Bhagavat upon the earth, the *avatāra*, is a function of the svarūpa and is thus eternal, real, and as untouched as the svarūpa itself by the phenomenal world. The Bhagavat can also assume an infinite number of forms simultaneously, without any transformation or change in the essential svarūpa.[6] "Though the *vigraha* can have many forms, different in phenomenal shape, there remains the one true svarūpa."[7] By such a power does Kṛṣṇa appear on

[6] CC *Madhya* 20:137 has: "In a single *vigraha* is his true, eternal form." *Vigraha* is thus any form that the deity may assume; see CC *Madhya* 9:141, 6:142, and the *ṭīkā* on CC *Ādi* 4:8, 9.

[7] CC *Ādi* 1:35–38.

the earth. And once upon the earth, by such a power is he able to be between each two Gopīs at the rāsa dance.

Bhāgavata 1:3:28 uses the phrase *Kṛṣṇas tu bhagavān svayam:* Kṛṣṇa is himself Bhagavān, the Bhagavat, the full godhead. To Jīva and the Bengal school, the person of the Bhagavat is Kṛṣṇa: "Kṛṣṇa is himself Bhagavān—his other name is Govinda. He is full of all divine qualities, and his eternal dwelling place is in Goloka."[8] Kṛṣṇa is not, as some would have it, a mere *avatāra* of Nārāyaṇa. "Some argue that . . . Nārāyaṇa is *svayam bhagavān,* who has become an *avatāra* in the form of Kṛṣṇa. . . . But Kṛṣṇa is the container of *avatāras,* and is *svayam bhagavān.* Kṛṣṇa is the container and refuge of all things; he is the highest god, and all the *śāstras* say this."[9] Kṛṣṇa is the controller of māyā, by which power he created the world. Creatures such as men are controlled by māyā, having been created by it: "Having control over māyā and being controlled by it: this is the difference between *īśvara* [i.e., Kṛṣṇa-Bhagavān] and the jīva. Do you conceive of the jīva as being undivided from *īśvara?*"[10] As the Bhagavat, Kṛṣṇa has its three aspects: Brahman the radiance, Paramātman the indwelling principle in

[8] *CC Madhya* 20:133. *CC Ādi* 2:74 explains the term *svayam bhagavān* as "he who has *bhagavattā*"—i.e., he who "has the quality of possessing all qualities"; see also *CC Ādi* 2:7. Kṛṣṇadāsa cites *Bhāgavata* 1:2:11 in support of his contention. Rādhāgovinda Nāth's commentary on the passage describes full godhood as "possessing infinite knowledge, infinite powers (śakti), infinite strength (*bala*), infinite devinity or splendor (*aiśvarya*), infinite energy (*vīrya*), and infinite magnificence (*tejaḥ*). . . . He is fully God who possesses none of the lower material qualities, but infinite immaterial qualities."

[9] *CC Ādi* 2:58–89.

[10] *CC Madhya* 6:148. The context of the passage is a discussion between Caitanya and the then *advaitin* Vāsudeva Sārvabhauma.

man, and the infinitely qualified full Bhagavat: "Brahmā is his splendor-aspect, an unqualified brightness, brilliant and blinding as the sun to the naked eye. Paramātmā is another aspect of Kṛṣṇa, the *ātmā* of *ātmās*; in this aspect, Kṛṣṇa is the crest-jewel of all things."[11] These two are contained in Kṛṣṇa the full (*pūrṇa*) Bhagavat. Each of these three can be gained by a different path. Brahman, the philosophical absolute, is gained by intellectual knowledge (*jñāna-mārga*). Paramātman is gained by the path of physical and mental discipline (*yoga-mārga*). But the full Bhagavat can be gained only by bhakti: "The unqualified Brahman is revealed by the *jñāna-mārga*. By the *yoga-mārga* the true indwelling form appears. But by the bhakti of the path of love [*rāga-bhakti*] one gains Bhagavān himself in Vraja. . . . Without bhakti none of these approaches [*sādhana*] can give results, and bhakti by itself can give all results."[12] "In bhakti is the full perception of Kṛṣṇa; his true, eternal form is in a single *vigraha*."[13]

The second point touches further on this notion of bhakti. As a way of realization, bhakti deserves, and will receive, a section of its own; but it is relevant here to note the following: The *svarūpa-śakti* of Kṛṣṇa has three aspects, corresponding to its three essential characteristics—those of *sat*, *cit*, and *ānanda*. *Ānanda* is the most important of these. Kṛṣṇa's power to give and to receive bliss is his most supreme power. The śakti of his *ānanda*-aspect is called his *hlādinī*-

[11] *Ibid.*, 20:135–36. See also the Sahajiyā text *Āgama*, p. 97.

[12] *Ibid.*, 24:60 ff. The text describes *paramātman* as "the true indwelling form of the divinity" (*antarayāmi īśvararūpa*).

[13] *Ibid.*, 20:137.

śakti. "*Hlādinī* causes Kṛṣṇa to taste *ānanda,* and by *hlādinī* he nourishes his bhaktas."[14]

Kṛṣṇa is the svarūpa of the Bhagavat; and as the means of Kṛṣṇa's giving and receiving pleasure (*ānanda*) is Rādhā, so Rādhā is his *hlādinī-śakti.* Rādhā is thus inseparable from the svarūpa of Kṛṣṇa. The highest aspect of the svarūpa consists of Rādhā and Kṛṣṇa in an eternal relationship of love. The importance of this love, seen as union by the Sahajiyās, is crucial. To the orthodox also, as the jīva is a part of the Bhagavat, he also possesses in some small way the power to give and to receive bliss; he has the qualities of Rādhā, who is, then, in her *prema-bhakti,* representative of him. When *prema-bhakti,* unselfish and devoted attention to Kṛṣṇa's pleasure, is the attitude of the worshiper, he is released from the power of māyā and stands directly before the svarūpa; he experiences the ultimate joy, the *ānanda* of Kṛṣṇa, the *mahābhāva.* "The essence [*sāra*] of *hlādinī* is prema; the essence of prema is *bhāva;* the highest state of *bhāva* is called *mahābhāva.* The true form [*svarūpa*] of *mahābhāva* is Rādhikā-ṭhākurāṇī."[15] By bhakti the worshiper demonstrates the element of *hlādinī-śakti* in him, and by it he is in a relationship of ever increasing pleasure to Kṛṣṇa. The Vaiṣṇavas carry this to one of two possible conclusions. Stressing the fact that the jīva is the same *but different from* the Bhagavat, they conclude that the eternal pleasure of the released jīva is that of Rādhā the worshiper of Kṛṣṇa in *viraha,* in prema, not that of eternal union with him.

[14] *CC Ādi* 4:53.
[15] *Ibid.,* 4:59 f.; see also *Āgama,* p. 108.

Men are of two types—those who are inclined toward Kṛṣṇa and those who are not. The latter, being naturally beyond the pale, are of no particular interest. When the former, by their attitude of prema, please Kṛṣṇa, he is disposed to grant his grace to them; then their salvation is assured. This notion of grace (*kṛpā*) is strong among the orthodox: "No one can know the truth of *īśvara*, except by his grace; he who gains the merest drop of the grace of *īśvara* can know the truth. Though you be guru of the world and possess all knowledge of the *śāstras*, and though there is no scholar who is your equal, if you do not have a drop of the grace of *īśvara*, you know nothing of his truth."[16] This seems to conflict somewhat with the theory that the svarūpa of Kṛṣṇa can in no way be connected with the phenomenal world, *māyā-śakti* being entirely extraneous to Kṛṣṇa's true self. The Vaiṣṇavas, however, have an answer.

There are on the earth certain saintly men, bhaktas who have already been released from the bondage of māyā and are directly under the control of the *svarūpa-śakti*. Even though they themselves no longer feel the effects of māyā, they remember what the bondage is like, and they have pity on the jīva who is struggling for release. Such a man is a proper guru. Such a man is able to channel the power of the svarūpa directly to the earth, for purposes of grace and of salvation. While Kṛṣṇa is able arbitrarily to assume a phenomenal form and appear upon the earth as an *avatāra*, such appearances are not always arbitrary. As the *Bhagavad-gītā* says, an *avatāra* comes upon the earth to bring peace to a

[16] *CC Madhya* 6:81–84. Kṛṣṇadāsa claims support from *Bhāgavata* 10:14:29.

troubled world, to bring good to the world of men.[17] Though Kṛṣṇa cannot have awareness of any trouble in the world, he comes in answer to a summons from the bhakta who is released. Kṛṣṇa appeared upon the earth as Caitanya at the urging of his bhakta Advaita Ācārya:

Seeing all the people with faces averted from Kṛṣṇa, seeing people immersed in worldly affairs, [Advaita] was very sorrowful. He reflected upon a course of salvation for the people, how all these people could be saved. "If Kṛṣṇa incarnates himself and propagates bhakti, then the people will be saved." So the *ācārya* prayed that Kṛṣṇa incarnate himself; he performed Kṛṣṇa-*pūjā* with *tulasī* and Ganges water. He summoned Kṛṣṇa with a loud outcry, and Vrajendrakumār was attracted by the shout.[18]

Kṛṣṇa can be controlled by his bhaktas, for, demonstrating their *hlādinī-śakti,* they give him the pleasure that is the primary function of his true nature.[19]

Sahajiyā variations on the theme. This theology the Sahajiyās found most congenial, though they leaned more heavily than did the orthodox on the non-difference side of the difference–non-difference theory. Given their presumption of the importance of man's material nature, they analyzed this a bit more closely. And given their presumption

[17] *Bhagavad-gītā* 4:7–8.

[18] *CC Ādi* 13:67–71. *Tulasī* is a plant sacred to Kṛṣṇa and was used by the Vaiṣṇavas in worship. Vrajendrakumār is Kṛṣṇa.

[19] This is by no means an unusual idea and is perhaps related to the notion common in the history of Indian religion that the divine powers can be subjected to one's will by proper austerities and the proper execution of ritual. In this case, Kṛṣṇa is "indebted" to the bhakta who serves him, and is obliged to repay the debt. *CC Ādi* 3:84 has: "He who gives *tulasī*-water to Kṛṣṇa puts Kṛṣṇa in his debt; Kṛṣṇa thinks to repay that debt."

of man's personal divinity, they ignored, for all practical purposes, the Vaiṣṇava theory of grace.

The essence of Tāntric thought is that man is a microcosm. He contains within himself all the elements of the the universe; he is a part that contains all the elements of the whole. As in the Vaiṣṇava theory of the relationship between the jīva and the Bhagavat, there is a quantitative, not a qualitative, difference between the whole and its parts.[20] In man is truth, and through man it must be known. For although the world is real, its reality is hidden by a māyā as impenetrable as that which hides its true nature from the jīva. Thus people who wander about the world seeking knowledge and doing good works are merely deluded. The truth is right at hand: "Do not look afar for what is hidden nearby."[21] "Thus I say, grieving, that the people of this country [*jambudvīpa*] who have God within their own bodies, are charmed by the material world; they neither perceive nor understand the God within, and, as if they were drunk, they stumble along in *māyā*."[22] It is knowledge of the God within that leads one to the ultimate and blissful state, the state of sahaja. This knowledge is not in-

[20] S. B. Dasgupta, *Introduction to Tantric Buddhism*, p. 161. The correspondence between macrocosm and microcosm, of course, is also present in the Upaniṣadic idea and concept of *ātman*; see Anam Charan Swain, "A Study of Saṁkara's Concept of Creation," (doctoral dissertation, Harvard University, 1957), p. 10. This is one of the central teachings of the *caryā-padas*; see *ORC*, pp. 96–97.

[21] *VV*, p. 96. This is common in the *caryā-padas* (e.g., no. 5 has: "Knowledge is nearby; do not go to seek it afar.") and, as we shall see, in the poetry and thought of the Bāuls.

[22] From the anonymous *Jñānādi-sādhana*, *VSP*, II, 1633. See also *Bauddha gān o doha*, no. 41.

tellectual knowledge (*jñāna*), but is the immediate knowledge of the heart: "He who is the *mānuṣa* is known in the heart, within, not by rational judgment."[23]

All things are unified within the microcosmic self. There are seeming dualities in the world, such as man and woman, human and divine, self and not-self. But such dualities are only seeming, and the first step toward restoring the natural and normal state of unity is the realization of this.

The Vaiṣṇavas consider the relationship of Rādhā and Kṛṣṇa in a number of differently significant ways. Kṛṣṇa is *ānanda* and Rādhā is his *hlādinī-śakti.*[24] And in much the same way, Kṛṣṇa is the visible form (*mūrti*) of rasa and of passionate love (*śṛṅgāra*), while Rādhā is the ultimate emotion (*mahābhāva*) connected with these. "Kṛṣṇa is the *mūrti* of rasa, the manifestation of *śṛṅgāra.* The true form of Rādhā is *mahābhāva.*"[25] This, to the Sahajiyās, is a projection of an inner reality.

One of the nicer perceptions of the Vaiṣṇavas, and one of the most complex, is that Rādhā and Kṛṣṇa, in true, basic, or "own" form (svarūpa) are one, in the sense that śakti and *śaktimān* are one, but that they became divided into two separate and individual forms (rūpa) in their līlā in the earthly Vṛndāvana, in order that they might taste more fully

[23] *SS* pada 30, attributed to Nandalāla. The *Jñānādi-sādhana* (*VSP*, II, 1634–35) modifies this to say that one aspect of Kṛṣṇa, in this case the *paramātman,* can be known by intellectual means, but that Kṛṣṇa, himself can be known only by a combination of intellectual, emotional, and physical means. The *Prema-vilāsa* of Yugala-dāsa (*VSP, II,* 1665) goes to the opposite extreme and says that all the pain and confusion of mankind comes from striving vainly after Kṛṣṇa with the mind.

[24] *CC Ādi* 4:181.

[25] *Ibid.,* 4:60.

the sweetness of one another. The CC tells us that "Rādhā and Kṛṣṇa are thus eternally one in svarūpa; they became two forms [rūpa] in order to taste the ultimate sweetness [rasa] of their līlā."[26] The implications of this might at this point merely be suggested. They are, first, that the rūpa participates fully in the qualities of the svarūpa, that the rūpas Rādhā and Kṛṣṇa are at the same time the svarūpa Rādhā-Kṛṣṇa. Otherwise, how could Kṛṣṇa, for example, experience fully both his own pleasure in receiving Rādhā's love and Rādhā's pleasure in giving to and receiving love from him? The second notion is corollary to this: the moment in time when Rādhā and Kṛṣṇa took form in the earthly Vṛndāvana is a kind of micro-time. The līlā of Rādhā and Kṛṣṇa in the earthly Vṛndāvana is a finite form of what goes on eternally in the heavenly Vṛndāvana. Thus, any given moment of the līlā, including the moment of union, is a capsule of eternity.[27] This is at the core of Sahajiyā doctrine.

The Sahajiyās say that the visible form of man or woman is rūpa. The svarūpa (Kṛṣṇa and Rādhā, male and female, or the material and non-material elements of man) is mingled with the rūpa in a condition of unspecified but absolute intimacy. The nature of this mingling is incomprehensible to the human mind and has to be explained by analogy; the relationship of svarūpa to rūpa is that of its scent to a flower.

[26] *Ibid.*, 4:85.

[27] This is also at the core of the bhāva-rasa theory: if the bhakta takes on the relationship (*bhāva*) demonstrated by any of the intimates of Kṛṣṇa (i.e., Yaśodā, Nanda, Balarāma, gopīs, gopas, etc.) at any point of the *Bhāgavata* story, he can, when he is in direct relationship to the svarūpa, experience the pleasure of that relationship infinitely (rasa).

"The scent of the flower is the nature of the flower; who can separate one from the other?"[28] "The rūpa and the svarūpa are completely united. They are intermingled one with the other."[29] The svarūpa contains divine joy (rasa), and the rūpa participates intimately in this: "That which is called the svarūpa is the container of rasa; and the two are one."[30] The svarūpa is Rādhā and Kṛṣṇa in blissful union. The svarūpa is also rūpa and svarūpa, man and God, in blissful union. The svarūpa can, and indeed must, be known through the rūpa: "Absorption in the rūpa, devotion to the rūpa—all is contained in the rūpa. He who understands this profoundly is one with the svarūpa."[31] The svarūpa, Rādhā-Kṛṣṇa, is full of rasa. It is this to which the worshiper should devote his attention: "If you worship the svarūpa and sacrifice to the svarūpa, if you know the svarūpa as the ultimate of all things [*sāra*] . . . you swim in a sea of rasa, which glitters when you touch it. In whom this rasa is manifest, his body is svarūpa."[32] This rasa is in the body: "When one knows that the līlā of Rādhā and Kṛṣṇa is manifested [in the body], that they taste līlā in their rūpas, that everything is contained in this highest rasa, that the body is full of this rasa, he tastes that rasa."[33]

The Sahajiyās were especially concerned with the relation-

[28] *SS* pada no. 68, attributed to Narahari.
[29] *Ibid.*, no. 42, attributed to Caṇḍīdāsa.
[30] *Ibid.*, no. 43, attributed to Caṇḍīdāsa.
[31] *Ibid.*, 44, anonymous.
[32] *Ibid.*, 37, attributed to Caṇḍīdāsa. See also pada 57, also attributed to Caṇḍīdāsa, which has: "If one understands the svarūpa and then performs *sādhana*, he is saved."
[33] *Dvīpakojjvala* (*Dīpakojjvala*[?]), Calcutta University MS 564, f. 13; the text is quoted in part in *ORC*, p. 148.

ship of material (*bhūtātmā*) to non-material (*jīvātmā*) elements within the rūpa, as well as with the relationship of the rūpa to the svarūpa. All of these are, in some intellectually incomprehensible way, one. As the rūpa and svarūpa are bound up with one another, so within the rūpa are the *jīvātmā* and *bhūtātmā* bound up with one another. There is thus a continuity between the material body and the highest form of the svarūpa, which is bliss.

The jīva or *jīvātmā*, which is connected to the svarūpa by *paramātmā*, is by its nature pure, untouched and unaffected by māyā. The material aspect of the rūpa, affected by māyā, is the *bhūtātmā*, which consists of the universal elements—earth, water, fire, air, and space.[34] "The *bhūtātmā* is a part [*aṁśa*] of the *jīvātmā*. . . . It is the elemental [*bhautika*] part of the self. . . . It is in all parts of the body. . . . It is the sensory organs . . . the material nature of all things . . . the means and awareness of sensory perception."[35] As a part (*aṁśa*) of the *jīvātmā*, the elemental part of the rūpa is involved with the svarūpa in the same way as the jīva is involved with the Bhagavat. The material body participates in reality, though it is not itself the ultimate and supreme reality. Or, to put it another way, *bhūtātmā* and *jīvātmā* are body and spirit, sometimes termed *prakṛti* (material nature) and *puruṣa* (spirit). The indwelling divine principle, *paramātmā*, is made up of these two in (sexual) union (*mithuna*): "*Jīvātmā* and *bhūtātmā* are *puruṣa* and *prakṛti*; *prakṛti* and *puruṣa* make up the form of *paramātmā*. *Para-*

[34] *Ātma-tattva*, p. 151. The Nyaya-vaiśeṣika philosophy accepts four elements as basic (earth, *kṣiti*, water, *ap*, fire, *tejas*, and air, *marut*); the fifth, *ākāśa*—sky or space—is considered as all-pervasive.

[35] *Sahaja-tattva* (*VSP*, II), p. 1657.

mātmā is the lord of all things and the life in all creatures; in eternal *mithuna* he is in repose."[36]

The *bhūtātmā* is that aspect of the *jīvātmā* which is the means of sensory awareness. It is the part which is drawn to the world, that causes desire, and that is controlled by māyā. In the conquest of māyā, it is thus the *bhūtātmā* that the worshipper has to control. If the senses are not controlled, the jīva cannot escape its bondage:

He is not able to escape, for the five are with him. If he is not indifferent to them, he cannot escape. If he remains concerned [*vikāra*], he goes only to death.

To him who is indifferent [*nirvikāra*], the world is of no concern, but while the five are with him, he cannot attain this. The five can be controlled in a little time, for they have but one language and one heart.[37]

When they are controlled, the jīva knows its nature as svarūpa, and enjoys infinite and eternal bliss. *Bhūtātmā* is the lowest point in the continuum that leads to the highest reality. *Bhūtātmā* is *prakṛti,* material nature, bound up with pure spirit, *puruṣa,* in eternal union. The highest reality is known through *bhūtātmā.* The progression is like this: "In the eight elements are the experience of the body.[38] These

[36] *DBhS,* p. 132.

[37] *Amṛtarasāvali,* p. 179. The terms *vikāra* and *nirvikāra* may need some comment, for there is a seeming contradiction here. *Vikāra* means "change from a natural state or condition"; thus *nirvikāra* indicates lack of such change. I would read the lines against the background of the definition of sahaja as "that which is natural": the *jīvātma* is by its nature pure, unaffected by māyā, indifferent to pleasure and pain, by its nature a participant in the ultimate bliss of the svarūpa. Change of this state implies concern with the world.

[38] *Prema-vilāsa* of *Yugalakiśora-dāsa* (*VSP,* II), p. 1664. The text does not explain why it sets the number at eight instead of the more usual six.

six [i.e., the five senses plus the mind] are the joy of joys [*ānandera ānanda*]. They steal the minds of all. They are united with *prakṛti*."[39] "Nīlacandra-rekhā [i.e., *prakṛti*] said —'From me comes everything. The body is of me, being is of me, experience is of me. Beauty rests in me and is experienced in my eyes. . . . The quality of rasa is in my lips, and from my lips the people of the world taste rasa."[40] *Sādhana*, the process of realization, begins in the body: "The rūpa is not to be thought of as material. . . . The rūpa is the immaterial highest truth. The basis of *sādhana* is in the material aspect of the seeker [*sādhaka*]."[41]

The world is an attractive place and draws the senses. But when the jīva is released from māyā and knows the svarūpa, he realizes that it is Kṛṣṇa's nature which is the most attractive thing of all. Kṛṣṇa is the ultimate in beauty, taste, smell, and touch.[42] Thus, when Kṛṣṇa is perceived, the jīva is drawn automatically to him.

The relationship between *jīvātmā* and *paramātmā* is cru-

It is possible that there is a connection with the fact that there are eight people in Tāntric circle-worship (see Renou and Filiozat, *L'Inde classique*, II, Sec. 1220). The *Ānanda-bhairava* (p. 138) identifies eight *nāyikās* with the eight parts of the body; there are traditionally eight *sakhīs*, companions of Rādhā, who also become the eight members of the Tāntric circle. The same text (p. 128) again mentions the number eight, this time seeming to refer to the objects of the six senses plus *nāyikā* (female) and *nāyaka* (male). Basu's note on the passage quotes the *Nigūḍhārtha-prākāśāvalī* to the effect that *nāyikā* and *nāyaka* here mean *jīvātmā* and *paramātmā*; we have seen that the text speaks of these as being in love-union. The number eight is also used in connection with Śiva (*Mahābhārata* 3:1939) to indicate the five elements plus mind, ego, and *prakṛti*. Kṛṣṇa is also spoken of as having an eightfold nature: *Bhagavad-gītā* 7:4.

39 *Ānanda-bhairava*, p. 152.

40 *Ibid.*, p. 137.

41 VV, p. 43.

42 *SS* pada 41; cf. *Rādhārasa-karikā*, *VSP*, II, 1660.

cial and is the subject of a large part of the difficult and devious allegory called the *Amṛtarasāvalī*.[43] The part of the allegory relevant here is as follows: There was a lotus pond. The pond was within the earth. It was in the keeping of a watchman called Sarvadeva. Sarvadeva had five followers, or guardians of the pond. There were ten others, whose leader was called Savā. One night these ten went to steal nectar from the lotus pond, but Savā was captured by the watchmen. But at dawn he escaped:

Savā was a prisoner when the moon arose. The earth remained in darkness for fifteen *daṇḍas*.[44] Then came the dawn, and with its light the prisoner escaped. He was freed by his own qualities. His imprisonment had been false, for he had not known himself. For many ages he had drifted without consciousness of self. The demon māyā, in the form of a shadow, had punished him. When the moon of the eternal *ānanda* [*nityānanda*][45] arose, the

[43] The *Amṛtarasāvalī* is a relatively late Sahajiyā text, dated by Sen (*BSI*, I, 419) as B.S. 1199 (A.D. 1793). Concerning its author, Sen says: "The Sahajiyā Mukunda-dāsa, it is known, was a follower of the Sāi group of Sahajiyās. It is known from Balarāma-dāsa's *Sārāvalī* that the author of the *Amṛtarasāvalī* was Mathurā-dāsa, one of Mukunda-dāsa's pupils." The *Sārāvalī* has: "That the *Rasāvalī* was written by Mathurā-dāsa is certain; the signature line is: 'The *Amṛtarasāvalī*, manifested by the pupil of Śrīmukunda-svāmi, Mathurā-dāsa by name.' " This *bhaṇitā* does not occur in the printed text I have used. The *Nigūḍhārtha-prakāśāvalī* of Gaurīdāsa mentions the *Amṛtarasāvalī* as being one of the first four Vaiṣṇava-sahajiyā works; it can perhaps be assumed that this means in quality rather than in time. The other three are the *Āgamasāra*, *Ānandabhairava*, and *Amṛtaratnāvalī*. The *Nigūḍhārtha-prakāśāvalī* (text in *PCSC*, p. 180) has: "The *Āgama* is the first [*āge*], and after it the *Ānandabhairava;* and following these the *Amṛta-ratnāvalī* and the *Amṛtarasāvalī*, an ocean of rasa." Tradition has it that the book was written by Mukunda-dāsa himself (*PCSC*, p. 199); but our text makes it clear that the author was a pupil of Mukunda-dāsa; the author, however, remains anonymous. *SS*, p. 190, has: "So, at the order of Mukunda, I wrote the book."

[44] A *daṇḍa* is the sixtieth part of a day, or twenty-four minutes.

[45] Or "the Nityānanda moon," a pun to parallel the one in the following

darkness was driven away. And who can describe the qualities of that moon which brings consciousness [*caitya*]?[46]

Fortunately, the somewhat more intelligible text *Nigūḍhārtha-prakāśāvalī* comments on and interprets this allegory. According to its understanding, the lotus pond, *sarovara,* is "the place where *paramātmā* is established."[47] The pond is within the earth—i.e., within the body, the body being microcosmic. Sarvadeva is *paramātmā-kandarpamohana, paramātmā* as the god of love (Kandarpa and Mohana are two of the names of Kāma-deva), and his five followers are Kāma's five flower arrows.[48] Savā is the *jīvātmā,* and his nine followers are the five *jñānendriyas* (senses through which knowledge is gained) and the four *karmendriyas* (work or action senses). The nectar of the pond within the body is rasa, and the act of stealing it is the attempt to know the divine bliss in an improper manner. The darkness, the shadow of māyā, is ignorance of the truth of one's own nature, and the dawn is the dawn of consciousness. Thus the *jīvātmā* is by nature free, being the same in essence as the *paramātmā.*[49] *Jīvātmā,* however, being also involved with *bhūtātmā,* is subject to the control of māyā, whereas *paramātmā* is not. The *jīvātmā* longs for the nectar of the lotus pond, the rasa of the true bliss of the svarūpa of Kṛṣṇa. But the *jīvātmā* is ignorant and, under the influence of māyā, tries to attain this bliss improperly. Once the *jīvātmā* passes

line: "Caitanya moon." Padas often speak of Caitanya and Nityānanda as moons rising over Nadiyā to drive away the darkness of the mind.

46 *SS,* pp. 163–67.

47 *Ibid.,* p. 163.

48 *Ibid.,* p. 164, nn. 1, 2.

49 *DBhS,* p. 132.

beyond the control of māyā at the dawn of consciousness, once the aggregate of the senses is controlled and superseded, the *jīvātmā* is released from its imprisonment. Thus, desire for rasa, together with proper use of the bodily senses, makes one realize the unity of the jīva with the *paramātmā*, and thus with the svarūpa or Kṛṣṇa.

Thus the cycle is completed. The highest nature of the svarūpa of Kṛṣṇa is bliss. The jīva, as a part of the svarūpa, also has as its highest nature bliss. Bliss is the characteristic of Rādhā and Kṛṣṇa in union. Rādhā and Kṛṣṇa are united in the svarūpa, in which the rūpa participates. Hence the ultimate divine and eternal joy of the union of Rādhā and Kṛṣṇa are known through the rūpa, in the body.

THE PLACE OF CAITANYA. Given all this, it is not hard to see why the Sahajiyās regard Caitanya as their case in point. Even to the orthodox Vaiṣṇavas, Caitanya is Rādhā and Kṛṣṇa in one body: "In the body of Caitanya the two are one, undivided."[50]

The story of the Caitanya-līlā of Kṛṣṇa is told by the Sahajiyā texts in various ways. The *Āgama*, for example, says that the gods, the *deva*s, came to Kṛṣṇa and complained that the Kali Age on earth was an age of wickedness. So Kṛṣṇa said to Rādhā, "Let us both become *avatāras*." But Rādhā said, "That is not my desire; all I require for my happiness is to stay with you here in the eternal Vṛndāvana." And, remembering her pain of separation in the previous *avatāra*, when Kṛṣṇa left her in Vṛndāvana to go to Mathurā, she said, "I could not bear another period of separation from

[50] CC *Ādi* 7:111, *ṭīkā*.

you." But Kṛṣṇa said, "There will be no *viraha* [i.e., pain of separation]; in our earthly līlā in Vṛndāvana we were one soul in two bodies. In this *avatāra* we will be one even in body—you externally, me internally. Thus will I, in the most complete way possible, taste your love."[51]

There were other reasons for the Caitanya-*avatāra:* the establishment of the special dharma of the Kali Age (bhakti) and the salvation of jīvas.[52] But all the texts agree that Rādhā and Kṛṣṇa became a single body in order to taste in the most intimate way possible the joys of union. The VV says that Kṛṣṇa was not wholly satisfied with his *avatāra* in Vṛndāvana, that his pleasure was not sufficiently complete: "With his companions of Goloka, the Lord has līlā in Vṛndāvana. But to fulfill his desires, he came to Nadiyā."[53] Or, says the *Kaḍacā* of Svarūpa: "Kṛṣṇa was born in the womb of Śacī with the emotions of Rādhā in order to feel for himself how deeply he was loved by her, to realize how charmingly fascinating was his beauty, which made Rādhā mad with love, and, lastly, to taste the pleasure which was experienced by Rādhā when united with him."[54] Or, according to *Amṛtarasāvalī:* "He had not tasted the purest form of prema; because of this, Kṛṣṇa took birth in the womb of Śacī."[55]

This doctrine of the dual incarnation is such a natural one for the Sahajiyās that it is impossible not to wonder whether

[51] *Āgama,* pp. 123–24.
[52] *Ibid.,* p. 123. The passage is based on the *CC:* see, for example, *Ādi* 4:14 f., 89 ff., etc.
[53] VV, p. 94.
[54] Translation by Basu, *PCSC,* pp. 22–23.
[55] P. 158.

or not it originated with them, being taken over later by the orthodox Vaiṣṇavas. There are arguments pro and con, none of them being overwhelmingly convincing. The facts suggest, however, that the doctrine might have been inspired by the old Sahajiyā notion of the unity of seeming opposites in the body, current in the *caryā-padas* long before the development of it by the Bengal Vaiṣṇavas.

The doctrine of the dual incarnation seems to be a peculiar development of the Bengal variety of Vaiṣṇava thought. Caitanya as an *avatāra* or as Kṛṣṇa himself was not of overwhelming importance to the Gosvāmins of Vṛndāvana. They revered him, but their theological speculations were more essentially geared to the Kṛṣṇa of the *Bhāgavata-purāṇa*.[56] There is no recognition of the dual incarnation in Caitanya in their writings. As we have already seen, it was Rāmānanda Rāya, called a "Sahaja-vaiṣṇava" by Kavikarṇapura and a practitioner of a typically Sahajiyā technique of chastity, who first emphasized the Rādhā-aspect of Caitanya. Or, at least, the first recognition of the Rādhā-aspect of Caitanya is attributed to Rāmānanda by Kṛṣṇadāsa, who, although a product of the Vṛndāvana school of theology, first states the dual incarnation theory with its full theological implications in his *Caitanya-caritāmṛta*.[57] As De points out, however: "It must, however, be noted that the Rādhā-bhāva of Caitanya is not an entirely original conception of Kṛṣṇadāsa Kavirāja, but is also referred to in Prabodhanānanda's *Caitanya-candrāmṛta* and in the contemporary padas of Vasu Ghoṣ, Narahari Sarkar . . . and others."[58]

[56] See *VFM*, p. 330.
[57] *CC Madhya* 7:278–81, 287–88.
[58] *VFM*, p. 70, n. 1.

It is clear that Caitanya's meeting with Rāmānanda, as related in *CC Madhya* 7, was in many ways a turning point in his life. Rāmānanda explains to Caitanya the meaning of his Rādhā-*bhāva,* and from this time until the end of his life, Caitanya is more and more subject to fits of wild enthusiasm and depressed longing for his Kṛṣṇa. It is to Rāmānanda that Caitanya first reveals his true form as Rādhā-Kṛṣṇa: "Then, smiling, the Lord [i.e., Caitanya] showed to him his true form [svarūpa]—Rasarāja [i.e., Kṛṣṇa] and Mahābhāva [i.e., Rādhā], the two in one form [rūpa]."[59] This is repeated by the Sahajiyā text *Vivarta-vilāsa:* "First he showed to Rāmānanda his *saṃnyāsī*-form; then Caitanya revealed his true form as Rādhā-Kṛṣṇa."[60] Rāmānanda feels that the *śṛṅgāra*-rasa or *madhura*-rasa, the ultimate experience of passionate love, is the highest possible experience: "*Śānta, dāsya, sākha,* and *vātsalya*—all are contained in *madhura-rasa.*"[61] He describes Kṛṣṇa as the new Kāma-deva, whose worship is in the Sahajiyā mantra or ritual formula called the *kāma-gāyatrī:* "In Vṛndāvana is the new unmanifested Madana, whose worship is in the *kāmagāyatrī* and *kāmabīja.*"[62]

A reasonable reconstruction of the history of the development of the theory is that Kṛṣṇadāsa acquired from his gurus in Vṛndāvana the notion of Rādhā and Kṛṣṇa in the intimate relationship of śakti to śaktimān, applied it to Caitanya on the basis of the perceptions of the pada-writers of Bengal, and put it into the mouth of Rāmānanda without,

[59] *CC Madhya* 8:233.
[60] VV, p. 142.
[61] *CC Madhya* 8:67.
[62] *Ibid.,* 8:109.

or, as seems to me more likely, with justification for doing so.

The reasons why the pada-writers felt that Caitanya was in part Rādhā are not hard to see. That he was Kṛṣṇa very few seemed to have any doubt: "The truth about Caitanya-gosvāmi is that he is himself the *svayam-bhagavān* Kṛṣṇa Vrajendranandana."[63] He was Rādhā because he exhibited the passion typical of Rādhā: "His limbs are supported by the limbs of his companions—he cannot walk. From time to time he slips to the earth, fainting, his body so weak that he cannot hold it up. Fallen to the earth, he gazes up at the faces of his companions, saying "O lord of my life, where are you?" In the fever of his former *viraha,* he has no peace."[64] And his golden color was that of Rādhā: "White, red, and golden—these three types of splendor did Śrīpati [i.e., Kṛṣṇa-Viṣṇu] take in the Satya, Tretā, and Kali Ages. In the Dvāpara Age he was blue-black colored. This is witnessed in all the *śāstras,* Āgamas, and Purāṇas. The propagation of the Name [of Kṛṣṇa] is the dharma of the Kali Age; it is for this that the golden-colored *avatāra* Caitanya has come."[65]

The Sahajiyās thought of Caitanya as the *sahaja-mānuṣa;* they considered him a guru who taught the Sahajiyā doctrine. The VV says that the doctrine originated with "Svarūpa Gosvāmin," but was revealed by Caitanya: "The Sahajiyā-dharma, having come from Svarūpa-gosvāmin, was made known to the *rasika-bhaktas* by Mahāprabhu [i.e., Caitanya], who revealed and uncovered it."[66] A text called the *Rasaka-*

[63] CC *Ādi* 2:102.
[64] A pada of Jñāna-dāsa (*Padakalpataru,* no. 1879); see Dimock, "Place of Gauracandrikā," p. 162.
[65] CC *Ādi* 3:29 ff.
[66] VV, p. 2.

dambalakalikā points out that Caitanya revealed the Sahajiyā doctrine both by his teaching and by his dual nature, but that the truth was interpreted and put forth by others. The "others" include, interestingly enough, the great Gosvāmin Rūpa, thus again acknowledging the debt of the Sahajiyās to the possibly unwitting theologians of Vṛndāvana: "Prabhu [i.e., Caitanya] propagated prema [i.e., Sahajiyā doctrine]. . . . Svarūpa taught the meaning of rasa to Rāmānanda. . . . Rūpa Gosvāmin taught the truth about the self; Rūpa, in his grace, taught all the truths of the profound and hidden meaning of the Vraja-rasa. . . . Rūpa Gosvāmin knew the *rāga-dharma* of Vraja, the inner meaning of Caitanya."[67] This is seconded by the *Rativilāsa-paddhati*: "So thinking, he became an *avatāra* in Navadvīpa, and constantly preached the nature of rasa. . . . Svarūpa, Rūpa, and Raghunātha, these three tasted in their hearts the profound nectar of *bhāva*."[68] Sahajiyā poets frequently became a little lyrical about it: "Waves of charm emanate from Caitanya's body. He whose body a drop of that great sea touches is mingled with it."[69] Or, again: "Worship Caitanya, say 'Caitanya'—take Caitanya's name; he who worships Caitanya is indeed blessed, and apart from the mercy of Caitanya there is no salvation."[70] Caitanya, Rādhā-Kṛṣṇa, in ecstasy in life and forever, is the guru of the world: "In Navadvīpa, Kṛṣṇa tasted his own sweetness. He took the dress of a *saṃnyāsin*, he tasted his own sweetness as Prabhu, the golden one. . . . Kāma-caitanya is the guru of the

[67] *Rasakadambakalikā*, pp. 20–22; quoted in *PCSC*, p. 161, n. 1.
[68] *Rativilāsa-paddhati*, pp. 31–33; quoted in *PCSC*, p. 161, n. 1.
[69] *VV*, p. 52.
[70] *SS* pada 10, attributed to Nityānanda-dāsa.

world. One gains what one desires—Caitanya is the tree of wishes."[71]

Caitanya swam in a sea of bliss; a sea of the rasa of the love of Rādhā and Kṛṣṇa, united in himself. The joy he knew can be known by any man. But what was natural to him, others must struggle to attain.

2. THE NATURE OF MAN

Pots of beer and voluptuous women may not have been the end that most Sahajiyās had in view. And although man has in him a divinity that can, at least in his own eyes, put him above all scandal and reproach, he is also a creature who has at least one foot firmly imbedded in the clay. The Sahajiyā view is, realistically, that until a man learns to jump, he will lift one foot only to find the other stuck.

The world is a very attractive place. Its forms and colors draw the eye, its sweetness draws the smell and taste, its women draw the desires of man to a very alarming extent. Man, being man, is fairly susceptible: "Desire, infatuation, lust, anger, delight in pleasure . . . these, as much as hunger and thirst, are the constant companions of the body."[72] Sexual attractiveness and desire, says the VV reasonably, are as much a part of human nature as sweet juice is of the sugarcane.[73] For after all, if such illustrious personages as Brahmā, Mahārudra, and Parāśara, the father of the sage Vyāsa, were lustful, in fact so lustful that they pursued

[71] VV, p. 51.

[72] *DBhS*, p. 131; see also VV, p. 62.

[73] VV, p. 101. The word for "juice" is rasa, its literal translation; both meanings of rasa are implied.

their own daughters, what can you expect of unreconstructed man?[74] The problem is not that man is subject to such desires, for they represent an unbounded energy which can be turned to profit. The problem is that the energies of an ignorant man are directed toward the wrong goal: the pursuit, conquest, and knowledge of women. They must be redirected toward the pursuit, conquest, and knowledge of the self.

THE FUNCTIONS OF CHASTITY. It might be reiterated that there are two doctrinal standards involved in this discussion. The first is that which makes equivalent the flesh and evil: Manichaean Christianity and, in a somewhat more indirect way, the more orthodox Vaiṣṇavism. Given this standard, the solution of the problem of the flesh is a very simple one: deny it. By denying the flesh one sublimates its energy, causing it to flow along more true, or "spiritual," channels. The second standard, that of the Sahajiyā, posits a unity of flesh and spirit, of human and divine. It seems to the Sahajiyās also that the flesh is not the end; but to them it is the most immediate, though somewhat risky, means of knowing the unity of which the flesh is only a part. The Sahajiyās accept the flesh, still attempting to affirm the spirit.

Caitanya, when his role was that of an ascetic, absolutely and roundly condemned any association with women, as we have seen. Not only was he himself of a strongly celibate bent, but the indications are that he demanded the same

[74] *Ānanda-bhairava*, p. 153. Rādhāgovinda Nāth, in his commentary on *CC Antya* 2:115, nicely understates the case in saying that lust causes a "restlessness of the mind not easily brought under control."

kind of asceticism of his followers. There is a story in the *CC* of how Choṭa Haridāsa, one of Caitanya's associates in Puri, paid some attention to a woman of that city, going so far as to accept alms from her; because of this Caitanya refused ever to look upon his face again. He said: "I can never again look upon the face of an ascetic [*vairāgī*] who associates with women. The senses are hard to control, and seek to fix themselves on worldly things. Even the wooden image of a woman has the power to steal the mind of a sage. . . . There are contemptible people, false ascetics, who gratify their fickle senses by acquaintanceship with women."[75] The way to control the senses is to deny them completely. Lust destroys the most rigorous of ascetics. Even so, some of Caitanya's followers considered his attitude a little harsh, as did Choṭa Haridāsa himself, who seems to have committed suicide. In any case, the *CBh* attests the fact that Caitanya, in his ascetic role, did not expect of others that which he did not do himself: "He never smiled at women, and when he saw a woman, even from a distance, he would turn aside."[76]

Caitanya's uncompromising celibacy, the celibacy of the traditional ascetic, is found and praised in many of his followers. The *CC* tells us of a more austere Haridāsa (the Haridāsa whipped through twenty-two market places) who was the prototype of a rigid, though curiously gentle, chastity:

There was, in the district in which Haridāsa was living, a zamindar named Rāmacandra Khān. This zamindar was antagonistic

[75] *CC Antya* 2:115 ff. The passage uses the term *prakṛti* for "woman"; its literal meaning is "material nature," and it has a special meaning for the Sahajiyās. In part, Kṛṣṇadāsa is paraphrasing *Bhāgavata* 9:19:17: "the senses attract strongly even the wisest of men."

[76] *CBh Ādi* 4:19. The term is *parastrī*, "woman belonging to another."

toward Vaiṣṇavas, and was greatly angered by the reverence and respect which the people showed toward Haridāsa. He therefore tried all kinds of ruses to lower Haridāsa in the eyes of the people, but nothing seemed to work. And finally, he summoned a young and very beautiful prostitute and ordered her to seduce Haridāsa and make him unchaste. The girl went, and found Haridāsa in the midst of his devotions. He said to her: When I finish my prayer I shall do as you desire. But he prayed all through the night, repeating the name of God. And so it went the next night, and the next. And finally the name of Kṛṣṇa, heard so often by the waiting girl, planted in her the seeds of bhakti, and she herself became a devout Vaiṣṇava.[77]

We have noticed that the perceptive Dāmodara saw and pointed out to Caitanya the possible misinterpretations which would be put upon Caitanya's having as a pupil a boy with a young and beautiful widow for a mother; the danger of such misinterpretations must have pushed the natural Vaiṣṇava tendency toward asceticism even further. Caitanya makes it perfectly obvious that he does not care to be associated with those deviant Vaiṣṇavas who associate with women in public.

The Sahajiyās also saw clearly that the senses have to be controlled and directed. But their methods of control, their technique of chastity, was not one of denial; it was one of transformation.

The old homeopathic principle says that poison is destroyed by poison; one rids oneself of a painful memory by dwelling on it, not by denying that the event that caused it ever existed. We have already noticed Rāmānanda's interesting version of this, by which he treated his two beautiful dancing girls with remarkable intimacy, himself remaining

[77] *CC Antya* 3:94 ff.

chaste. A similar case is that of the philosopher Viśvanātha Cakravartī, of whom the *Narottama-vilāsa* tells the following tale:

After some days Viśvanātha, at the order of his guru, left Śrīkhaṇḍa . . . and, having married, he went to live in Vṛndāvana. At the command of his guru, Viśvanātha went to lie with his wife, who was a very beautiful girl. . . . He lay with her on the bed, but Viśvanātha was transformed, and he did not touch her, as it had been his custom to do. He lay with his wife according to the instructions of his guru . . . and thus he controlled his senses.[78]

Thus, by controlling one's sexual desire, the will is brought to bear, and one's response to a stimulus is controlled by constant exposure to that stimulus. If one is continually exposed to a given sexual situation, passion gradually drains away; desire loses its significance, perhaps even being replaced by boredom. Nirmal Kumar Bose, a scholar of great perception as well as secretary to Gandhi during the last few years of the latter's life, makes this interesting observation:

In order to follow more fully the discipline known as brahmācārya, Gandhi adopted a curious mental attitude which, although rare, is one of the established modes of subordination of sex among spiritual aspirants in India. It was by becoming a woman that he tried to circumvent one of the most powerful and disturbing elements which belong to our biological existence.[79]

To the matter of "becoming a woman," we shall have occasion to return. The technique to which Bose refers was Gandhi's sleeping in the same bed with a young woman

[78] *NV*, pp. 200–201.
[79] Nirmal Kumar Bose, *My Days with Gandhi*, p. 3.

without touching her sexually. This is not only, as Bose puts it, "reminiscent of the Tantras," but is in fact the same Sahajiyā technique employed by Rāmānanda, Viśvanātha, and others.

A second assumption underlying the Sahajiyā attitude regarding the function of chastity is that loss of semen is loss of power. This is a notion common in much of India, and Carstairs discusses it as it occurs in Rajasthan:

> This concerned the making, storing, and expenditure of a man's semen (*viriya*) in which resides his strength. Everyone knew that semen was not easily formed; it takes forty days, and forty drops of blood, to make one drop of semen. . . . Everyone was agreed on one point, that the semen is ultimately stored in a reservoir in the head, whose capacity is twenty *tolas* (6.8 ounces). Semen of good quality is rich and viscous, like the cream of unadulterated milk. A man who possesses a store of such good semen becomes a superman. "He glows with radiant health," said Shanker Lal. He excels all normal men in strength and stamina, both moral and physical.[80]

Exposure to sexual stimulation arouses this power; controlled, the power is like steam in a boiler, no longer random. Practically, this means that the Sahajiyā trains himself to have ritual sexual intercourse without seminal discharge. And theoretically, by the admission that man is subject to desire, the Sahajiyās affirm the natural equilibrium between the attractiveness of the world and the attraction of the senses. This equilibrium is to be more than accepted; it is to be used. Desire, called kāma, is dangerous only when it

[80] G. Morris Carstairs, *The Twice-born*, pp. 83–84.

is considered as the end. The truth is that kāma is the beginning.

PRAKṚTI AND PURUṢA. Nirmal Kumar Bose wrote that Gandhi sought to control his passions by "becoming a woman." Though perhaps even psychologists and physiologists might admit that, given a certain predisposition, such a transmutation is possible, Bose's remark is casual enough to give a moment's pause. The questions are, of course, "why" and "how."

The question of homosexuality aside, as leading into a logical maze not wholly relevant, if a man becomes a woman, he presumably no longer considers a woman's body desirable. There is also the textual argument that the proper attitude of the worshipper toward Kṛṣṇa is that of the Gopīs, which the Sahajiyās took quite literally. The jīva is in the same relationship to the svarūpa as the Gopīs to Kṛṣṇa: the same, yet with an aspect of difference that allows the Sahajiyās to speak of a coming-together of two parts. The jīva is a Gopī, or Rādhā. One is, and should consider oneself, a woman, in relation to the sole male of the universe, to Kṛṣṇa. There is in fact a whole school of lyric writing based on this concept—the so-called *nāgara-bhāva* padas of Narahari Sarkār, whom we have noticed as one of the founders of the Sahajiyā school at Śrīkhaṇḍa.[81] Thus, says a Sahajiyā text, "assume the Gopī-*bhāva* . . . and incessantly [let the mind] dwell upon the body of Kṛṣṇa. Each in his own way will enjoy the pleasure of coition. The Gopī-

[81] See Chap. III, n. 71; see *BSI*, I, 289.

bhāva does away with maleness in sexual relationship."[82] When the worshipper becomes a woman, he is purified, and can enter into ritual intercourse without desire, without kāma: "The altar of beauty, the fulfillment of all passion is Rādhā. In union with a woman, if a man becomes a woman, he is purified."[83]

How a man becomes a woman is equally easy for the Sahajiyās to explain. The notion that the body contains both Rādhā and Kṛṣṇa leads more or less naturally to a recognition of what Jung called the "anima" element of masculine nature—"the representative of the female minority hidden below the threshold of consciousness."[84] Man is a sort of hermaphroditic creature, and the two sides of his nature, in terms borrowed from ancient views of the dualism of matter and spirit, are called *prakṛti* (female) and *puruṣa* (male): in the self is *prakṛti* and in the self is *puruṣa*.[85]

Although the svarūpa of the individual, and thus the rūpa, contains both male and female, it seems as if the sex of the body is determined by a preponderance of one or the other aspect. *Prakṛti* and *puruṣa* are spoken of as having two different rūpas, each containing rasa: "In the self is *prakṛti* and in the self is *puruṣa*; they are in two rūpas, and in both is rasa manifested."[86]

The rūpas are here thought of as two parts of a whole;

[82] *VV*, p. 50.
[83] *SS* pada 32.
[84] "Dogma and Natural Symbols," in *Psychology and Religion*, p. 42.
[85] *DBhS*, p. 138. The text goes on to say that *prakṛti* and *puruṣa* are the two elements of rasa, that bliss is latent in the two divided forms.
[86] *Ibid.*

if there were not two parts, there could be no coming-together into union. Unity can be considered the ultimate static state, but the process of the realization of this unity is dynamic.

> *Prakṛti* and *puruṣa* are the container and contained. Apart from them, nothing remains, even for a moment. They were manifested for purposes of play [*khela*]; by their natures they experience passion and rasa. . . . the body contains both of these, in greater or lesser parts. One body contains the two, making their loveplay, divided in their love only for pleasure or by a lovers' quarrel.[87]

There are two possibilities then, for the realization of unity. The first is the union of male and female rūpas, making one whole. Secondly, since every individual has within him both male and female elements, it is possible for him to realize unity entirely within himself. The second of these possibilities, the higher of the two, gives the notion of "becoming a woman" a new dimension. If one has an overabundance of *puruṣa* in his system, and is thus male, in order to pass beyond the point at which he needs a woman as an aid to the realization of blissful unity and to reach the point where he can realize it entirely within himself, he has to neutralize his maleness and balance male and female within himself. He has, so to speak, to raise the concentration of his *prakṛti* to equal that of his *puruṣa;* it seems that, to gain equilibrium within the self, equal halves are needed to make the whole. Thus: "Having abandoned his male body, he becomes the *prakṛti-svarūpa.* Know therefore the *svarūpa* of Rādhā; it can be known within the heart.

[87] *Ibid.*, p. 145.

When one becomes *prakṛti* by union with *prakṛti* it is not by means of his masculine body. God is hidden, but if one is purified, one can be saved, my brother."[88] When one is purified, kāma no longer remains. The worshiper cannot want a woman to satisfy himself, for he is no longer a man.

KĀMA AND PREMA. One of the things which makes the Vaiṣṇava-Sahajiyā doctrine interesting is that because of its debt to the Vaiṣṇavas it is more than a mere outline of a mechanistic system. Basically, the Sahajiyā teaching is simple enough: man is divine; all that he has to do is acknowledge that fact, learning to shed that part of him which keeps him from realization of his true, infinite, and blissful Kṛṣṇa-nature and, when the material husk is shucked off, to enjoy an eternity of pleasure. But, as the Sahajiyās were the first to admit, the path to this goal is slippery and right next to an abyss that extends all the way down to hell. As we have already noticed, one of the slipperiest places is greased with man's desire, kāma.

The Sahajiyās enter into something of a paradox by accepting the Vaiṣṇava notion that one must enter upon his search for eternal bliss with an attitude of selfless love. For the Vaiṣṇavas themselves there is no paradox, for the worship of Kṛṣṇa, near him and yet apart from him, is their goal. Worship is pleasing to Kṛṣṇa only if the worshiper, like the Gopī, has no thought of self. In such a case, the worshipper gets his reward from Kṛṣṇa's pleasure; the bhakta's joy increases as Kṛṣṇa's pleasure grows. This selfless attitude of love is prema. But given the Sahajiyā posi-

[88] *SS* pada 56, attributed to Caṇḍīdāsa.

tion, to the extent that one is Kṛṣṇa, one finds himself in the embarrassing condition of offering selfless love to himself. Fortunately, the Sahajiyās do not try to carry their argument this far but content themselves with saying that prema means that desire has been directed away from the self and toward its proper goal. It is generally agreed by Vaiṣṇavas of all types that if kāma, desire for the satisfaction of the senses, remains, egoism and vanity also remain. And where egoism and vanity remain, the self can never be known. Kāma must be transformed.[89]

The classical example of prema is that of the Gopīs and especially of Rādhā. The Gopīs were willing to sacrifice their position in society, their homes and families, their chastity, in the extremity of their love or Kṛṣṇa. The Gopīs longed for Kṛṣṇa, but their desire was a desire to satisfy him.

> The prema of the Gopīs is . . . a pure and spotless prema, with no element of kāma in it. The manifestations of kāma and prema are as different as iron and gold. . . . Kāma is the desire for the satisfaction of the self, but prema is the desire for the satisfaction of the senses of Kṛṣṇa. The sole object of Kāma is the pleasure of the self, but prema has as its only object the pleasure of Kṛṣṇa. . . . So abandon all else and worship Kṛṣṇa; serve him in prema, with his pleasure as your sole object.[90]

An attitude of prema is necessary. But the ways in which the Vaiṣṇavas and the Vaiṣṇava-sahajiyās define the difference between kāma and prema are revealing. To the Vaiṣ-

[89] Gratification of sexual desire is a dangerous form of egoism, and VV, p. 109, says that "if one takes a woman [for pleasure], his own soul is surely lost; his soul is destroyed, and he gains only hell." Even the desire for liberation (*mukti*) is basically selfish, for it gratifies the ego. VV, p. 99, says that Kṛṣṇa's "anger toward the selfish bhakta is very great; he who pleases himself by the conquest of his senses is destined for hell."

[90] *CC Ādi* 4:139 ff.

ṇavas, the difference is qualitative: they are as different as iron and gold. Kāma is a mere instinct, prema is a result of the grace of Kṛṣṇa: "If Kṛṣṇa grants his grace to any fortunate man, he teaches from within that man, as an indwelling guru. Then, when there is faith, devotion [bhakti] toward Kṛṣṇa, and association with holy men, the fruit is prema, in which the material world fades away."[91] The Sahajiyās, somewhat more alchemically inclined, feel that kāma and prema are not qualitatively different, but that kāma becomes prema by a slight rearrangement of motive and object. Say the Sahajiyās: "Prema is derived from kāma, but the motives of the two are different."[92]

To the Sahajiyās, prema becomes merely the desire to know the truth. When they speak of the prema of the worshiper toward Kṛṣṇa, they speak symbolically. And to the Sahajiyās prema is, far from being a result of Kṛṣṇa's grace, in no way exclusive. Every human being has a body and is as a result subject to kāma. Thus every human being has the potential for prema as well: "In whom there is a suggestion of kāma, prema is born."[93]

The sexual ritual must be to the worshiper as the road to the traveler: the road is the means, not the destination.[94] The bee uses the flower as a source of honey; when the honey has been made, the bee has no more use for the flower.[95]

91 *CC Madhya* 22:29 ff.

92 *VV*, p. 105.

93 *Ibid.*, p. 55.

94 *Caṇḍīdāser padāvalī* (BSP edition), No. 786; the passage is: "The practice of the *rāga-sādhana* [i.e., the sexual ritual] is as the road for the traveller."

95 *Prema-vilāsa* of Yugala-dāsa (*VSP*, II, 1665): "The honey-bees . . . gather honey from many flowers, and afterwards have no further use for the flowers."

The *Ānandabhairava* puts it unequivocally: "Kāma is the passion of the body. He who has his bodily passion in mind will never be saved from such a sin, no matter how many births he passes through. He will suffer from birth to birth and he will go to hell."[96] The transformation of kāma to prema is the transformation of man to woman. It is for this that the Sahajiyā trains himself so arduously.

As we have seen, the notion of *bhāva* is at the core of the worship of all Vaiṣṇavas; it is based on the principle that the Vṛndāvana-līlā can actually be re-created in the life of the worshiper by his taking on the personality of one of Kṛṣṇa's intimates in Vṛndāvana. Constant thought, remembrance, reflection, and action lead to becoming. This is also the essence of the Sahajiyā idea of transformation, though it is termed by them *āropa.*

Āropa, in more usual philosophical thought, means the attribution of the qualities and nature of one subject to those of another, an "illusory imposition," as S. N. Dasgupta terms it.[97] To the Sahajiyās, the "imposition" of the character and nature of Rādhā upon one's own is anything but illusory. It is, quite to the contrary, a recognition of reality. *Āropa* is the way in which *prakṛti* and *puruṣa* are balanced; it is the way in which the svarūpa is known through the rūpa; it is what makes the difference between a *sādhaka* and a libertine. "If he ignores *āropa,* he will go to hell."[98] *Āropa* is the necessary and delicate process by which the Sahajiyā is taught to raise both feet from the clay.

[96] P. 148. Another possible reading is: "He will suffer birth after birth"—*janme janme bhoga bhuñjaye.*

[97] *History of Indian Philosophy,* III, 142.

[98] *SS* pada 68, attributed to Narahari.

3. MAN AND THE UNIVERSE

THE PLACE OF THE HIDDEN MOON. If the *avatāra* of Kṛṣṇa in the earthly Vṛndāvana described in the *Bhāgavata-purāṇa* is essential to the svarūpa of the Bhagavat Kṛṣṇa, if Kṛṣṇa is able to appear in the phenomenal world without any effect on his non-phenomenal nature, it is equally reasonable that all those who are in intimate relation to him in the earthly Vṛndāvana are also essential to his svarūpa and are on the earth as parts of Kṛṣṇa's *avatāra*. Rādhā and the Gopīs are his śaktis, inseparable from his true self: "The Gopīs, beloved of Kṛṣṇa, are his *svarūpa-śaktis* . . . they are identical with him."[99] And CC *Ādi* 13 tells us that before Kṛṣṇa took the form of Caitanya, he caused certain of his bhaktas in the eternal Vṛndāvana to take human form as Caitanya's mother, father, brother, friends, and teachers. There is no reason not to extend this still further: the whole paraphernalia of the heavenly Vṛndāvana takes phenomenal form as Kṛṣṇa does; and, like him, it does so without affecting its essential non-phenomenal nature. In Vaiṣṇava thought, Kṛṣṇa's surroundings, both objects and persons, are considered extensions of Kṛṣṇa's self, and are collectively called Kṛṣṇa's *dhāman*. The *dhāman*, then, makes a simultaneous appearance on the earth with Kṛṣṇa; like him, it participates simultaneously in both phenomenal and non-phenomenal worlds. The earthly Vṛndāvana, the Vṛndāvana described in the *Bhāgavata*, is identical with the heavenly Vṛndāvana, and Kṛṣṇa exists simultaneously in both

[99] Rādhāgovinda Nāth's *ṭīkā* on *CC Ādi* 1:41.

places, together with his *dhāman:* the river Yamunā, the Gopas and Gopīs, the cows and trees and flowers.

All this being part of the svarūpa, the Sahajiyās say that it is all contained within the self. They allegorically describe the eternal Vṛndāvana in the following way.

In the eternal Vṛndāvana there is neither night nor day; there is continual pleasure; flowers bloom eternally; there are trees, under which one may cool oneself and rest; honey creepers grow in profusion, and the bees are intoxicated by the fragrance of their white and golden flowers; there is no death, but eternal youth.[100] Another text says that the eternal Vṛndāvana is far away, yet within the fourteen worlds; in it there is no old age or death; it is inhabited by youths, knowers of the rasa contained within themselves, knowers of the ways of *prakṛti* and the splendor of *puruṣa.* It is a place where there is no coming or going, no becoming—where everything is stable and where therefore there is no deception or falsity:[101] "The place is divine and imperishable, and remains from age to age. There is no movement, no destruction. The sun . . . the wind . . . the moon . . . do not move, and all mistiness [of vision] is destroyed."[102] It is in this place that the eternally young Kṛṣṇa has perpetual pleasure with his Rādhā: "Know then the eternal svarūpa of Kṛṣṇa. His body, of supreme excellence, is eternal bliss. Whatever he desires, that desire is fulfilled; he is eternally young, eternally taking his pleasure in Vra-

[100] *Āgama*, pp. 107–8.

[101] This is of course the state of sahaja described by the *caryā-padas*; see for example *caryā* no. 7, of Kānhu-pā.

[102] *Amṛtarasāvalī*, pp. 186–87.

japur [i.e., Vṛndāvana]."[103] For in youth is both passion and prema: "In youth, passion fills the whole world."[104] "The time of youth is the svarūpa of prema."[105] The young lovers experience eternal *mahābhāva,* the highest state of love, embodied in Rādhā: "The lovers both experience eternal *mahābhāva;* there is no greater truth than this. In their *bhāva,* Rādhā and Kṛṣṇa, the two, are one. The qualities and beauty of each eternally steal the other's thoughts."[106]

In this place, the bliss of the *sahaja-mānuṣa* grows eternally, and is never sated:

In external Vṛndāvana, the immaterial *puruṣa,* treasure-house of rasa, truth, and bliss, has līlā within himself, and still is never satisfied. The eternal truth, eternally renewed, of which the bhaktas drink eternally—I will take my pleasure from this store, and I shall sip this nectar, this *sudhā*-drink.[107]

In this eternal world . . . there is no coming or going. From the outside it cannot be seen; it is the place of the hidden moon, it can only be known within. It resides in the lotus of the six petals.[108]

[103] *Āgama,* p. 99.
[104] *CC Ādi* 4:102.
[105] *Ādyasārasvatakārikā,* p. 4, quoted by Basu in *SS,* p. 99 n. Basu comments that "those who worship the *prema-līlā* of Kṛṣṇa remain as eternal youths, since it is at that time of life that seeds of prema are nourished in the heart."
[106] *VV,* p. 66.
[107] *SS* pada 34, attributed to Kṛṣṇadāsa. A view is that the līlā is eternal because the desire of Rādhā and Kṛṣṇa for one another is eternal, never able to be satiated. On the contrary, a taste of the supreme rasa increases the desire for another taste. See VV, p. 122. The pada of "Kṛṣṇadāsa" quoted here goes on: "My sweetness and the prema of Rādhā . . . both are growing constantly, and neither is ever exhausted; my sweetness is eternally renewed."
[108] *Ānanda-bhairava,* p. 136.

The eternal Vṛndāvana, the projection of the self, the sahaja, the secret place, "the place of the hidden moon," is the place of the eternal pleasure of Rādhā and Kṛṣṇa. The conceit is that a stream of rasa flows perpetually from the eternal Vṛndāvana to the earth, manifested as the stream of rasa flowing to and between men and women.[109] This stream is a most wonderful stream: it is clear, without a trace of mud, flowing between two banks that are high and rocky. It is a fountain of youth, and bathing in the stream increases beauty. If one bathes therein, union with the divine is certain.[110] Like the līlā of Rādhā and Kṛṣṇa, which is its source, it is eternally flowing.[111] It is a stream so broad that it has no other shore.[112]

The eternal Vṛndāvana is known within the *sahaja-mānuṣa* as he worships the united Rādhā-Kṛṣṇa, says the *Sahaja-tattva*.[113]

[109] S. B. Dasgupta (*Śrīrādhār-krama-bikāśa*, p. 254) says: "In the eyes of the Vaiṣṇava-sahajiyās the idea of union was the highest idea. In this union is *mahābhāva*—the sahaja. The sahaja is . . . the acme of prema. The sahaja is the ultimate truth contained in the universal Brahma egg; from it the world arose, in it everything is contained, and in it destroyed. This sahaja was the substance of the 'eternal country' [*nityā-deśa*]. . . . Thus, 'Vṛndāvana' and 'mental Vṛndāvana' was the *guptacandrapur* of the Sahajiyās. . . . *Guptacandrapur* is the place of the pleasure of Rādhā and Kṛṣṇa; from their eternal pleasure, a stream of *sahaja-rasa* flows eternally."

[110] See for example *Amṛtarasāvalī*, pp. 166 ff., 171 f.

[111] *Sahaja-upāsana-tattva* of Taruṇīramaṇa (*SPP*, IV, No. 1), quoted in *RKB*, p. 255.

[112] *RKB*, p. 255, quoting the *Sahaja-tattva* "of Mukunda-dāsa," Manindrakumār Nandi edition, p. 58.

[113] *VSP*, II, 1655 ff. The author of the text is Rādhāvallabha-dāsa. The MS from which D. C. Sen has printed the text is, according to him, datable A.D. 1822; Sukumār Sen (*BSI* I, 423) dates the work itself B.S. 1195 or A.D. 1789, and has this to say about the author: "The poet Rādhāvallabha-dāsa (or Rādhā-dāsa) was a pupil of Śrīnivāsa-ācārya. Among the pupils of Śrīnivāsa there were three Rādhāvallabhas, among them Rādhāvallabha Cakravartī, whom Rāmagopāla-dāsa mentions in his

Let us speak about Vṛndāvana. Vṛndāvana is manifested in [two] ways. What are they? The Vṛndāvana of the mind, and the eternal Vṛndāvana. [The eternal Vṛndāvana] is the līlā-Vṛndāvana; its lord is the lord of Gokula, fully Bhagavān, possessing all divine qualities. . . . It is the eternal place, where the eternal Rādhā and Kṛṣṇa exist, each the receptacle for the sweetness of the other: that is the eternal Vṛndāvana. What of the Vṛndāvana of the mind? It is Kṛṣṇa-bhakti, and is manifested in the mind of the worshipper as the two who have become one in love.[114]

The eternal Vṛndāvana is seen only by him who has eyes to see: "[Vṛndāvana is] the crest-jewel of the earth, a forest full of wishing-trees; to material eyes it seems an illusion. It manifests its true form [only] to the eyes of prema."[115] It is hidden by māyā, but is nonetheless real. The music of the flute is not less real, says the VV, because one cannot see the flute-player:

He who is devoted to the immaterial body has knowledge of the self; he understands. . . . If it were not manifest, how could one worship? Without the existence of Vraja, there could be no worship. . . . All jīvas become intoxicated by the drama of māyā, but all things come to him who is intoxicated by the joy within himself. . . . He who desires the pleasures of the body is not able to be steadfast; his heart is a nest of worms, who performs sādhana adversely [i.e., with the pleasure of the body as his aim]. The sound of the flute is heard, but the player may not be seen.[116]

Rasakalpāvallī . . . who wrote a few padas of lamentation and translated the *Vilāpakusa-māñjali* of Raghunātha-dāsa" (p. 441).

[114] *Ibid.*, p. 1656.

[115] *CC Ādi* 5:17–18.

[116] VV, p. 73.

MAN IS THE UNIVERSE. Man is the universe in the sense that in him is the eternal Vṛndāvana. He is the universe also in the more pragmatic Tāntric sense that he is made up of the same elements which make up the universe, in the same arrangement. Nothing real stands between him and the infinity of space and time. And as the vertical cosmographic extremes of the continuous universe are hell and heaven, so those of the body are the organs of base sexual enjoyment at the lowest point; and pure consciousness, truth, and bliss —the brain—at the highest.

The body is made up of several vertically arranged successive sections, called *padmas* (lotuses) or *sarovaras* (lotus ponds). Thought about the locations and functions of these *padmas* is borrowed by the Sahajiyās directly from the Tantras: only the terminology sometimes differs.

The *padmas* or *sarovaras* are distributed along the spinal column. Their relative positions and functions can be glimpsed by noting the extremes: the lowest *padma* is related to purely sexual activity. The highest, located in the brain (according to Carstairs' informants, it might be remembered, the storehouse of semen), is related to the realization of the purely non-physical ultimate. The *Ātma-tattva*[117] lists the *padmas* as follows.

[117] The *Ātma-tattva* text used for this study is in the anthology *Vaiṣṇava-granthāvalī*, pp. 151 ff. Sukumār Sen, in his *Bāṅgālā sāhitye gadya*, p. 7, gives the opening lines of a work called *Deha-kaḍacā*, which are very similar to those of the *Ātma-tattva*. Sen ascribes this work to the pen of Narottama-dāsa, which would place the work chronologically in the early seventeenth century. Interestingly, the text called *Camotkāra-candrikā*, ascribed to Kṛṣṇadāsa, has the same opening lines as the *Deha-kaḍacā* (see Asiatic Society MSS 3614 and 5363: *Descriptive Catalogue of the Vernacular Manuscripts in the Collections of the Royal Asiatic Society of Bengal*, by Haraprasād Śāstrī, pp. 102–3). The relevant lines are:

There are four lotuses in the body. The first is the four-petalled lotus, located in the anus. This is the dwelling-place of the *jīvātma.*[118] There is a six-petalled lotus, located at the base of the penis, the dwelling-place of the *bhūtātmā.* There is a ten-petalled lotus, of which each petal has ten petals, located in the *kuṇḍali*-place,[119] the dwelling-place of *param-*

Deha-kaḍacā: tumi ki / āmi jība / tumi kona jība / āmi taṭastha jība / thāken kothā / bhāṇḍe. . . .

Camotkāra-candrikā: tumi ki / āmi jība / kona jība / taṭastha jība / thāka kothā / bhāṇḍe. . . .

Ātma-tattva: jība kayti / ki ki / sthula jība / taṭastha jība / baddha jība. . . .

S. K. De, in his *History of Bengali Literature in the Nineteenth Century,* pp. 464–65, connects the *Deha-kaḍacā* with a Sahajiyā text called *Ātma-jijñāsa,* and relates both texts to a "bare dry fatiguing aphoristic" genre peculiar to Sahajiyā philosophical texts. De says specifically: "The first work that calls for mention in this group is the *Deha-kaḍacā* attributed to Narottama-ṭhākura (text published in the *SPP* for B.S. 1304, no. 1, pp. 39–46). . . . The text of this MS . . . seems to be almost identical (making due allowance for trifling scribal and other variations) with that of the *Ātma-jijñāsa* ascribed to Kṛṣṇadāsa (*SP* MS No. 1474)." He mentions as other works of the same type the *Āśraya-nirṇaya, Ātma-nirūpaṇa, Svarūpa-barṇana,* and *Rāgamayī-kaṇā,* all Sahajiyā works ascribed to Kṛṣṇadāsa. Our anonymous *Ātmatattva* can be classed here.

118 The term used is *guhyadeśa,* "the secret place," suggesting the hidden place which is the abode of Rādhā and Kṛṣṇa in union. This is the *mūlādhāra-cakra* of the Tantras, located between the anus and penis and representing the gross sexual urge and function. See Woodroffe, *Shakti and Shākta,* p. 641.

119 The specific location is not given. The term *kuṇḍalinī,* "coiled" suggests the doctrine of *kuṇḍalinī-śakti,* the "serpent-power" of the Hindu Tantras. There is a slight difference between the Tantras and the present text, however, the Tantras conceiving of the *kuṇḍalinī-śakti* as lying coiled in the *mūlādhāra-cakra.* It is the purpose of Tāntric *sādhana* to raise this serpent power through the four or six *cakras* to union with the ultimate principal (Śiva), who resides in the *sahasrāra-cakra* in the head. Woodroffe (*Shakti and Shākta,* pp. 653 ff.) has this to say about it: "From the Mahākuṇḍalinī the universe has sprung. In her supreme form She is at rest, coiled round and at one . . . with the Shivabindu. She next uncoils Herself to manifest. . . . The body may . . . be compared to a magnet with two poles. The Mūlādhāra, in so far as it is the seat of the Kuṇḍalinī Shakti, is that static pole in relation to the rest of the body,

ātmā. There is a burning lotus (*ujjvalapadma*),[120] of which the number of petals is not specified, although it is said that each of its petals has twelve petals. This is the dwelling-place of the *ātmārāmeśvara,* who contains bliss within himself.[121] The ascending importance of the lotuses lies in the fact that experience in *sādhana* is transformed from physical to purely spiritual. The power of the individual ascends in *sādhana* toward ultimate union and bliss in the uppermost lotus.

The *ātmās* which dwell in the lotuses have qualities and functions. The *jīvātmā* is blood-red in color, is sustained by water, and has as its function (*karma*) the "bearing of the burden."[122] The *bhūtātmā* is bright yellow in color, is sustained by food, and has as its *karma* the increasing or fostering of the six *ripus*, the "enemies" of realization: *kāma* (desire), *krodha* (anger), *lobha* (lust), *moha* (infatuation), *mada* (intoxication with pleasure), and *mātsarya* (malice). The *paramātmā* is the color of lightning, is sustained by the wind, and has as its *karma* the various mental activities, and consciousness. The *ātmārāma,* the self-desiring, is the color

which is dynamic. . . . This static Shakti is affected by the Prāṇāyāma and the other Yogic processes and becomes dynamic. Thus, when completely dynamic, that is, when Kuṇḍalinī unites with Shiva in the Shahasrāra, the polarization of the body gives way. The two poles are united in one, and there is the state of consciousness called Samādhi."

120 Dasgupta (*ORC*, p. 118) points out that in the *Sādhana-mālā* it is said that the producer of *mahāsukha* (supreme pleasure) resides in the navel and has fire as her nature: "When roused by Yogic practice she becomes ablaze in the region of the navel." She then moves upward through the *cakras*, burning everything, produces bliss in the *sahasrāra-cakra,* and returns to lie dormant again in the navel.

121 Kṛṣṇa, containing Rādhā within himself?

122 *Bhārabahana:* the burden is not specified.

of the moon, is sustained by the nectar of the name Hari (i.e., Kṛṣṇa), and its *karma* is to keep the word "Hari" constantly in the mind.[123] The *ātmārameśvara* has the form and color of the sun,[124] is also sustained by the nectar of the name, and has as its *karma* the worship of Kṛṣṇa, wisdom, strength, knowledge, and above all the tasting of rasa.

The text goes on to discuss the five *prāṇas* (breaths) that live in these lotuses, and then, in detail, the relationship of the physical body to the rest of the universe.[125] It is at this point very close to pure Tāntrism. The text continues: From the creative union of *prakṛti* and *puruṣa* there arise the three qualities *rājasa* (passion), *tāmasa* (darkness or ignorance), and *sattva* (truth). From *rājasa* the five elements are born: earth, water, fire, air, and space. These also have qualities and dwelling places. The qualities of earth are odor and light color (*śukla*); its dwelling-place is in the nose. The qualities of water are rasa[126] and pale or golden color (*gaura*), and its dwelling-place is in the lips. Fire is omitted in the text. The qualities of air are touch and dark color

[123] The *ātmārāma* is not assigned a lotus dwelling-place, an omission for which no explanation is given.

[124] Sun and moon are symbols used in Buddhist and Hindu Tantras for the "nerves" of the left and right, called *iḍā* and *piṅgalā*. This is another statement of the essential unity. Dasgupta (*ITB*, p. 170) says: "The *iḍā* and *piṅgalā* are outside the spinal cord and proceed from the left and right testicles respectively and pass on to the right and left of the *suṣumnā* (the central nerve) in the bent form of a bow. The *iḍā* is also called the moon, of white color, and the Śakti; the *piṅgalā* is called the sun, of red color, and the *puruṣa*. *Suṣumnā* is of the color and nature of fire."

[125] We shall notice a whole series of equivalences based on the number five: the five elements of the universe and of the human body, the five senses, the five arrows of Kāma the love god.

[126] Rasa is also literally "juice."

(*śyāma*—the color of Kṛṣṇa), and its dwelling-place is in the eye. The qualities of space are sound and smoke-color, and its dwelling-place is in the ear.

From *tāmasa* arise the ten senses, the five *jñānendriyas* (knowledge-senses) and the five *karmendriyas* (activity-senses). The five *jñānendriyas* are in the nose, tongue, eye, skin, and ear, and they experience smell, taste, heat and cold, sight, and sound. The five *karmendriyas* are tongue (speech), hand, foot, anus (*payu*), and sexual organ (*upastha*). The speech-sense enables one to speak good or evil words, the hand-sense to hold substantial things, the foot-sense to come and go, the anus-sense to pass feces, and the genitals to pass sperm and urine.

From *sattva* arise ten *devatās*, each of whom controls and guards one of the senses, directing them, assumedly, toward their proper purposes. By the aggregate of these equivalences, the cosmic nature of man is stated.

The account given by the *Ānanda-bhairava* is not as complete as that of the *Ātma-tattva*, though it describes in more detail the lotuses of the body. In this text, the number of lotuses is, however, set at three, and they are described in descending order. In the head is a thousand-petalled lotus, floating in a lotus pond (*sarovara*). The truth is contained in this lotus pond, and the water from it flows down and fills the lotus ponds below: the stream of rasa that, Sahajiyā fancy has it, flows from the eternal Vṛndāvana to earth. The water fills the lotus pond that is in the belly. In this pond is union of the rūpa and svarūpa; in it floats a hundred-petalled lotus, on which the svarūpa rests. Somewhere below the lotus pond of the belly is another pond, and in it grows a lotus of eight petals. This is sometimes called the lotus of the thigh (*ūru*).[127] This pond is gloomy and dark. It is the lake of the physical aspect of the worshipper, before he has been transformed.

The VV account of the subject (pp. 93 ff.) is much the same as that of the *Ānanda-bhairava*, except that, as in the *Ātma-tattva*, the lotuses are four in number. Their locations are not given, but it is said that they are in ascending order. The first and lowest lotus has six petals.[128] In this lotus the līlā of Rādhā and Kṛṣṇa is taking place. Above this is a lotus of eight petals, in which are hidden the eight *sakhīs*, the companions, of Rādhā.[129] Above this is a hundred-petalled lotus, in which is the knowledge of the truth of the guru; wise men take refuge in this lotus. In the highest place of all is the lotus of a thousand petals, in which the Lord himself resides. One who knows the truth of these lotuses, says the text, knows the most profound form of the līlā of Rādhā and Kṛṣṇa.

The *Sahaja-tattva* account is very sketchy. The text names

127 See *Shakti and Shākta*, p. 637.

128 The more usual number is four or eight. The reason given by the *Amṛtarasāvalī* for the number six is, somewhat cryptically, that six *nāyikās* dwell in the six-petalled lotus. The six senses, as some texts count them, are used in *sādhana;* six is thus to those texts the lowest significant number. In general, the significance of the number of petals is obscure. Woodroffe, in his *Shakti and Shākta*, p. 641, says that in the Tāntric texts the number of petals is determined by the number and position of the *naḍis* (channels or "nerves" passing through a particular *cakra*). The numbers given in most Tāntric texts are 4, 6, 10, 12, 16, 2, and 1,000, in that order. The Sahajiyā texts all agree about the thousand-petalled lotus in the head, but disagree among themselves and with the Tantras as to the rest. There is no reason given for any of this in any text I have consulted.

129 The eight members of the Tāntric circle. The sakhīs of Rādhā are parts of her in the same way in which the śaktis are parts of the *śaktiman;* thus all women participate in the qualities of Rādhā.

six lotuses, being those of the foot, thigh, navel, heart, hand, and face or head. It is said that Brahmā has his abode in the thousand-petalled lotus and that two hundred other lotuses cover his jeweled couch. In the two eyes, Rādhā and Kṛṣṇa rest, each on a lotus of a hundred petals: Rādhā is in the left eye and Kṛṣṇa in the right. The *paramātmā* is seated on a jeweled throne in the region of the navel, and he comes and goes in the body through the nostrils.[130]

Other Sahajiyā texts present roughly the same picture, in varying degrees of completeness and obscurity. The details are not always clear, nor are they intended to be. But their general meaning is obvious enough.

The Tantras draw still more elementary parallels between the human body and the universe. Some go so far as to attempt to locate seas, mountains, rivers, and other geographical features, within the body.[131] The *Ātma-tattva* details the identity of the elements of the universe with those of the body. The Tantras, like the Sahajiyā texts, vary in their statements on the number and location of the *cakras*, as they term the *padmas*. But the principle is the same: the *cakras* are of ascending importance, the basest at the seat of sexual passion, the highest in the head, where, the *Ṣaṭ-cakra-nirūpaṇa* says, the union of Śiva and Śakti (to the Sahajiyās, Rādhā and Kṛṣṇa) takes place.

The Buddhist Tantras locate four *cakras* along the spinal column, the first in the navel, the second in the heart, the third in the throat, and the highest in the head. The Hindu Tantras (as witnessed by the *Ṣaṭ-cakra-nirūpaṇa*), however,

[130] *VSP*, II, 1655–58. The reference is to control of the breath as an essential part of Yogic discipline.

[131] See *ITB*, p. 161. For an example of this in Sahajiyā literature, see *Ānanda-bhairava*, p. 133.

list six in addition to the *cakra* of the head, which is called *sahasrāra*. These seven are the *mūlādhāra*, located between the anus and the penis, the color of which is red; the *svādhiṣṭhāna*, located at the base of the penis, which is vermilion in color; the *maṇipura* (called *maṇa* by the *Ānanda-bhairava*), located in the navel, which has the color of cloud; the *anāhata*, with twelve petals, located in the heart, and of reddish color: the *viśuddha*, of sixteen petals, located in the throat, which is the color of smoke; the *ājñā*, located between the eyebrows, of two petals and unstated color; and the *sahasrāra*, of a thousand petals, located in the head, and white in color.

To the Sahajiyās, the body is full of rasa, of the bliss of union, or, speaking purely physiologically, of semen. The place of rasa at the beginning of *sādhana* is in the lowest lotus, the seat of sexual passion. By *sādhana*, rasa is raised from lotus to lotus along the spinal column, until it unites with the thousand-petalled lotus in the head; there, in pure experience and pure consciousness of Rādhā and Kṛṣṇa in union, of the svarūpa, is full and eternal realization of their bliss. Here there is no longer even the seeming distinction of human and divine; here man knows completely the divine *ānanda* within himself.[132] His consciousness has moved from physical, especially sexual, sensation gradually upward to a

[132] The other way of viewing this unity, suggested but not much stressed in the Sahajiyā texts, is the unity of left and right. The VV, for example (p. 90), mentions rather in passing that "*puruṣa* is the right and *prakṛti* is called the left." The Tantras, however, lay stress on this view of unity. Dasgupta mentions in *ORC*, pp. 107 f.: "We have seen that the Bodhicitta [the sahaja, the supreme bliss] is constituted of two factors, viz. Śūnyatā and Karuṇā, or Prajñā and Upāya. Among the nerves of the body, which are innumerable, thirty-two are more important, of which again three are the most important, two by the sides of the spinal cord and one in the middle; with these two side nerves are identified and cardinal

blissful state of pure abstraction from all things physical, a state of *samādhi.* Rāmakṛṣṇa, who, while not himself a Vaiṣṇava-sahajiyā, was nonetheless a Tāntric of a sort, writes of this height of experience. By substituting the term rasa for *kulakuṇḍalinī* and the terms Rādhā and Kṛṣṇa for Śakti and Śiva in the following excerpt from his teaching as reported in the *Śrīśrīrāmakṛṣṇa-kathāmṛta,* we have a good summary of the Vaiṣṇava-sahajiyā doctrine in the matter:

> There are the *īḍā, piṅgalā,* and *suṣumnā* channels, and within the *suṣumnā* there are six lotuses. The lowest of these is the *mūlādhāra.* Then come the *svādhiṣṭhāna, maṇipura, anāhata, viśuddha,* and *ājña.* These are [also] called the six *cakras.*
>
> When the *kulakuṇḍalinī* is awakened, it passes gradually through the *mūlādhārā, svādhiṣṭhāna,* and *maṇipura,* to the *anāhata* lotus which is in the heart, and there it rests.
>
> Then the mind moves away from [the gross physical senses]. There is perception, and a great brilliance is seen. The *sādhaka,* when he sees this brilliance, is struck dumb in wonder.
>
> The *kuṇḍalinī* moves through the six *cakras,* and, coming to the *sahasrāra,* is united with it. Then there is *samādhi.*
>
> These *cakras* are also called *bhūmis.* The heart is the fourth of these, and in it is the *anāhata* lotus, with twelve petals.
>
> The *viśuddha cakra* is the fifth *bhūmi.* When the mind rises here, it is anxious to hear and speak of *īśvara.* Its place is in the throat, and its lotus has sixteen petals.
>
> Then the sixth *bhūmi,* and here is the *ājñā cakra,* with two petals. When the *kulakuṇḍalinī* rises here, the form [rūpa] of *īśvara* is seen. But a slight veil remains—it is as if one sees a

---

principles Prajñā and Upāya, and the middle nerve, which is the meeting-place of the other two nerves, is spoken of as the path of Sahajā. . . . It may be said that the two nerves represent the principle of duality, and the middle nerve . . . the principle of absolute unity."

light within a lantern, and thinks that the light itself can be touched, but the glass intervenes.

Then the seventh *bhūmi*, where the lotus has a thousand petals; when the *kuṇḍalinī* comes here there is *samādhi*. In this *sahasrāra* Śiva, full of *sat*, *cit*, and *ānanda*, resides, in union with Śakti. . . . In *samādhi*, nothing external remains. One cannot even take care of his body any more; if milk is put into his mouth, he does not swallow. If he remains for 21 days in this condition, he is dead. The ship puts out to sea, and returns no more.[133]

Thus the ascent of the soul, from the basest of mortal worlds to the most blissful of eternities. Or, in parallel physiology, thus the semen flows upward through the middle channel to the lotus in the brain. Instead of discharging semen wastefully, the practitioner can in intercourse redirect this vital force, both giving and receiving within himself. The *Kaḍacā* of Svarūpa puts it this way: "If he controls himself in the process of *sādhana*, he becomes full of Brahmā [i.e., assumedly, that he enjoys a state of bliss like that of union with Brahmā]. Even if he has a hundred women, there will be no discharge of semen. Then the material *rasika* has become a possessor of the true knowledge."[134] This accomplishment, of course, takes considerable discipline and training, including the course on how to become a woman. Given an equivalence of human and divine, a

[133] *Śrīśrīrāmakṛṣṇakathāmṛta*, IV, 141–42.

[134] Text in *PCSC*, p. 74. There is also a passage in the *VV* (p. 62) in which it is said that in the process of *sādhana* the semen ascends into the head. See also *ORC*, pp. 109–28. For a discussion of the concept in a different setting, see Henri Maspero, "Les procedes de 'nourir le principe vital' dans la religion taoiste ancienne" in *Journal Asiatique*, CCXCIX (1937). The similarity here is perhaps due to the influence of Indian Tāntrism on China.

physiological act has cosmic characteristics and consequences. The Sahajiyā doctrine, as Dasgupta says, "views our whole being in all its physical, biological, and psychological aspects from an ontological point of view. And when everything is thus viewed from the ontological perspective, human love acquires an ontological significance."[135]

[135] *ORC*, p. 158.

6) Principles of Sādhana

1. VARIOUS AIDS TO ATTAINMENT

THE AUTHORITY OF THE ŚĀSTRAS. According to one commonly accepted view in Indian philosophy, there are eight possible sources of knowledge. These are perception (*pratyakṣa*), inference (*anumāna*), testimony (*śabda*), analogy (*upamāna*), assumption (*arthāpatti*), non-recognition (*abhāva*), equivalence (*saṃbhava*), and tradition (*aitihya*).[1] Jīva Gosvāmin rejects seven of them, retaining only *śabda*, the testimony of scripture—revelation.

It is a part of a basic conservatism of most religions that truth is seen as past. One of the most usual arguments made by religious systems in India is that their ideas are to be found in older systems, but that in the older systems these

[1] *VFM*, 2d ed., pp. 257–58.

ideas were improperly or incompletely interpreted. There is an instructive story told by Kṛṣṇadāsa of how the scholar Vāsudeva Sārvabhauma expounded the *advaita-vāda* precociously to Caitanya for seven days. Caitanya patiently waited for him to finish, and then, according to Kṛṣṇadāsa, put the ax to his argument by saying that he had misinterpreted the Vedas. Caitanya seems to have been fond of doing things like this, for we are also told that he was able to defeat a paṇḍit who had performed the rather impressive feat of reciting one hundred extempore Sanskrit verses on the beauty of the Ganges merely by finding poetic flaws in one of them.[2] In any case, when Vāsudeva had finished his argument, Caitanya said:

> I understand the meaning of the texts clearly, but your explanation has bewildered me. The language of the texts states their meaning clearly, but you say that the true meaning is hidden. You do not explain the primary meaning, but try to hide it behind a secondary meaning. . . . In all jīvas there is bone and there is excrement. These are not essentially different from conch-shell and cow-dung. Yet conch-shell and cow-dung are purifying, while bone and excrement are defiling. The word of the Vedas is the only thing that makes the difference between them.[3]

Therefore, says Caitanya, one cannot reason by analogy, and one cannot look for secondary meanings. There is often difference of opinion, of course, on just what the primary meaning is. Caitanya accepts revelation as authority, including, assumedly, that of the Vedas. For the Gosvāmins, reve-

[2] CC *Ādi* 16:28–104.
[3] CC *Madhya* 6:121–28.

lation is through the *śāstras;* but for practical purposes, as the commentator Viśvanātha suggests, to them the term *śāstra* means the *Bhāgavata-purāṇa:* "By the term *śāstra* is meant exclusively the *Śrīmād-bhāgavata,* which enjoins acts of devotion."[4] For Kṛṣṇa revealed himself through the *śāstras*: "To the māyā-trapped creature, knowledge of Kṛṣṇa does not come easily. In his mercy toward the jīva, Kṛṣṇa made the Vedas and Purāṇas. He causes the jīva to know him through the *śāstras,* and through the guru, and in the ātmā."[5] So bhakti is the teaching, the primary meaning, of the *śāstras*: "The gaining of Kṛṣṇa is the *sambandha* of the Veda-*śāstra* . . . bhakti is its *abhidheya* . . . prema is its *prayojana.*"[6]

Vaiṣṇavas of all sorts consider that there are two general types of bhakti. The first is an external, ritual activity based on the injunctions of the *śāstras* (*vidhi*) and is called *vaidhi-bhakti.* The second is the internal, passionate relationship of the released jīva to Kṛṣṇa and is called *rāgānuga-bhakti. Vaidhi-bhakti* is for that very great majority of persons who are neither by nature in direct relationship to Kṛṣṇa nor yet released from māyā by completion of the disciplines: "Those who do not possess *rāga,* worship according to the injunc-

[4] The commentary *Bhaktirasāmrtasindhu-bindu* on Rūpa's *Bhaktirasāmrtasindhu,* p. 14; see *VFM,* p. 128.

[5] CC *Madhya* 20:106 ff.

[6] CC *Madhya* 20:109–10. The three terms are technical ones collectively called *anubandha,* introductory statements to a literary or philosophical work. There are usually either four or six in all. The *Nyāya-bindu-ṭīkā* of Dharmottara, as Daniel H. H. Ingalls has pointed out to me, defines them in this way: "The *viśaya* is the subject-matter of the text. The *abhidheya* (or *abhidhana*) is what the text proposes to say about the subject matter. *Sambandha* is the connection between the subject matter and the explanatory text, what result the study of the text will produce. *Adhikārī* is he who is entitled to study the text. And *prayojana* is the purpose of the text."

tions of the *śāstras*. This is called *vaidhi-bhakti*, and is propounded in all the *śāstras*."[7]

The Tāntric tradition had for centuries been opposed to the Vedas and had provided a counterpoint of non-Vedic authority and ritual in Indian religion, as Sir John Woodroffe has pointed out.[8] In respect to this attitude toward the Vedic *śāstras*, the Sahajiyās took after the Tāntric side of the family: "The *sahaja-mānuṣa* is on the farther shore of Vedic regulation. In custom and in behaviour he recognizes neither Veda nor Viṣṇu. The truth of the *mānuṣa* is very wonderful; who can express it, or really know it?"[9] Or, most powerfully,

The *sādhu* said: You have been previously taught that the Vedas and the other *śāstras* were produced from the mouth of Parameśvara, and that the Vedas and the other *śātras* define what is dharma and what is not; tell me what you have found to be true in the Vedas and the other *śāstras*, and what you have found to be false. The untutored jīva replied: When Kṛṣṇa-parameśvara showed to me that which is false, I understood that the Vedas and their *śāstras* all are false, and that the dharma which the Brahmans and others follow is all false, and that attachment to mother and father is false, and that the ego is false.[10]

[7] *CC Madhya* 22:59.

[8] *Shakti and Shākta*, p. 504.

[9] *SS* pada 24, attributed to Vidyāpati. This attitude toward the Vedas is not confined to the Tantras, though it may be one way in which the Tāntric tradition influenced the mainstream of Indian religious life, through the bhakti schools. We have noticed its expression in the *Bhāgavata* itself; it is an attitude, as Jadunāth Sinha points out in his article "Bhāgavata Religion: The Cult of Bhakti," in *CHI*, IV, 146, that is frequent in texts dealing with bhakti from the time of the Upaniṣads. *Kaṭha-upaniṣad* 2:23 and *Muṇḍaka-upaniṣad* 3:2:3 have: "The self cannot be realized by the study of the Vedas, nor by intelligence, nor by deep learning; it can be realized only by him whom it chooses or favors; to him the Self reveals its own nature."

[10] *Jñānādi-sādhana*, *VSP*, II, 1636.

Not only are the Vedic *śāstras* false, but they are downright dangerous, for they delude people and make them flounder around in māyā: "The Brahman, in reading the *śāstras*, falls into a great pit. . . . Following the *śāstras*, he does various things, but, floundering in māyā, he cannot realize their meaning."[11] The jīva "wanders aimless in māyā, and he dies in shame and hatred, deluded by the Vedas."[12] That is fairly outspoken.

But even in this regard, the Sahajiyās are not without a trace of their Vaiṣṇava inheritance. The untutored jīva says that the *śāstras* have been falsely interpreted, but he does not deny that they were written by Parameśvara-Kṛṣṇa. And the Sahajiyā texts freely attest their reverence for the writings of the Gosvāmins and their pupil Kṛṣṇadāsa; these works, of course, are said to teach the Sahajiyā doctrine. Anyone who thinks differently is not reading them properly. "Investigate thoroughly the books which the Gosvāmins wrote, and gain through them a knowledge of what is to be worshiped."[13] As Kṛṣṇadāsa acknowledged Vṛndāvana-dāsa the author of the *Caitanya-bhāgavata* as the new Vyāsa,[14] so the Sahajiyās put Kṛṣṇadāsa himself on a level with that sage and legendary writer of the *Bhāgavata-purāṇa:* "As Veda-vyāsa wrote of the līlā of Kṛṣṇa, so Kṛṣṇadāsa wrote of the inner meaning of Caitanya."[15]

The Sahajiyās, while condemning roundly the Vedic *śāstras,* accept the Vaiṣṇava *śāstras* and the *vaidhi-bhakti*

[11] *Āgama,* p. 106.
[12] VV, p. 89.
[13] *Rādhārasa-karikā,* VSP, II, 1671.
[14] In many places. See, for example, *CC Ādi* 13:48.
[15] VV, p. 20.

based upon them, up to the point at which one goes beyond *vaidhi-bhakti* to direct knowledge of Kṛṣṇa. When he knows Kṛṣṇa directly, the bhakta has no further interest in the *śāstras*. "If one does not have Kṛṣṇa, he must honor the injunctions of the *śāstras*. But when he knows Kṛṣṇa, even what is not proper according to the *śāstras* becomes proper."[16]

VAIDHI-BHAKTI: THE ORTHODOX VIEW. S. K. De observes that because *vaidhi-bhakti* is based on the injunctions of the *śāstras*, it is "conditional," being "based upon fear of transgression; and as fear enters as an element of guiding devotional practices, this method must be regarded as somewhat formal and mechanical. As a preliminary stage, however, it is indispensable for some individuals before they can pass on to higher and more spontaneous Rāgānuga Bhakti."[17] The two, *vaidhi* and *rāgānuga*, may thus be considered as a kind of sequence: "Now hear some of the signs of him who follows *vaidhi* and of him who follows *rāgānuga*; for certain people are followers of one, and certain people followers of the other. In knowledge gained by *rāga* there is nothing false; and by *vaidhi* worship one gains *rāga*, and knows the sweetness [*mādhurya*]; that is certain."[18]

Since the Sahajiyās accept in principle the distinction between the two kinds of bhakti, we might look first at the characteristics of the two as they are outlined in the orthodox texts. The CC says that there are two types of *sādhana*,

[16] *DBhS*, p. 124.
[17] *VFM*, p. 283, in discussing Jīva's *Bhakti-saṃdarbha*.
[18] *VV*, p. 102.

inner (*antara*) and outer (*bāhya*). *Bāhya-sādhana* is the performance of various ritual acts of worship (*vaidhi*), while *antara-sādhana* is the service of Kṛṣṇa in Vraja—the realization of the released jīva (*rāgānuga*). It is phrased this way: "*Bāhya* and *antara*—there are these two kinds of *sādhana*. *Bāhya* is such activity as the *sādhaka* listening to *kīrtana*; *antara* is within the heart of the *sādhaka*, in his perfected body: day and night he serves Kṛṣṇa in Vraja."[19] Rūpa Gosvāmin makes the distinction in a similar way, while elaborating on the categories: he says that there are three types of bhakti, namely, *sādhana-bhakti*, *bhāva-bhakti*, and *prema-bhakti*. *Sādhana-bhakti* is divided into *vaidhi* and *rāgānuga*: "*vaidhi* is where the impulse to devotional acts comes entirely from the Vaiṣṇava *śāstra* . . . and where the state of *rāga* is not reached."[20] *Bhāva-bhakti* is a "further maturing of the Sādhana Bhakti . . . based on inward emotion (*bhāva*), which has not yet reached the stage of love or Preman."[21] *Prema-bhakti* is of course the final stage of the development, the expression of which is pure prema.

The CC, following the *Haribhakti-vilāsa* in the matter, describes the *śāstra*-based devotional acts as being sixty-four in number.[22] Among these are:

Gurupadāśraya, having the feet of the guru as a refuge. The guru must be a Vaiṣṇava (*HBV* 1:40 and 4:144). He

[19] CC *Madhya* 22:89 f.
[20] *VFM*, p. 128.
[21] *Ibid.*, p. 132.
[22] CC *Madhya* 22:58 ff. As the *ṭīkā* on the passage states, these devotional acts are described more fully in Rūpa's *Bhaktirasāmṛtasindhu* and yet more fully in the *HBV*, which is the standard work of Vaiṣṇava ritual, prescriptions, and proscriptions.

must be of a recognized Vaiṣṇava community or tradition, of which there are four: Śrī-sampradāya, Brahmā or Madhvācarya-sampradāya, Rūdra or Viṣṇusvāmi-sampradāya, and Sanaka or Nimbārka-sampradāya. The community of the guru's guru must have been the same. The guru must be of the *bhāva* toward Kṛṣṇa appropriate to the nature of the pupil. The guru must be skilled or learned in the *śāstras* and *smṛti,* especially in the *Bhāgavata.* He must be able to inspire worship, bhakti, and love. And, finally, he must give no instruction to a non-Vaiṣṇava.

Taking the *bīja-mantra* (*dīkṣā*) from the guru.

Service of the guru (*guruseva*).

Saddharma-śikṣāpṛccha, the learning of the true dharma.

Sādhumārgānugamana, following a righteous path, or the way of a holy man.

The abandonment of pleasure, in love for Kṛṣṇa.

Living in a place sacred to Kṛṣṇa.

Following the (bhakti) path through to its conclusion.

Fasting on the *ekādaśī* day, a day sacred to Vaiṣṇavas.

Respect for the earth, the peepul tree, cows, Brahmans, and Vaiṣṇavas.

Driving away and keeping clear of all antagonistic faiths and improper forms of service; prohibitions are riding in a conveyance when going to the temple, not serving the image of the god at festival times, not making *praṇāma* (obeisance) before the visible image of the god, making *praṇāma* with one hand, lying down before the image, eating before the image, and abusing anyone in the presence of the image.[23]

[23] There are thirty-two such offenses listed "from the *Āgama-śāstra*" and twenty-three others quoted from the *Varāha-purāṇa.*

Refusal to associate with non-Vaiṣṇavas.

Abjuring argument and all contention.

Holding profit and loss as the same.

Not being overcome by pain or sorrow.

Not condemning gods or *śāstras* because they are other than the Vaiṣṇava ones.

Not giving anxiety to anyone by word or deed.

Listening (*sravaṇa*) to *kīrtana,* the praises of Kṛṣṇa in song or prayer.

Performing *kīrtana.*

Remembering Kṛṣṇa and meditating upon him (*smaraṇa*).

Being respectful to all things worthy of respect.

Services to Kṛṣṇa, such as fanning the image, making a bed for the image, cleansing and censing the temple (*lepa*), cleansing the eating utensils, gathering flowers and *tulasī,* for the temple.[24]

Worship of Kṛṣṇa (*pūjana*) by offerings of flowers, *tulasī,* sandalwood, and various offerings (*naivedya*).

Becoming (i.e., taking on the *bhāva* of) a servant of Kṛṣṇa (*dāsya*), a friend of Kṛṣṇa (*sākhya*), a parent of Kṛṣṇa (*vātsalya*), or his lover (*mādhurya*).

The offering of one's whole self to Kṛṣṇa.

Singing and dancing before the image.

Prostration before the image.

Elevation of the image.

Following the image in procession.

Pilgrimage to the holy places of the Vaiṣṇavas.

The reading and repetition of prayers and mantras.

[24] The term used here for these acts collectively is *paricaya. Bhāgavata* 7:5:23, on which the point is based, calls them *padasevana.*

Worship with incense and sweet-smelling garlands (*dhūpamālyagandha*).

Taking the consecrated food (*mahāprasāda*).

Ārati: the waving of lights, *tulasī*-leaves, the conch shell, and other sacred objects before the image.

The observance of such important festivals as Jhulana, Dola, and Rathayātra.

Gazing at the image.

Dedication of beloved objects to Kṛṣṇa.

Meditation (*dhyāna*) on and service of everything that belongs to Kṛṣṇa, especially the *tulasī* plant, Vaiṣṇavas, Mathurā, and the *Bhāgavata-purāṇa.*

But, says Kṛṣṇadāsa, the last five are the best:

Association with holy men (*sādhusaṅga*).

Performing *nāmasaṃkīrtana,* the singing of the names and praises of Kṛṣṇa.

Listening to the reading of the *Bhāgavata.*

Dwelling at Mathurā.

Honoring and serving the image.

For in these five is the birth of prema: "The best *sādhana* is in these five parts. Through even a little of these five, Kṛṣṇa-prema is born."[25] There are also long lists of things it is proper for a Vaiṣṇava to avoid, which are not especially relevant here.[26]

[25] *CC Madhya* 22:75.

[26] De (*VFM*, p. 130) lists ten *nāmāparādhas* (offenses against the name of Kṛṣṇa) in addition to the various *sevāparādhas* (offenses in worship) listed above, which he finds in the commentary on *Bhaktirasāmṛtasindhu.* These include such things as "unwillingness to listen to the Mahātmya of the Name" and "equalizing the Nāma-mahātmya to the merit of other pious acts."

Another discussion of the acts of *vaidhi*-bhakti is in Jīva's *Bhakti-saṃdarbha.*[27] In that text Jīva mentions eleven elements of ritual devotion, as opposed to the nine given in *Bhāgavata* 7:6. They are *śaraṇāpattiḥ,* having Kṛṣṇa as the only refuge, *guru-seva,* devotion to the guru; *śravaṇa,* listening to the reading of *Bhāgavata* and to the stories of Kṛṣṇa; *kīrtana,* singing the praises and the names of Kṛṣṇa; *smaraṇa,* the act of remembering or concentration that "consists of fixing one's thought on the name, form, or [līlā] of the deity" (De). *Smaraṇa,* which is especially important because it is the crucial step in the worshipper's assumption of a *bhāva* in relationship to Kṛṣṇa, is divided into five subcategories, including *smaraṇa-sāmānya,* "the act of fixing the mind in a general way" (De); *dhyāna,* special concentration in an uninterrupted flow; and *samādhi,* which is the point at which the object of thought is the sole occupant of the mind. The remaining elements of ritual devotion are *pada-seva,* which includes many of the ritual acts enumerated by the CC, *arcanā,* which includes other formal acts such as the putting of the Vaiṣṇava signs on the body, *vandanā,* which is, as in Kṛṣṇadāsa, the gesture of respect and homage. The last three that Jīva mentions are more properly states than ritual actions. They are *dāsya,* the feeling toward Kṛṣṇa as a servant toward his master; *sākhya,* the relationship of the worshipper to Kṛṣṇa as friend to friend; and, finally, *ātma-nivedana,* the complete and utter surrender of the self to Kṛṣṇa.

It is significant that Kṛṣṇa-dāsa feels that prema can be born through performance of the five most important acts

[27] VFM, pp. 280 ff.

of *vaidhi-bhakti.* Through external rituals people can attain that state of self-denial and inner calm that is prerequisite to the development of *rāgānuga.*

Rāgānuga is the state that lies beyond mere devotional acts, a state beyond all striving, in which the jīva confronts the svarūpa directly. S. K. De describes its relationship to *vaidhi:*

> Passionate souls soon pass beyond outward rule and form to an inner and more esoteric way of realization, based upon the cultivation of the inward feelings of devotion. . . . Rāga is defined as the natural, deep, and inseparable absorption (*svārasikī tanmayī parāviṣṭatā*) in the desired object (*iṣṭa*), namely, Kṛṣṇa. The Rāgānuga is distinguished from the Vaidhi inasmuch as in the Vaidhi the realization is in the injunction (*vidhi*) of the Śāstra, but here it is through the greed (*lobha*) of realizing the feelings of the people of Vraja. . . . One desirous of this way of realization will adopt the particular Bhāva . . . of the particular favorite of Kṛṣṇa according to his or her Līlā, Veśa, and Svabhāva, and live in the ecstacy of that vicarious enjoyment. . . . It is indeed not achieved by the direct injunction of the Śāstras, but it does not also arise spontaneously within one's own self. It is engendered by external effort, by elaborately imitating the actions and feelings of those connected with Kṛṣṇa in Vraja . . . but it is governed by no mechanical Śāstric rules whatever, even if they are not necessarily discarded; it follows the natural inclination of the heart, and depends entirely upon one's own capacity for devotion.[28]

VAIDHI-BHAKTI: THE SAHAJIYĀ VIEW. The VV tells us that the Gosvāmins, following Caitanya's teaching, used both *vaidhi* and *rāgānuga* forms of worship, but knew that the

[28] *Ibid.,* p. 130.

true meaning of the līlā of Caitanya can be found only in *rāgānuga:* "The Gosvāmins wrote of both an emotional method and a ritual one. The dharma of the Gosvāmins themselves was of the bhāva kind, and in this is the true meaning of Prabhu. He described the injunctions of the *śāstras* as the way of ritual, and instructed Sanātana in both."[29]

Vaidhi and *rāgānuga* are also called *aiśvarya* and *mādhurya,* i.e., "majesty" and "sweetness." The VV, following Kṣṛṇadāsa, makes it quite clear that in Kṛṣṇa's own opinion *mādhurya* is by far the superior variety; one who worships in a *vaidhi* (*aiśvarya*) fashion is conceiving of Kṛṣṇa as some sort of supreme being, while he who worships in the *rāgā* or *mādhurya* way has toward Kṛṣṇa the love that pleases him. Kṛṣṇa says: "All the world has *vaidhi-bhakti* toward me, but through *vaidhi-bhakti* [alone] no one can gain the bhāva of Vraja. All the world can know my majesty, but toward that cold majesty there can be no prema, and prema is my desire. He who worships [exclusively] in *vaidhi-bhakti,* in awareness of my majesty, goes to Vaikuṇṭha [i.e., the lower heaven] and gains the four types of *mukti.*"[30] Or, put another way, *vaidhi* can bring happiness, but happiness is not the purpose of *sādhana:* "He who performs *vaidhi* works performs the highest of meritorious action, and in meritorious action there is happiness. But that happi-

[29] VV, p. 40.
[30] *CC Ādi* 3:14 ff., quoted by Ākiñcana-dāsa in VV, p. 103. A discussion of the four types of *mukti* is given in *CC Ādi* 5:26 ff.: *sārṣṭhi* is having the same type of majesty as the divinity being worshipped; *sārūpya* is having a form like that of the divinity; *sāmipya* is existing in a place near the divinity; and *sālokya* is being in one place with the divinity.

ness is not the primary object . . . it is like a chain of gold, a decoration. There can be no union with the joined forms through merit, my brother. . . . He who performs only meritorious action makes the rounds of earth and heaven again and again."[31] In order to know Kṛṣṇa in the eternal Vṛndāvana, one must move on to the stage of *rāgā*. The VV, somewhat enigmatically, goes on: "Thus, that bhakta who worships in *rati-rasa* will reach the eternal Vṛndāvana. He will make the immaterial *rati-rasa* apparent, and will dwell with Kṛṣṇa."[32]

Kṛṣṇa manifested himself in the earthly Vṛndāvana in order to show people the way of *rāga:* "He manifested the *rāgamārga* . . . he taught it by his līlā."[33] For it was in the *rāga-mārga* that the Gopīs loved Kṛṣṇa, and their way is the best way of all. Though *vaidhi-bhakti* can lead to *rāgānuga* and *rāgānuga* to the realization of Kṛṣṇa, *vaidhi-bhakti* alone does not lead to realization of Kṛṣṇa: "Activity, repetition of mantras, physical discipline, intellectual knowledge, asceticism, meditation—this is *vidhi-bhakti,* and through it the *mādhurya* cannot be attained. [But] only he who follows the way of *rāga* and worships Kṛṣṇa in profound love can gain the *mādhurya* of Kṛṣṇa with ease."[34]

Most texts accept as characteristic of *vaidhi-bhakti* the sixty-four devotional acts that the *CC* enumerates: Rāgā-

[31] *Premānanda-laharī,* p. 6, quoted in *PCSC,* p. 4.

[32] VV, p. 103. There are two possible meanings, perhaps both being implied by Ākiñcana-dāsa. The first is that *rati* and rasa mean Rādhā and Kṛṣṇa. The passage then says that by making Rādhā and Kṛṣṇa manifest, in Sahajiyā *sādhana,* one gains eternal bliss. The second is that unmanifest and manifest, or apparent and unapparent (*prākṛta* and *aprākṛta*) refer to the *vaidhi* and *rāgānuga* modes of worship. The passage then says that only he who transforms *vaidhi* into *rāgānuga* can gain eternal bliss.

[33] *CC Ādi* 4:220.

[34] *CC Madhya* 21:100.

nuga "can be gained by honoring the sixty-four."[35] "I have taught the sixty-four modes of worship."[36] And, says the VV a little defensively: "So, although I have said that *rāga* does not arise from *vaidhi*, that *vaidhi* does not mean the sixty-four types of bhakti."[37] The *Premānanda-laharī* sums up the Sahajiyā position: "Therefore leave the *vaidhi*-path and worship only in *rāga*. If there is no *rāga* there can be no union."[38]

So the Sahajiyās accept the discipline of the sixty-four devotional acts. But such discipline merely brings the worshipper to the point where he can embark on a stage of bhakti completely foreign to the orthodox—the "new *vidhi*-bhakti," the training for the sexual ritual and the ritual itself. Consistent with their habit, the texts discuss these matters in the most oblique way, often making interpretation difficult.

> The internal [*antara*] and the external [*bāhya*]—in these two ways can the *sevaka* worship, and I will explain them. The new *vidhi-bhakti* is that of Rādhā, and without this bhakti Rādhā cannot be known. Who can worship her except through the mercy of a young woman; toward whom is her mercy, he can worship her. . . . This bhakti is of two kinds, the *vidhi-bhakti*, in which is union; this is a *sthāyi-bhāva* having as its container [*āśraya*] . . . the guru in the hundred-petalled lotus, and in the thousand-petalled lotus the perfection of *rati*.[39]

THE NECESSITY OF THE GURU. The Sahajiyās never allow us to forget that the sexual *sādhana* is a dangerous and slippery

[35] *Rāgaratnāvalī*, p. 7.
[36] *Rasasāra*, p. 37.
[37] VV, p. 102.
[38] *Premānanda-laharī*, p. 6, quoted in *PCSC*, p. 4.
[39] VV, pp. 81, 82.

path and that the *sādhaka* needs a steady and well-trained hand to lead him along it. Except for the guru, the *sādhaka* would not know the proper way to discipline himself. Without the guru, the *sādhaka* is apt to slip, and when he slips he falls all the way to hell (*SS* pada 9). Furthermore, the Sahajiyā doctrine is not meant for the ears of all; its transmission is up to those who themselves have reached the goal and is for only a few carefully chosen disciples. The guru is of vital importance to all esoteric cults. Of his place in the Tantras, Woodroffe writes:

There is in reality but one Guru, and that is the Lord (Ishvara) Himself. He is the Supreme Guru, as also is Devi his power, one with Himself. But He acts through man and human means. The ordinary human Guru is but the manisfestation on earth, of the Ādinātha Mahākāla and Mahākāli the Supreme Guru abiding in Kailasa. As the Yoginī Tantra . . . says, *guroḥ sthānam hi kailāsam.* It is He who is in, and speaks with the voice of, the earthly Guru. . . . The Tantra Shāstras are full of the greatness of the Guru. He is not to be thought of as a mere man. . . . Guru, it is said, can save one from the wrath of Shiva, but in no way can one be saved from the wrath of the Guru.[40]

The orthodox Vaiṣṇava worship was complicated but completely open, and in a way it is curious that the Gosvāmins have given the guru a most elevated place in their scheme of things. To Jīva, the guru should be looked upon as the divinity himself (*sva-gurau bhagavād-dṛṣṭi kartavya*).[41] It is more than likely that this is another indication

[40] *Shakti and Shākta,* pp. 491–92. Payne (*The Śāktas,* p. 57) gives the last statement in a somewhat different fashion: "If Śiva is angered, the preceptor is a deliverer; if the preceptor is angered, there is no deliverer." Payne refers to McCulloch, *MacDonald MSS,* p. 1.

[41] *Bhakti-samdarbha;* see VFM, p. 278.

of Tāntric influence. The *HBV*, which we have already seen to be deeply concerned with Tāntrism, says that the guru possesses the greatness of God, the supreme object of worship,[42] and that "the devotee should worship [his guru] first, because the *śāstras* ordain that the worship of the preceptor should precede that of the gods inasmuch as the preceptor is representative of all the gods."[43] Even more interesting is the fact that Jīva writes that any secret obtained from the Bhagavat by the released bhakta must be kept secret, and not divulged to anyone.[44] We must assume that he means anyone but carefully selected pupils.

Parallel to this, the notion is found, especially in Kṛṣṇadāsa, that the true meaning of the Caitanya-līlā is profound and mysterious and hidden: "Very profound and mysterious [*nigūḍha*] is this theory of rasa. Svarūpa Gosvāmin alone knows its meaning . . . Caitanya revealed the hidden meaning to him."[45] Or, again: "The crest-jewel of the Caitanya-līlā was in the treasure-house of Svarūpa, and Svarūpa placed it in the mouth of Raghunātha, and Raghunātha gave it to the bhaktas."[46] Kṛṣṇadāsa's remarks being as enigmatic as this, it is not strange that the Sahajiyās, and espe-

42 *HBV*, *vilāsa* 1:56 (pp. 30–31 of the Murshidabad edition) quotes the *Devitantra*: "Śiva said . . . There is no distinction between myself and the guru."

43 *VFM*, p. 353.

44 *Ibid.*, p. 288.

45 *CC Ādi* 4:137–38. In his commentary on the passage, Rādhāgovinda Nāth writes: "This is the reason for the writing of [the *CC*] . . . that the idea of the Caitanya-*avatāra* is very secret . . . no one except Caitanya himself knows it; Svarūpa Dāmodara was very close to Caitanya, and Caitanya told the secret to him. . . . Raghunātha-dāsa was for many years in the company of Svarūpa, and Svarūpa taught it to him." Raghunātha knew Svarūpa at Puri, as we have noticed.

46 *CC Madhya* 2:73–74.

cially Ākiñcana-dāsa, took the opportunity to say that this "mysterious and profound" meaning is the Sahajiyā one. Ākiñcana-dāsa extends the line of the transmission of the true meaning from Raghunātha to Kṛṣṇadāsa to Mukunda to himself. And the writer of the *Amṛtarasāvalī* can say that Kṛṣṇadāsa's book is really about Sahajiyā doctrine, but hidden from the eyes of ordinary and uninstructed men.

The Sahajiyās had of course more valid reason to keep their teachings secret, and thus for the elevation of the guru as one who has himself successfully negotiated the dangerous path of *sādhana,* and who can therefore reveal the true meaning of the esoteric texts.

To the Sahajiyās too, the guru is not merely to be respected; he is to be worshipped: "Guru, Kṛṣṇa, Vaiṣṇava—worship these three; by their grace your desires will be fulfilled."[47] "Worship the guru; then will Vrajendra-nandana fulfill your desires."[48] Nothing is possible if the guru is not worshipped: "If you do not meditate upon your guru's feet, the wealth of prema will disappear."[49] It is by the help of the guru that the ultimate is known: "He who knows the source of this *rati* is transformed by *āropa* and knows the svarūpa. If he knows this, by the mercy of the guru he reaches the condition of perfection [*siddhi*]."[50]

Woodroffe said that to the Tāntrics, the guru is *īśvara* himself. To the orthodox Vaiṣṇavas, the guru is Kṛṣṇa: "In the form of guru, Kṛṣṇa distributes his grace to his bhaktas. Know then the *śikṣā-guru,* the true form of Kṛṣṇa, indwell-

47 *SS pada* 2, signed "Dīna-narottama."
48 *Ibid.*, 4, attributed to Narottama-dāsa.
49 *Ibid.*, 7, attributed to Vṛndāvana-dāsa.
50 *Ibid.*, 57, attributed to Caṇḍīdāsa.

ing in bhaktas."[51] And to the Sahajiyās, the guru is Kṛṣṇa or the released bhakta, the *sahaja-mānuṣa* who has realized himself as Kṛṣṇa. "Kṛṣṇa, himself Bhagavān, is in the form of guru. Hear these words, they are proven by the holy *Purāṇa:* Kṛṣṇa is himself the guru, within the self. In the rūpa of a Vaiṣṇava he is the wishing-tree of all desires."[52] Kṛṣṇa the guru is indwelling in the jīva; thus, true knowledge and realization can be transmitted immediately and inwardly. "When Kṛṣṇa grants his grace to any lucky person, he teaches from within the self, in the form of indwelling guru."[53] To the Sahajiyās, Kṛṣṇa is not the *śikṣā-guru,* the guru who instructs the devotee after his initiation, but the *dīkṣā-guru,* the guru who gives the devotee the mantra that he is to repeat and meditate upon. Again the Sahajiyās take after their Tāntric forebears, to whom, Woodroffe has said, "the Devi herself is Guru."[54] For to the Sahajiyās, Rādhā is the *śikṣā-guru:* "The *dīkṣā-guru* is Kṛṣṇa, the lord of the world. Rādhā teaches, as the *śikṣā-guru.* . . . The mantra is the true form of the *dīkṣā-guru* Kṛṣṇa; the *śikṣā-guru* Rādhā is of one *ātmā* with him."[55] To the interesting idea that the mantra is Kṛṣṇa's form we shall have occasion

[51] *CC Ādi* 1:27–28. See also *CC Madhya* 19:133.

[52] *SS* pada 2, signed "Dīna-narottama."

[53] *CC Madhya* 22:30. Dasgupta (*ORC,* p. 102) says in regard to the Sahajiyās: "The only way of knowing the truth is, therefore, to seek the grace of the guru who, and who alone, can make a man realize the Supreme Reality. It is believed that the true preceptor in his non-dual state identifies himself with the disciple and performs from within the disciple all that is necessary for the latter's spiritual uplift."

[54] *Shakti and Shākta,* p. 505.

[55] *VV,* p. 41. The text (p. 49) continues in this vein: "Know Rādhā and Kṛṣṇa within, the *śikṣā* and the *dīkṣā* gurus; knowing both, worship both svarūpas . . . two gurus, one body wonderful in form . . . such worship is a well of rasa, my brother."

to return. What is of concern at the moment is Rādhā as the *śikṣā-guru*. The Tāntrics say that all females are in some sense embodiments of the Devi. "For this reason, all women are worshipful."[56] Rādhā is guru, as well as the *prakṛti* that defines a woman as female, as well as the woman as ritual sexual partner who teaches the *sādhaka* to know the divine bliss in the *vaidhi* sexual ritual before he passes on to know the joy of union with her within himself. There is a tradition that the ritual partner of Caṇḍīdāsa was a washerwoman named Rāmī; Caṇḍidāsā writes: "The washerwoman of that country is the queen of rasa; in her heart is the svarūpa of Rādhā. You, [O Rāmī], are my guru in *sādhana*; you are the wishing-tree of rasa, and I am your slave."[57] Thus Sahajiyā reasoning has inscribed another of its circles. The *dīkṣā-guru* is Kṛṣṇa, and the *śikṣā-guru* is Rādhā. Both dwell within the worshiper, in svarūpa. Both gurus are necessary for the completion of worship. Through the mantra, the Kṛṣṇa-guru, as we shall see, he knows himself to be identical with the universe. Through the Rādhā-guru the worshiper is brought along the path of ritual *sādhana* to infinite bliss.

2. SVAKĪYĀ AND PARAKĪYĀ

THEOLOGICAL IMPLICATIONS AND THE HISTORY OF THE DOCTRINE. The Sahajiyās, obviously, were obliged to give a great deal of thought to women. But again, in their analysis, they had a good model to follow, for the Vaiṣṇavas, with their penchant for classifying Rādhā's moods and states for pur-

[56] *Shakti and Shākta*, p. 505.
[57] *Caṇḍīdāsa-padāvali*, p. 152.

poses of their lyrics, presented the Sahajiyās with a ready-made and fairly elaborate scheme. We have already noticed in passing one classification which was significant for the Sahajiyās, that of svakīyā and parakīyā (see Chapter I, Section 1c). The analysis is more complicated and is of some interest and relevance.

The classifications svakīyā (or *svīyā*) and parakīyā are, like the poetic classifications of the stages of love adapted by the Vaiṣṇavas, old and familiar ones in Sanskrit poetic theory, as are their subclassifications.[58] Svakīyā and parakīyā women are, in that theory, two basic types toward whom love can be directed; a third, *sāmānyā* or *veśyā*, a courtesan, is for all practical purposes ignored by the Vaiṣṇavas. The appropriateness of such classifications to the analysis of the type of poetry in which the Vaiṣṇavas excelled is clear, as is their relevance to a descriptive analysis of the attitudes and emotions of a worshipper toward Kṛṣṇa.

The Vaiṣṇava theologians tied themselves into knots because of the stories in the *Bhāgavata* of the love between Kṛṣṇa and the Gopīs, for it is said that the Gopīs, at the time when they were involved in love affairs with Kṛṣṇa, were parakīyā women, women belonging to others. Even though the context was that of divine līlā, such behavior was against accepted standards of morality. Ways had to be found in which the Gopīs could be made out, in the last analysis, to be svakīyā. This required no little skill, and Rūpa and Jīva Gosvāmin gave it all they had. Rūpa, for example, begins

[58] De, discussing the *Ujjvalanīlamaṇī*, in which these theories are fully developed, remarks (*VFM*, p. 156) that "each of these two kinds of heroine . . . is classified again, in accordance with the scheme of classical Poetics, into the adolescent and artless (Mugdhā) the youthful (Madhyā)."

by saying that anyone who loves a parakīyā woman "transgresses the limits of dharma"; Kṛṣṇa, because of his nature as God, could not have done that.[59] Furthermore, he goes on, the Gopīs had been married to Kṛṣṇa, though not by the generally accepted rites: "They were really svakīyā, by virtue of the Gandharva rites, though the marriage was never in manifested form."[60] Or, he says, giving us another alternative, even though the Gopīs were the wives of others, their marriages had never been consummated; their husbands, the Gopas, had been deceived by the power (māyā) of Kṛṣṇa into believing that their wives had been lying with them: "Even though the Gopīs were the wives of other men, they had never had intercourse with their husbands. Even at the time of their trysts with Kṛṣṇa, Kṛṣṇa by his power of māyā arranged to have forms of the Gopīs beside each of their husbands, so that they would think 'My wife is with me.' "[61] And, he says, even though critics have "spoken lightly of the Upa-pati" (i.e., the unmarried lover), they have had in mind not Kṛṣṇa but the ordinary man.[62]

Jīva fared slightly better in his attempts at justification. In the *Kṛṣṇa-saṃdarbha* of his *Ṣaṭ-saṃdarbha* he argues as follows: The term *jāra* (lover) used in the *Bhāgavata* in regard to the relationship of Kṛṣṇa to the Gopīs is a symbolic expression; it refers to an attitude, not to a physical fact. It is more in keeping with the *rasa-śāstra* as well as with rea-

[59] *Ujjvalanīlamaṇī, nāyaka-bheda* 11 (pp. 14–15).

[60] *Ujjvalanīlamaṇī, Kṛṣṇa-vallabhā* 5 (p. 19). Gandharva marriage is love marriage undertaken by mutual consent, with no ritual witnessed by a third party.

[61] *Ibid.*, 19–20 (pp. 79–80). The theory is based on *Bhāgavata* 10:33:37.

[62] See *VFM*, pp. 154 f.

son to regard the Gopīs as svakīyā, for desire for what is not one's own only brings trouble, and no rational man, of course, considers a course of action in which trouble is inevitable. Furthermore, the *rasa-śāstra* does not approve of parakīyā union. It is not only contrary to proper dharma, but it obstructs the attainment of pure rasa. So Kṛṣṇa could not have indulged in it. And, following Rūpa, if the Gopīs call the Gopas "husband," this is because of Kṛṣṇa's *māyā-śākti* and has no relationship to truth. And, finally, the Gopīs are the *svarūpa-śāktis* of Kṛṣṇa. They are intrinsic to him. How then can they be parakīyā? Jīva, followed by Kṛṣṇadāsa, unpacks this last argument a little further: even a theoretical distinction between svakīyā and parakīyā is possible only in the manifest earthly līlā, the *prakaṭa* līlā. In the eternal Vṛndāvana the Gopīs are not manifested at all, but are the unmanifest śaktis of Kṛṣṇa.[63]

Kṛṣṇadāsa of course follows, in the main, Jīva's arguments. He acknowledges the *Bhāgavata*'s statement that Kṛṣṇa was the lover of the Gopīs. Kṛṣṇa, in fact, was able to be with sixteen thousand women at once because of the power of his svarūpa to be manifest in an infinite number of forms without effect on his true nature: "One *vigraha* can have many forms: still, in essence, there is no division—his svarūpa remains one. So it was when Kṛṣṇa made love to his wives [queens: *mahiṣī*]; each of them had full experience of him."[64] But it is not true that the Gopīs were parakīyā. Kṛṣṇa has three śaktis, the most important of which is *hlādinī*. This *hlādinī-śakti* has different forms according to

[63] For additional arguments, *ibid.*, pp. 264–68.
[64] CC *Ādi* 1:35 f.

the time of manifestation and the dwelling-place of Kṛṣṇa. In Vaikuṇṭha the *hlādinī-śakti* is represented by Lakṣmī and Kṛṣṇa's other wives. In Dvāraka it is his *mahiṣīs,* his queens. And in Vraja it is the Gopīs. "The śakti of Kṛṣṇa is manifested in three ways—the first is Lakṣmī and the others; the second is the *mahiṣīs*; in Vraja it is the Gopīs who are foremost among all to Vrajendranandana, who is *svayam-bhagavān.*"[65] If Lakṣmi and the others are svakīyā, so are the Gopīs.

Kṛṣṇadāsa also approaches the matter from a slightly different angle. All Kṛṣṇa's consorts, in all ages and places, are in essence Rādhā, who is the epitome of *hlādinī-śakti.* As Kṛṣṇa is the "container of *avatāras,*" or as the jīva is a part of Kṛṣṇa, so the three classes of Kṛṣṇa's consorts are parts (*aṁśa*) of Rādhā:

> She whose body, mind, and senses are filled with Kṛṣṇa-prema is Rādhā, the śakti of Kṛṣṇa himself and his companion in līlā. . . . We have seen that the consorts of Kṛṣṇa are of three kinds—Lakṣmī and the others, the second the *mahiṣīs,* and above them all his companions in Vṛndāvana. All these consorts emanate from Rādhā. As Kṛṣṇa the *avatārī* becomes an *avatāra,* so from Rādhā the container of parts these three classes emanate. . . . Her physical form is the Gopīs; they are her bodily manifestations and the sources of rasa. Without many consorts Kṛṣṇa could not experience the joy of rasa; therefore she has many manifestations. The svarūpa of Kṛṣṇa is filled with *prema-rasa,* and his śakti is one with him.[66]

The śaktis being intrinsic, Kṛṣṇa's līlā was with himself.

Despite the clear position of the Gosvāmins, however, in the course of the history of the Vaiṣṇava movement in

[65] *Ibid.,* 1:40 ff.
[66] *Ibid.,* 1:61 ff.

Bengal itself dominance shifted from the svakīyā position to the parakīyā one—perhaps implying a gain in strength of the Sahajiyā wing, but not necessarily implying that the full Sahajiyā doctrinal position was accepted by all Vaiṣṇavas in Bengal proper. Kṛṣṇadāsa had left the question open by presenting both positions in his CC. In a scholarly desire to include everything, he gave the arguments of Rūpa and Jīva Gosvāmin and then went on to speak qualifiedly for the parakīyā position and to say that Caitanya himself had believed in it. "Thus, *madhura-rasa* is its name, and it is divided into two bhāvas—svakīyā and parakīyā. The greater enjoyment of rasa is in the parakīyā-bhāva, and its place is only in Vraja."[67]

Kṛṣṇadāsa is careful to point out that what is possible for Kṛṣṇa is not necessarily possible for mortal men. But it is curious that he even suggests the superiority of the parakīyā point of view, when his teachers were so strongly of the svakīyā persuasion. It is always possible, though I think it not very likely, that there are interpolations in the text. It is more likely that Kṛṣṇadāsa advanced the parakīyā position despite his teachers. There are indications that the parakīyā doctrine developed in Bengal proper, the area in which Kṛṣṇadāsa's work was designed to circulate, and that it was widely accepted in that area at about the time when Kṛṣṇadāsa wrote. The early padas are almost all written from the parakīyā point of view. The evidence of the *Karṇānanda* of Yadunandana-dāsa, a text of the early eighteenth century, while quite late, is suggestive.[68]

Yadunandana-dāsa himself clearly favors the parakīyā

[67] *Ibid.*, 4:41–42.

[68] The *Karṇānanda* is a rather difficult text to place doctrinally. I have

doctrine and attributes its promulgation, interestingly, to the familiar Sahajiyā line of transmission of the true meaning of the Caitanya-līlā, namely, Caitanya to Svarūpa to Rūpa to—and here he deviates—Śrīnivāsa Ācārya. The inclusion of Śrīnivāsa at the expense of Raghunātha-dāsa is significant. Of Śrīnivāsa, Yadunandana-dāsa probably knew a great deal. Śrīnivāsa was the father and guru of Yadunandana's own guru Hemalatā-devī, at whose request he wrote his book. Śrīnivāsa himself was a pupil of Jīva Gosvāmin at Vṛndāvana, though, like Kṛṣṇadāsa, he was more oriented toward Bengal, and with his contemporaries Narottama and Śyāmānanda was instrumental in the spread of the Vaiṣṇava movement there. If Yadunandana-dāsa says so, it is probably true that Śrīnivāsa did preach the parakīyā doctrine, having broken with the authority of his guru Jīva. Yadunandana-dāsa tries to repair the break by claiming that Jīva also held a parakīyā position. Quoting a passage from the *Stavāvalī,* he says: "He who understands only the external meaning of this passage calls it svakīyā in teaching; but the real and inner meaning is parakīyā. Superficial people who do not know what is in the depths of the heart of Jīva Gosvāmin count him among those of the svakīyā persuasion. But he who understands the real meaning of the book knows that it is parakīyā. All who realize this are absorbed in bliss."[69]

found no Sahajiyā writers who quote or refer to the book as a Sahajiyā text, yet it has certain Sahajiyā characteristics, as will be seen. It is quite possible that Yadunandana was a Sahajiyā. The Sahajiyā text *Hīrāvalītattva* has come down in his name (*BSI*, p. 401), and his guru, as we have seen, was a woman, Hemalatā-devi, a daughter of Śrīnivāsa. The *Karṇānanda* gives its date as *śaka* 1629 (A.D. 1707).

[69] *Karṇānanda,* p. 88.

The question was no mere theological quibble, but was very probably the basic point of overt doctrine separating the orthodox and the Sahajiyā Vaiṣṇavas. As such, it exercised a good many people very considerably. At the time of Yadunandana's writing the question was by no means settled. At the beginning of his fifth *niryāsa,* Yadunandana tells us a story of how Jīva sent the manuscript of his *Gopāla-campū* to Śrīnivāsa Ācārya. Śrīnivāsa, when he got the book, was overjoyed, for he felt that it explained the Kṛṣṇa-līlā from the parakīyā point of view. But evidently the clarity of Jīva's explanation of the parakīyā position was not sufficient for Śrīnivāsa, for he compared the work to a box which looks like one thing (svakīyā) from the outside, but is quite another thing (parakīyā) within. At any rate, Śrīvyāsa Cakravartī, also called Vyāsa Śārma, read the book, but misinterpreted it and began to teach the svakīyā doctrine on the basis of it. Śrīnivāsa and his friend and pupil Rāmacandra were upset by this and sent a letter to Jīva himself. According to Yadunandana, Jīva replied, confirming the parakīyā interpretation of the *Gopāla-campū,* and saying that as the earthly Vṛndāvana-līlā is exactly representative of the līlā, which is taking place eternally in the heavenly Vṛndāvana, parakīyā-bhāva is a characteristic of the eternal līlā also (which would seem to be the opposite of Jīva's argument in the *Kṛṣṇa-saṃdarbha*). The letter in question, which seems to me to require some exegetical ability to apply to the situation at all, is given in the *Karṇānanda* text.[70] And so the controversy waxed hot.

On the surface, at least, the question was settled, in an

[70] *Ibid.*, pp. 90–93.

unusually direct fashion, in A.D. 1717—the date of the first of two most wonderful documents printed by D. C. Sen in his *Vaṅga-sāhitya paricaya.* In that year the contending parties agreed to have a formal debate on the subject at the court of the Nabāb Jāfāra (Zāfār) Khān: "And so it was decided to petition the illustrious and honored king, the Nabāb Jāphāra Khān, to decide."[71] Scholars came from all over Bengal and Orissa, and from Benares and Vikrampur, together with theologians and ascetics (*vairāgī*) from these regions, and for six months debated the following questions: the real meaning of the *Bhāgavata,* Caitanya's interpretation of it, the interpretations of the *bhakti-śāstras* of the Gosvāmins, and the *Bhāgavata* commentary by Śrīdharasvāmin. We are told that the scholars of the svakīyā persuasion were unable to uphold their position: "Those upholding the parakīyā position have won, and the parakīyā has thus been established as the true doctrine throughout Bengal [*gauḍa-maṇḍale*]." Those of the svakīyā persuasion, being defeated, acknowledged themselves as followers of Jīva Gosvāmin, Narahari Sarkār, Ṭhākura-mahāśaya (i.e., Narottama), Ācārya-ṭhākura (i.e., Śrīnivāsa), and Syāmānanda-gosvāmi: "The leading exponents of *parakīyā-dharma* having been sent here, and leaders of them having come from Vṛndāvana, we [the exponents of the svakīyā position] have been defeated. We therefore acknowledge ourselves as followers of these five: Jīva Gosvāmin.". . .[72] It is clear that by 1717 Jīva was widely accepted as a defender of the parakīyā doctrine, despite his own writings. It is possible that Jīva's

[71] *VSP,* II, p. 1642.
[72] *Ibid.,* p. 1639.

writings were not at this time widely circulated in Bengal and that people depended for their information on the position of the Gosvāmins upon the interpretations presented by such texts as the *Karṇānanda.*

The second part of this first document says that the writer, who seems to have been Kṛṣṇadeva Devaśarma of Jayanagara, who had come to the debate in order to try to establish the svakīyā doctrine, confesses that he has not been able to do this in the discussion of the various *bhakti-śāstras* and admits his defeat. Then follows a long list of witnesses to the proceedings. The list of svakīyā defenders, significantly, is headed by the title *śri oṃ advaita gosvāmī,* and the first name on it is Śrīkālacānd Devaśarma of Śāntipur: the line of Advaita Ācārya of Śāntipur remained solidly orthodox.

The date of the second document is A.D. 1732 (B.S. 1225), and, although much longer, contains the same type of information as does the first. It tells how various people had believed in the svakīyā position and had come to Bengal to defend it. Among the names of the parakīyā exponents is that of Rādhā-mohana-ṭhākura, who was a pada-writer of considerable talent of the Bengal school and a direct descendant of Śrīnivāsa. He had evidently carried on an extended controversy with the subscribers to the svakīyā doctrine and had been instrumental in bringing the whole question to court for settlement: "Rādhāmohana-ṭhākura, the descendant of Ācārya-ṭhākura, and with him [various others] . . . completed a discussion of many *śāstras,* in which discussion Rādhāmohana-ṭhākura . . . was not able to be defeated. The defeated scholars acknowledged their defeat and as students accepted the *parakīyā-dharma*, and . . . went back to their own countries."[73]

Even assuming that the precedence gained by the parakīyā doctrine was due to Sahajiyā influences within the Bengal school, there is no indication that Śrīnivāsa and the others were in their ritual practice anything but orthodox. But to the Sahajiyās, the parakīyā doctrine is more than an interpretation of a textual passage. If Kṛṣṇa's līlā was with parakīyā women, the parakīyā-līlā is what men must emulate.

The Sahajiyās established the correctness of the parakīyā argument in a variety of ways. The *Āgama* text, for example, outpoints the Gosvāmins by agreeing in the first instance that the relationship between Kṛṣṇa and the Gopīs in Goloka was indeed a svakīyā one, the relationship of śakti to *śaktimān*. But the text goes on: of all the śaktis of Kṛṣṇa, two were chief, and their names were Rādhā and Virājā. Virājā was very jealous of the love of Kṛṣṇa and Rādhā, her feeling toward Kṛṣṇa thus being shown to be not prema but selfish kāma. In the extremity of her jealousy she tried to drown herself. She was pulled out by Kṛṣṇa, who then decided that he and his hundred crores of śaktis would all make an appearance on earth in Vṛndāvana. He decided further that Rādhā and Virājā and the rest of the śaktis would take the shape of the wives of others (*parastrī*) so that they would be able to taste the ultimate sweetness, which comes only through the parakīyā-līlā. Rādhā became the Gopī Rādhā, Virājā became her chief rival Candrāvalī whose basic characteristic is kāma: "I will make you the wives of others. . . . Being the wives of others, you will gain

[73] *Ibid.*, p. 1643.

great happiness. . . . Among you, Virājā will be named Candrāvalī."[74]

The superiority of the parakīyā-bhāva is demonstrated not only by the fact that this was the relationship between Rādhā and Kṛṣṇa, but also by observations of human relationships. The Court of Love at Champagne comes to mind. The feeling of *viraha,* the pain and longing stemming from the separation of lover and beloved, is a measure of the depth of prema; it is intensified by the fact that one who really has prema will actively wish her separation from her lover if that separation pleases him. The Sahajiyās noted this and agreed that *viraha* is more intense in a parakīyā relationship than in a svakīyā one. In a parakīyā relationship nothing is certain, and *viraha* is more intense because each separation might be the final one. The *DBhS* puts it this way: "If there is no parakīyā there can be no birth of bhāva. It is in fear of separation that grief [*ārti*] and passionate longing [*anurāga*] grow. To svakīyās there is no fear of separation . . . and without *anurāga* there is no prema."[75] And again: "In a svakīyā relationship there is no fear of separation; that is why there is no birth of bhāva in it. *Anurāga* manifests itself in extra-marital [*aupapatya*] love; that was the cause of the supreme enjoyment of rasa in Vṛndāvana."[76] It is, as the Sahajiyās observed, one of the perversities of human nature that what is hardest to obtain seems most

[74] *Āgama,* pp. 112 f. The story here is probably based on that given in the *Brahmavaivarta-purāṇa* (XIV–XVI, 174 ff. of the Deva-sāhitya-kuṭi edition). For notes on the name *Candrāvalī,* see Sukumār Sen's *bhūmikā* to *Balarāmadāser padāvalī,* p. 12.

[75] *DBhS,* p. 131.

[76] *Ibid.,* p. 138.

enjoyable when it is obtained. A text called the *Ujjvala-candrikā* says that "the *loka-śāstras* say that which presents the greatest obstacles, in a situation in which one has a secret desire, and where fulfillment is hardest to obtain, is that situation *rati* and desire [*manmatha*] are the most intense. This is the opinion of the great sages themselves, in their *śāstras*."[77] Real passion, and thus real fulfillment, are possible only in the parakīyā-bhāva: "In parakīyā there is real passion [*rāga*], and the profound joy of rasa. In svakīyā there is no rasa, but merely a semblance of it."[78] As full realization in *rāgānuga* follows upon the struggle toward realization through *vaidhi*, through the injunctions of the *śāstras*, so, in a neat parallel, does full enjoyment of rasa in the parakīyā-bhāva succeed the semblance of full enjoyment as experienced in the married state, the svakīyā. As true love fades when parakīyā becomes svakīyā, so svakīyā can be changed to parakīyā, and true love caused to bloom, by extra-marital love.

Parakīyā is, then, a characteristic of the Gopīs, and therefore of the Rādhā whom the worshiper takes as a ritual partner and of the worshiper himself, as Rādhā. "As when a girl [*nāyikā*] sees an attractive man [*nāyaka*] and has a passionate desire for him—such should be the emotion with which one calls constantly for Kṛṣṇa. In this passion all thought of self disappears, together with the darkness of the mind."[79]

[77] P. 5, quoted in *PCSC*, p. 46, n. 2.

[78] *Rasaratnasāra*, p. 65, quoted in *PCSC*, p. 46, n. 2.

[79] *Karacā* [sic] of Govinda-dāsa, p. 60. This text is one of considerable interest. The book has the *bhaṇitā* of Govinda-dāsa of Kañcananagara, who says that he is a blacksmith (p. 87) who accompanied Caitanya on the

A parakīyā relationship is pure prema, and a svakīyā relationship has kāma as its characteristic: "He who enjoys a svakīyā woman is maddened with the lust for gratifying his own senses, and has intercourse with her out of love for his own body. There is no fear in a svakīyā relationship, for it is sanctioned by the Vedas. . . . Because of this sanction, one takes the svakīyā relationship for granted; there is no fear of separation, so one may act for his own pleasure."[80] Svakīyā love, says the *DBhS*, is meaningful only when procreation is the end in view; it is worthless for emotional or religious purposes.[81]

The two terms are thus extended to mean kāma and prema. The *Rāgamayi-kanā* says that Candrāvalī, who was certainly not a svakīyā woman in the literal sense of that term, in relation to Kṛṣṇa, was svakīyā because her desire for Kṛṣṇa was selfish: "In the place of Candrāvalī the river of

---

latter's pilgrimage to the south and west of India shortly after his *saṃnyāsa*. If this is true, the book has great historical value, for other biographies of Caitanya contain only the barest outline of that period of his life. But, as it happens, much doubt has been cast upon the authenticity of the work (*VFM*, p. 47, n. 1; *BSI*, pp. 271–72). Its authenticity has been questioned primarily on the grounds that some modern Bengali words, including some English loan words, are used in the text. The fact that no manuscript of the work has so far appeared has also made some scholars wonder about its genuineness: the work simply appeared in print in 1895. De (*VFM*, p. 47) offers an opinion which seems reasonable: that the work contains some authentic information, perhaps derived from oral tradition, which some writer or editor put into modern Bengali. If portions of the work are finally found to be authentic, it will put at the disposal of scholars a great deal of material relevant not only to the life and the personality but to the times of Caitanya. If it is a "black forgery," as one writer indignantly calls it, it is an interesting one: for whether authentic or spurious, whether sixteenth or nineteenth century, the devotional atmosphere of the book is great. It has at least that value.

80 *Ratnasāra*, pp. 6–7, text in *PCSC*, p. 55, n. 1.

81 *DBhS*, p. 137.

kāma flows; she drifts eternally upon it, and knows nothing else. She is maddened by her own kāma. . . . Those who, like Candrāvalī, are centered in themselves are in the svakīyā-bhāva."[82] And, by further extension, those who follow paths of worship other than pure *rāgānuga*, i.e., those concerned with *vidhi* as an end, or with *karma*, *jñāna*, or the Vedas, are also svakīyā: "Leave the practice of *jñana*, *karma*, and *vidhi*, and do not look toward the Vedic dharma—that is svakīyā worship."[83] "*Parakīyā-rati* is the source of the *mādhurya* relationship, while *rati* toward the majesty of God is svakīyā."[84]

Parakīyā is subclassified into two types corresponding to *vaidhi* and *rāgānuga* bhakti: external or ritual parakīyā (*bāhya*), sexual union in physical, rūpa, form, and inner or "secret" (*marma*) parakīyā, union in svarūpa without the aid of a woman. The transition is made by *āropa*: "By *āropa* that *marma parakīyā* is gained; in *bāhya* parakīyā one takes a female partner."[85] The *Premabhakti-candrikā* uses somewhat different terminology, but here too the distinction is that between *vaidhi* and *rāgānuga*. This text calls them *jñāni-parakīyā and suddha-parakīyā*. The characteristics of "the parakīyā have been heard from the mouth of Bhārata. . . . This was not *suddha-parakīyā*, but *jñāni-parakīyā*, parakīyā toward the Bhagavat by the *jñāna-mārga*. The *jñāni-parakīyā* is a dharma based in māyā."[86] *Jñāni-parakīyā* is thus based in material nature and is that path which leads

[82] P. 18, text in *PCSC*, p. 80, n. 1.
[83] *Ratnasāra*, p. 38, text in *PCSC*, p. 81.
[84] *Bhṛṅgaratnāvalī*, p. 14, text in *PCSC*, p. 85.
[85] VV, p. 78.
[86] *Premabhakti-candrikā*, p. 8, text in *PCSC*, p. 86.

only as far as the Brahma aspect of Kṛṣṇa. It should be left behind, and *suddha-parakīyā*, the *rāgānuga* path, should be followed.[87]

In sum, on the abstract level, parakīyā is the ideal condition of the worshipper, *rāgānuga* bhakti. On a more earthy one, the ideal partner for the ritual is a parakīyā woman, for parakīyā was the condition of Rādhā at the time when she and Kṛṣṇa enjoyed to the fullest each other's love.

THE NĀYIKĀ. We are not told much more about the type of woman who is ideal for the Sahajiyā ritual—she who is called the *nāyikā*. Assumedly, since all women contain Rādhā, anyone will do. Historically, it seems that many women of high caste and even of noble birth were associated with one or another form of the Sahajiyā. We have already noted one or two. B. Bhattacarya, in his introduction to the *Sādhana-mālā*, attributes the founding of the Sahajayāna movement to a woman of royal family.[88] Probably Winternitz is recording the same tradition when he writes:

> A great Tantra teacher, to whom a Sādhana is also attributed, is Indrabhūti (about 687–717 A.D.), the author of *Jñāna-siddhi* and numerous other Tāntric works. . . . He was a king of Uddiyāna. . . . Lakṣmīmkarā, who, in her *Advaya-siddhi* proclaimed novel, monistic doctrines, which were called Sahajayāna, and which are even at the present day prevalent among the Bāuls of Bengal, was a sister of Indrabhūti. She refutes asceticism, ceremonies, and the worship of images, and recommends only meditation on the body, in which all the gods dwell. Another prominent Tan-

[87] *Ibid.*, p. 9, text in *PCSC*, p. 93.
[88] Gaekwad's Oriental series, XXVI, pp. liv f., lviii ff.

tric authoress is Sahaja-yoginī Cintā (*c.* 761 A.D.), and indeed, it is no rare thing to find women among the writers of Tantric works.[89]

Nor is it rare to find women among Tāntric and Sahajiyā gurus. But there is no indication that the royal lady spoken of by Bhattacarya and Winternitz, if indeed she is one and the same, took part in sexual *sādhana* herself.

Even when *nāyikās* are mentioned by name in the texts, and they sometimes are, it is difficult to identify them in terms of caste or class. For, as Rameś Basu points out: "Although there are many female Tāntrics mentioned in the . . . literature, they are called by their guru-given names. Thus their caste and family are not known."[90] But there are indications that even if the sect was founded by a lady of high station, those who carried on her work were not always of equally exalted birth. In the curious passage alluded to before, in which Ākiñcana-dāsa lists the names of the women who were the ritual partners of the Gosvāmins, there are such indications:

Eternal obeisance to the lotus feet of the daughter of Ṣaṭhī, whose mind and body were devoted to Caitanya. All these *nāyikās* were of surpassing beauty, in nature and bodily form like the goddesses of Vraja [i.e., the Gopīs]. . . . Śrīrūpa performed *sādhana* with Mīrā, and Raghunātha Bhaṭṭa with Karnābāi, Sanātana Gosvāmi with Lakṣahīrā, whom he served with love; Lokanātha Gosvāmi with a Caṇḍāla girl and Kṛṣṇadāsa with a milk-maid, like those who lived in Vraja.[91]

[89] *History of Indian Literature,* II, 393.
[90] "Bauddha o śaiva ḍākinī o yoginīdiger kathā," in *SPP,* B.S. 1333 No. 1, pp. 38–39.
[91] VV, pp. 107–8.

Traditionally, the *nāyikā* of Caṇḍīdāsa was a washerwoman, as we have seen. As Ākiñcana-dāsa aptly recalls, the Gopīs themselves, being cowherdesses, were not of the highest caste.

It is interesting that the terms Ḍombī and Caṇḍālī, women of two casteless groups which bear the names Ḍom and Caṇḍāla, are found throughout the *caryā*-songs. These names, in the code of the *sandhyā-bhāṣā*, mean the *mūlādhāra-cakra* of the Tantras, the *cakra* that contains the "serpent power." And, for that matter, the VV passage noted above goes on to associate, in an obscure fashion, Kṛṣṇadāsa's milkmaid with the term *piṅgalā*, one of the tubes through which the semen rises, according to the Tāntric physiology. But it is certainly possible that the use of these names reflects a historical fact: that low-caste and non-caste women were preferred as *nāyikās*, perhaps thereby emphasizing the Sahajiyā contempt for the Vedic and Brahmanical tradition.

Of whatever caste she might have been the *nāyikā* was ideally a parakīyā woman. And, more than that, she was a married parakīyā woman. Following Rūpa and Jīva, and ultimately following Sanskrit poetic theory, Kṛṣṇadāsa divides parakīyā women into two classes, *kanyakā*, or unmarried women, and *paroḍhā*, women who have living husbands.[92] Of these two, obviously, *paroḍhā* is the higher category. For a *kanyakā* woman can marry and her love become svakīyā. *Paroḍhā* women have more to lose, and their lovers thus more to gain. The Gopīs were *paroḍhā*. "The pure *paroḍhā-bhāva* is the ultimate in prema, and the

92 See for example Rūpa's *Ujjvalanīlamaṇī*, *Kṛṣṇa-vallabhā* 8 and 24.

means of tasting the sweetness of Kṛṣṇa."[93] These, says the *Nāyikā-sādhana-ṭikā*, are the other signs of her:

> She is of the greatest beauty, and she has a husband at home. She is most wonderful, in beauty and in qualities. Suddenly, by *bhāva*, she will come to unite with him. Her beauty will pass through his eyes into his heart, and when it enters his heart it will draw his mind. There will be *sādhana* with her.[94]

All agree that she is beautiful, for desire must be aroused if it is to be used. Some become quite lyrical about it:

> The vessel of sahaja is fresh and young, and wounds with the arrows of her glance. She possesses all the marks of beauty, and the clothes and jewels upon her body are bright and colored. Her lips are full of nectar and her body such that a golden creeper cannot compare with it. Her *alakā* and *tilakā* [ornamental marks] are flattering to her body. Such a *nāyikā* is a *sahaja-nāyikā*; serve such a one and know her excellence and greatness.[95]

The marks of beauty are detailed still further by the *Bṛhat-premabhakti-candrikā*:

> The signs of a true *prakṛtī* are these: her thighs are unequalled by [the grace and roundness of] plantain trees, her breasts by [the fullness of] bel-fruit, her lips are redder than bimba-fruit, her teeth more beautiful than pomegranate seeds and her eyes than those of a deer; her walk is more graceful than an elephant's, her complexion puts to shame the *campaka*-flower and her scent the lotus, her nose is unrivalled by the *tila*-flower, her

[93] *CC Ādi* 4:44. The commentator Rādhāgovinda Nāth takes the position that Kṛṣṇa could not have been an *upa-pati* (extramarital lover) in his unmanifest or eternal form. For, says he, if the *parakīyā-līlā* had existed in the eternal Vṛndāvana, there would have been no reason for an earthly līlā at all.

[94] Fol. 1; Calcutta University MS 3906.

[95] *Nigūdārtha-prakāśāvalī*, p. 16; quoted in *PCSC*, p. 60.

ear by that of the vulture, her brow by the bud of the *bak*-flower, her voice by that of the nightingale,[96]

and so on. While these images are conventional, it is clear that the *nāyikā* has, together with other characteristics of the Gopīs, their physical attractiveness.

Rādhā is the prototype of the *nāyikā*, as Kṛṣṇa is of her masculine counterpart the *nāyaka*. Kṛṣṇadāsa says that "Kṛṣṇa-vrajendranandana is the crest-jewel of *nāyakas*—and of *nāyikās*, his consort Rādhikā."[97] And, as Rādhā is Kṛṣṇa's guru, so is the *nāyikā* guru of the *nāyaka*. Kṛṣṇadāsa says, quoting Kṛṣṇa: "The Rādhā-prema is guru, and I am the pupil."[98] The VV, quoting an unidentified source, says that the *nāyikā*, who is "maddened with the nectar of the moon," is the teacher (*śikhārinī*) of the Kṛṣṇa-līlā, and that in her "is the ultimate sweetness of the Kṛṣṇa-līlā. I serve and worship her, and I know her greatness."[99]

The *nāyaka* and *nāyikā* must be "alike." They must both have only religious ends in view when undertaking the *sādhana*. They must both be superior types of people. As Yugala-dāsa says, with a play on the word *sāmāna*: "If a man and woman are alike, there can be union. [Even] if she is a *sādhārinī* they can plumb the depths of rasa."[100] *Sāmāna* means "alike." It also suggests

[96] P. 55, quoted in *PCSC*, p. 62.
[97] *CC Madhya* 23:45. Kṛṣṇadāsa goes on to cite the authority of the *Gautamīya-tantra*, the *Bhakti-rasāmṛta-sindu*, and other works; cf. *VFM*, p. 137. According to Kṛṣṇadāsa, *nāyikā* and *nāyaka* are terms descriptive of conditions that give rise to rasa.
[98] *CC Ādi* 4:108.
[99] VV, p. 92.
[100] *Prema-vilāsa* of Yugalera-dāsa (*VSP*, II, 1666).

the third type [of whom], the Sādhāranī or Sāmānya or Veśya [i.e., courtesan], [who] is omitted [in the *Ujjvalanīlamaṇī*]. The Kubjā who is extolled for her feeling toward Kṛṣṇa . . . Jīva Gosvāmin would frankly regard as Sāmānyā, whose Dāsya [i.e., annointing Kṛṣṇa's body] was raised into Madhura Rasa. As her desire was for Kṛṣṇa, it was directed toward a worthy object, and therefore praised; but, being selfish and frankly sensual, it was deprecated in comparison with the love of the Gopīs, which was free from these traits.[101]

It can be assumed that Yugala-dāsa was trying too hard for his pun. For, as the forthright *Rasa-tattva-sāra* says, though "her eyes will be like lotuses and her complexion like a *campaka*-flower; she will not know three men, for she who knows three men is a prostitute."[102] The two she can know, it might be gathered, are her husband and her lover, who is her ritual partner. On the subject of sameness, the writer called Dvija-caṇḍīdāsa is explicit:

The man and woman should be of one type in order to worship in that *rati*. . . . The man should be of the *siṃha* class of men, and the woman of the *padminī* type. . . . If a woman of good type takes an evil man for *sādhana*, her heart will be torn like a flower by thorns. And if a man of good type takes a lesser woman as an object of *rati*, he will wander as if dead, as a man possessed by an evil spirit. So Dvīja-candīdāsa says.[103]

By *siṃha* and *padminī* Dvija-caṇḍīdāsa indicates the highest types of beings of their respective sexes.

One final point deserves mention. The implications

[101] *VFM*, p. 155. n. 3.

[102] P. 9, quoted in *PCSC*, p. 59.

[103] *Caṇḍīdāser padavālī* (BM edition), p. 161. The word that I have translated "class" is *jāti*, which very often means "caste"; I think, however, that the meaning here is more general.

throughout are that both male and female can attain the ultimate goal. Yet the texts that I have seen are without exception written from the masculine point of view. I suspect that this is for no more devious reason than that they are written, as far as it is possible to tell, by men. To the writers, who were not necessarily sensitive to feminist attitudes, woman is the fire of purification, the flower of limited usefulness, the guru who guides the *sādhaka* along his lonely way. But the theory says she is Rādhā, the recipient and enjoyer of Kṛṣṇa's love; she also contains Kṛṣṇa within herself, and so can know the infinite *ānanda*. The writers must be forgiven their purely first personal concern.

7) A Hint of Immortality

1. THE PROGRESS OF SĀDHANA

MOST SAHAJIYĀ TEXTS AGREE that there are three distinct stages in the *sādhaka's* progress toward his blissful goal. These are, loosely, the stage of preparation, the stage at which the sexual ritual is undertaken, and the stage after sexual ritual, when the *sādhaka* is beyond all mortal and external things, and pervades all time and all space. The three stages are called, respectively, *pravarta, sādhaka,* and *siddha.*[1]

Though the texts differ from one another regarding the precise characteristics of these states, the suggestions of the *Rādhārasa-karikā* might be taken as illustrative. This text says that the first stage is that in which the worshiper prac-

[1] VV, p. 129.

tices *vaidhi-bhakti* in the sense in which the orthodox Vaiṣṇavas mean it: by such disciplines as repetition of the names of Kṛṣṇa and learning mantras at the feet of the *dīkṣā-guru*. By such practices, it is said, the *sādhaka* gains the lowest of the heavens, Vaikuṇṭha. The second stage, that of *sādhaka*, is characterized by bhāva, the transformation (*āropa*) of the worshiper into one of the actors in the passionate drama of Vṛndāvana, i.e., Rādhā. Between this stage and the next, the worshiper, purified, practices the sexual ritual, which brings him to the final state of bliss, beyond ritual, and the enjoyment of the eternal and divine rasa. Specifically:

Pravarta, sādhaka, siddhi—these are the three stages of *rāga*. The mind is fixed upon guru, Kṛṣṇa, and Vaiṣṇava. The characteristics of the three are *nāma, bhāva,* and rasa. These three forms of *sādhana,* my brother, result in realization. The *svarūpa* of the *śāstras* is Kṛṣṇa the lord of Vaikuṇṭha, and if one is perfect in the mantras one reaches that place. The svarūpa of bhāva is Vrajendra-nandinī [i.e., Rādhā], and if one is perfect in bhāva, he gains Rādhā. The svarūpa of rasa is Yugala-kiśora [i.e., the blissful Kṛṣṇa] in Vraja, and if one tastes rasa he knows Kṛṣṇa the perfection of rasa. This is the true meaning of *pravarta, sādhaka,* and *siddhi.* In the *pravarta* state, one gains the feet of the guru. . . . In the *sādhaka*-state, one gains the *sakhīs* [i.e., the Gopīs]. And in the *siddha* state one gains the point of true service to Kṛṣṇa.[2]

The *Rasabhakti-candrikā* also describes the initial stage as characterized by repetition of the mantra of the name of Kṛṣṇa, but goes on to suggest that the state of the worshiper at this stage is *śānta-bhāva,* the attitude toward Kṛṣṇa as a majestic divinity rather than an intimate. With this is

[2] *Rādhārasa-karikā* (*VSP,* II, 1668–69).

connected the practice of the sixty-four ritual actions of *vaidhi-bhakti* under the tutelage of the guru and in association with holy men. The worshiper listens to the Vaiṣṇava *kīrtana* and takes part in it, thereby planting the seeds of prema and preparing himself to embark upon the otherwise disastrous sexual ritual. The *sādhaka* stage here is physical sexual ritual, in the purified bhāva state, and with guru as the *nāyakā* (Rādhā the *śikṣā-guru*). The characteristic of it is described as "the feet of the *sakhīs*," which has a double meaning. In Vaiṣṇava terms, the *sakhī*s are those Gopī-companions of Rādhā who had pleasure in serving the divine pair in their love meetings. In Sahajiyā terms, *sakhī* is also a name for the *nāyikā:* worship and service of the *nāyikā* are parts of the ritual. At this stage, the līlā of Rādhā and Kṛṣṇa is realized by the union in svarūpa of the *nāyaka* and *nāyikā.* The ultimate state of rasa is described in poetic and symbolic terms ("blackness" is, of course, the color of Kṛṣṇa's body): "Of the *pravarta* stage the characteristics are the taking of the name of Kṛṣṇa and *śānta.* Of the *sādhaka* stage, the characteristic is bhāva. Of the *siddha* stage, the characteristics are prema and rasa. The refuge of the *siddha* is at the feet of Rādhā and Kṛṣṇa; its characteristic is being among the *sakhīs.* Its *uddīpana*s are five: new clouds, black flowers, black bees, nightingales, and the throat of the peacock."[3] Tying all this back into the cosmic scheme, and a traditional scheme for theological texts, this work goes on to say that each of these stages has a characteristic time, place, and receptacle (*patra*). Those of the *pravarta* stage are not described. The *sādhaka* stage has as its time the Kali

[3] *VSP,* II, 1658–60.

Age,[4] as it place Navadvip, and as its vessel Caitanya. The *siddha* stage, as might be imagined, has eternity, Vṛndāvana, and Kṛṣṇa as the three. The text then offers an allegorical description of the worshiper's advance along an ascending path of religious awareness. The first step is desire (kāma), the second disappointment, the third sleeplessness, and so on until the seventh stage, at which the worshiper-lover becomes ill, the eighth, in which he becomes mad, the ninth, in which he loses consciousness, until finally, in the tenth, he no longer knows a difference between himself and Rādhā-Kṛṣṇa. The allegory is obviously to the progress of a love affair, and by describing *sādhana* this way, the writer is also giving a courteous nod of acknowledgment to the poetic fancies of the Vaiṣṇavas.

The *Rasasāra* further categorizes the process. Although it too recognizes the three stages, it says that the first, which it calls *taṭastha,* has four discrete characteristics: "In the first *taṭastha* stage, a feeling of reverence is aroused in the body; in the second, there is companionship with *sādhus*; in the third, one performs worship; and in the fourth, one takes on the bhāva of a *sādhaka.*"[5]

THE POWER OF THE NAME. The *Rāgamayī-kaṇā* says that the worship characteristic of the *pravarta* stage is the name of Hari.[6] Kṛṣṇadāsa, as we have seen, also considers that the repetition of the name of Kṛṣṇa is one of the five most important acts of *vaidhi-bhakti.* One name of Kṛṣṇa, some-

[4] Reading *kali* for *kala.*
[5] P. 4, quoted in *PCSC,* p. 8.
[6] P. 21, quoted in *PCSC,* p. 8

times even though uttered accidentally, has in it the power of salvation. "One Kṛṣṇa-*nāma* destroys all sin; it is the source of prema and the manifestation of bhakti."[7]

From the *nāma* comes the salvation of the whole world.[8] The notion is probably another of those taken over from the Tāntrics. The *DBhS* says, "the name and the possessor of the name are one."[9]

The power of the word, or, in Christian terms, the Word,[10] is one of the most important assumptions of many systems of Indian thought. The Sahajiyās consider it from two points of view: first, that a word is the thing which it represents, and, secondly, that even meaningless sound has meaning.

Although ideas about the efficacy of ritual formulas, the power of the spoken word, are central to the Tantras, they are also firmly rooted in more generally accepted systems of Indian thought, such as the Pūrva-mīmāṃsā. The basis of such thought, of course, is that the relationship between a word and its meaning is not arbitrary, but natural: the word and its referrent are in some sense one. Radhakrishnan writes that in the Pūrva-mīmāṃsā system "the Vedas are eternal, since the words of which they are composed are eternal. The relationship between the word and its meaning is natural

[7] *CC Ādi* 8:22.

[8] *Ibid.*, 17:19.

[9] *DBhS*, p. 123. There is another possible, though I think less likely, reading. *Nāmī*, which I have interpreted as "possessor of the name," might also refer to Rādhā, in which case the line would say that Rādhā and Kṛṣṇa are two forms but essentially undivided, making equally good doctrinal sense. But the context of the passage is the power of the name, and I lean toward the interpretation given.

[10] See Thomas Aquinas, *Summa Theologica*, question XXXIV, "The Person of the Son," and article XIII, "The Names of God."

and not created by convention."[11] This is the reason for the sanctity of the Vedas and the great power inherent in them. Nor is this an idea peculiar to India. Stories of medieval witchcraft and alchemy in Europe abound with sorcerers whose power lies in their knowledge of the name of some supernatural being, giving them control of him. Malinowski recognizes the principle in so-called primitive religions, in his essay on "The Problem of Meaning in Primitive Languages": "A word has some power over a thing. . . . It participates in the nature of a thing, that it is akin or even identical in its contained 'meaning' with the thing or with its prototype. . . . The word gives power, allows one to exercise an influence over an object or an action."[12] And the notion is prominent in Judaism, as George Foote Moore points out: "It was a universal belief in the age that the names of gods in incantations and adjurations put the power of those gods at the command of the magician. . . . Moses killed the Egyptian (Ec. 2.14) by pronouncing the Name over him."[13] And this accounts for the powers of such magicians as Simon Magus and Jesus, the latter possessing his miraculous abilities, a curious legend says, including his ability to fly, because he had stolen the written true names of angels from Egyptian temples and had secreted them about his person.[14] Such also was the belief of the Sahajiyās: the repetition of the name assists the worshipper to realize the svarūpa of Kṛṣṇa within himself, "awakening," so to speak,

[11] *Indian Philosophy,* II, 389.
[12] In *Magic, Science, and Religion,* pp. 228 ff.
[13] *Judaism,* I, 426.
[14] Arnobius, *Adv. nat.* 1:43.

Kṛṣṇa within him. The *Ānanda-bhairava* says that "having said and having understood Hari . . . the uttering of the name in the mouth brings the experience of him within."[15] The name has the power to transform the senses: "By the word 'Hari' the senses are conquered—desire, anger, lust, . . . all are conquered."[16] Or, "in the mantra of the name of Hari all sin is destroyed; the aspirant cannot become a *sādhaka* as long as sin remains. When one becomes a *sādhaka* there is nothing which is other than himself, for if anything external remains he is turned back to the *taṭastha* stage."[17] The VV complicates the matter slightly, saying that Rādhā is known by the repetition of one of the names of Kṛṣṇa, and Kṛṣṇa himself is known by another: "By the word 'Hari' Śrīrādhikā is known, and he who says 'Kṛṣṇa' knows Kṛṣṇa the son of Yaśodā."[18] The reference is to the devotional formula of the orthodox Vaiṣṇavas, repetition and variations on the phrase *harekṛṣṇa.*

The worshiper is taught a mantra by his *dīkṣā-guru,* and thus the *sādhana* is initiated.[19] At each stage of the sexual discipline, as we shall soon see, mantras are to be repeated, from a few to several hundred times, thus causing increasing realization of the presence of the divine svarūpa within. The most frequent mantras are called the *kāma-bīja* and *kāma-gāyatrī.* These pure Tāntric or Sahajiyā formulas are, interestingly, mentioned in the writings of the Gosvāmins. Gopāla Bhaṭṭa, in his *HBV*, says that they are appropriate

15 *Ānanda-bhairava,* p. 135.
16 *Ibid.,* p. 145.
17 *Rasasāra,* pp. 1–2.
18 VV, p. 120.
19 *Ibid.,* p. 41.

mantras for a Vaiṣṇava guru, using as his authority the *Gautamīyā-tantra.*[20] The *Prema-vilāsa* of Nityānanda-dāsa says that Jīva Gosvāmin, when he was initiating Śrīnivāsa Ācārya at Vṛndāvana, gave him the *kāma-bīja* as a mantra.[21] And Kṛṣṇa was considered by Kṛṣṇadāsa as the new Kāmadeva, the new god of love, whose worship was by the *kāma-gāyatrī* and *kāma-bīja*: "A new invisible Madana is in Vṛndāvana, and his worship is by the *kāma-gāyatrī* and *kāma-bīja.*"[22] Kṛṣṇadāsa says, in a statement that must have delighted the Sahajiyās, that the *kāma-gāyatrī* is the svarūpa of Kṛṣṇa: "The mantra *kāma-gāyatrī* is the svarūpa of Kṛṣṇa. . . . Its letters cause Kṛṣṇa to rise like the moon, and . . . fill the three worlds with desire for him.[23]

One *kāma-gāyatrī,* in a near, serious, and almost blasphemous parody of that Vedic *gāyatrī* found in *RV* 3:62:10, goes as follows: "*kāmadevaya vidmahe puṣpabāṇāya dhīmahi tan no'nangaḥ pracodayāt.*"[24] The VV begins to explain its significance in this way: "In the word *kāmadevāya* is that receptacle of the well of rasa; in the word *vidma* is gained a glimpse of what is truly taking place; the word *he* is a prayer for the presentation of the body and the senses; in the word *puṣpabānāya* are the two lotuses; by the word *dhīmahi* is meant the graduation of *sādhana.*"[25] In each

[20] *Vilāsa,* I, pp. 56–58 of the Murshidabad edition.

[21] P. 66.

[22] *CC Madhya* 8:109.

[23] *Ibid.,* 21:104.

[24] "We meditate on the god of love, whose arrows are flowers, so that the bodiless one may compel it." *Tat* refers to rasa, to semen. There are many formulas called *kāma-gāyatrī,* as we shall see.

[25] VV, pp. 152–53. For a discussion of the adoption of Vedic mantras by the Tantrics, see Chintaharan Chakravarti, *The Tantras—Studies on Their Religion and Literature,* pp. 5–6.

word of the mantra there is increasing assimilation of the svarūpa, realization of the identity of the self and the infinite reality. We might stop a moment to elaborate on this crucial concept.

It is the commonly accepted idea in the West that the relationship between a word and its referrent is purely arbitrary, that the name of an object and the object itself are not the same entities, or that an object does not naturally evoke the name which represents it. In other terms, a word is a symbol, not a sign. On the other hand, it is true that, although the response is conditioned, a name does call its referrent to mind. There is no need at this point to do more than recognize the fact that differences in conditioning among individuals will evoke differing responses to the same name.

It is also commonly accepted that the meaning of the verbal symbol will vary with the environment in which it finds itself. The Sanskrit aestheticians recognize this fact and point to the differing symbolic value of the word "spears" in different environments: "The spears are long," and "The spears entered the city." The latter, of course, evokes a powerful image of massed troops, an image which extends beyond that of the simple denotative "spear."[26] Or compare these three utterances: "The lamb is in the field." "You are a lamb." "He is the Lamb." The distinctions are various. The reference of the first is clearly to a small woolly animal and to nothing beyond that. This is the primary level

[26] For a discussion of this and the whole *dhvani* theory of levels of meaning in Sanskrit poetry, see Daniel H. H. Ingalls, *An Anthology of Sanskirt Court Poetry*, pp. 17 ff.

of symbolic value. The second utterance is quite a different thing. Unless the speaker happens to be addressing a lamb, the reference is to the person addressed having certain qualities of a lamb, primarily gentleness. This is the secondary level of symbolic value. The third utterance includes the symbolic values of the other two, but is like them limited to a particular context: here the context of the Apocalypse or of a poem by Blake. The reference is of course to the Christ, as the sacrificial lamb (level 1) and as possessing the gentleness of that creature (level 2).

Ordinarily, one has to pass through the first and second levels of symbolic value to reach the third. The word "Lamb" (except for the gratuitous orthographic clue, the initial capital letter) has, apart from context, no meaning except for the primary one. And even if the context were religious, the word "Lamb" would have no value on the tertiary level if the other two levels were not there. Thus, although the relationship between the symbol "lamb" and the small woolly animal might be arbitrary, the symbolic value of the word "Lamb" is not arbitrary but possesses the values "sacrifice" and "gentleness." The suggestion of the Sahajiyās is that it is possible to go directly to level three, that of religious and emotional value, without passing through the second level of symbolism. In other words, the Sahajiyās want to pass from the word itself to religious realization.

In terms of ordinary, everyday word symbols, this transition is clearly not possible, for the associations of ordinary words are too immediate. This is a principle recognized by many religions that use unordinary languages for ritual purposes: Sanskrit for Hindu and Buddhist ritual, Latin for the

Mass. One of the purposes of this is to avoid the association of words with everyday objects and thoughts, and to put the worshiper immediately into a religious context.

One of the characteristics of nonsense verse is a desire to get around the level of meaningful reference to an unconscious level on which language is unrelated to anything except an emotional state, a desire to induce an emotional state without having to take account of conditioning or of intellectual values of any kind. In this situation, the only non-linguistic values are environmental. Nonsense verse, apart from the environment "poetry," is meaningless. Within the context "poetry," however, it is meaningless only on the primary symbolic level; it is meaningful on the tertiary, non-intellectual level. This is, to the Sahajiyās, also the rationale of the *bīja-mantra,* the "seed" of realization.

When the *sādhaka* has progressed far enough, says the *Rāgamayīkaṇā,* the *bīja-mantra* takes the place of the full one. For the adept, this seed is enough, for it contains the universe. In the *bīja-mantra* the godhead itself reposes, as the fruit tree reposes in its seed. J. S. Hauer sums it up: the guru starts to train his pupil by giving him the mantra and teaching him to concentrate on the sounds and the significance—not the etymological meaning—of it. The result, says Hauer, is the inner appropriation by the student of the contents of the formula, in Sahajiyā terms the godhead itself.[27]

For the formula must be, in the ordinary sense of the

[27] *Die Dharani in nordlichen Buddhismus und ihre Parallelen in der sogennanten Mithrasliturgie,* pp. 6 ff.

word, meaningless. Dasgupta quotes Vasubandhu's *Boddhi-sattva-bhūmi* to the effect that meaninglessness is the meaning of the mantra.[28] Only if the *mantra,* in other words, has no relationship to any intellectual process, will the student be able to appropriate its power immediately. The mind cannot get in the way: by *jñāna,* intellect, the worshipper can know only a lesser form of God.

The Sahajiyā *bīja-mantras* are, accordingly, such meaningless agglomerations of sound as *klīṃ* (the *kāma-bīja*), *hrīṃ, drliṃ.* But these contain massive power; they contain the full godhead: "In the *bīja klīṃ* is Kṛṣṇa; in *hrīṃ* is Rādhā; and in the *bīja drliṃ* is the guru."[29] In the *kāma-bīja* is the universe: "The *bīja* has five "letters"—*ka, la, ī, ṃ,* and the sign of nasalization [*bindu*]. These five are the five elements: *ka* is the earth, *la* the water, *ī* the fire, *ṃ* the wind, and *bindu* is the sky. . . . And in realized form, *ka* is Kṛṣṇa, *la* Rādhā, *ī* is bliss [*hlādinī*], *ṃ* is rūpa, and *bindu* is Vṛndāvana."[30] Through the *bīja* the worshiper appropriates the universe. Through the *bīja* he covers all of space and exists through all of time. As the semen rises through the lotuses, all consciousness of time and space are wiped away. The semen reaches the thousand-petalled lotus in the brain, where Rādhā and Kṛṣṇa reside, and there is only eternity

[28] *ITB,* p. 66.
[29] VV, p. 153.
[30] *Ātma-tattva,* p. 151. *Amṛtarasāvalī,* p. 155, and VV, p. 137, make very similar statements. And, most interestingly, Gopāla Bhaṭṭa, in *HBV,* p. 58, writes: "From the *kāma-bīja klīm* the universe is created, so says the *Śiva-śrūti:* from the letter *ka* water arises; from the letter *la* the world is born; from *ī* fire comes, from *nada* the wind, and from *bindu* comes the sky."

and pure bliss. The drop of water, trembling so long on the lotus leaf, returns to the vast and bottomless sea.[31]

THE NĀYIKĀ-SĀDHANA-ṬĪKĀ. The reader will have noticed, perhaps with some irritation, that I have discussed *āropa,* the technique of transmuting kāma to prema, and the general discipline necessary for the transition from physical sex to abstract and complete bliss, in general terms, in terms of the philosophical and psychological bases of the Sahajiyā rather than their practical application. Unfortunately, an outsider's knowledge is limited by the texts available to him; and the texts available to me are philosophical and psychological justifications, not manuals. Obviously, the innermost secrets of the cult were not written down, or, if they were, were otherwise carefully guarded. If one wished to know more, he would, I fear, have to become an initiate. That being so, most of us will have to remain content, if frustratedly so, with such incomplete descriptions and oblique statements as those which have gone before. The text that follows might redress the balance a little.

There is a little manuscript in the possession of the Bengali Manuscripts Library of Calcutta University called the *Nāyikā-sādhana-ṭīkā.* Its colophon tells us that it was written by Rūpānuga-dāsa, in the Bengali year 1266 (A.D. 1860). It is not entirely clear whether it is supposed to be a commentary (*ṭīkā*) on some other text or not; it is encouraging to think that it might have been so intended, for this would help to explain some of its mysteries. The writer says that "he who publicizes these things, I know, is lost and will cer-

[31] *Sahaja-tattva* (VSP, II, 1656–57).

tainly go to hell." In some respects, the writer need not have worried, for his text is sufficiently murky to prevent any but an incomplete understanding of the ritual he expounds. For the rest, we must take our chances.

I have chosen this manuscript to translate, insofar as I can, in full, for two reasons. First, it is short enough to be manageable, while giving a reasonably complete account of the ritual. Secondly, a section of the text is given in M. M. Bose's *PCSC*, providing an opportunity for me to check, for this section at least, my reading of the scribe's sometimes difficult hand. It should not be thought that this text is representative of the best in Sahajiyā writing or thought; it is too mechanistic and even crass. As I have tried to suggest, however strange or, to some, offensive the Sahajiyā ritual is, the thought of the Sahajiyās can be exalted and their poetry graceful. The mechanics described below represent only one aspect of their doctrine.

(f.1.) Glory to ŚrīśrīRādhā-Kṛṣṇa. Thus is written the *Nāyikā-sādhana:* (1) *sādhana,* (2) *smaraṇa,* (3) *āropa,* (4) *manana,* (5) *dhyāna,* (6) *pūjā,* (7) *japana,* and (8) *ārādhana.* Of these, the *bīja* and *gāyatrī,* and the *āropa,* are discussed.

[1. *sādhana:*] When desire arises for the rasa which is in the rūpa, one should meditate in his mind on the *nāyikā* lovely and desirable. By his meditation upon that container of rasa, she will suddenly appear, and he will gain sight of her. These are the signs of the *nāyikā:* she is of greatest beauty and has a husband at home; her qualities are equal to her beauty, most wonderful.[32] By *bhāva* she will come, suddenly, and be joined with him. Her beauty will pass through his eyes and into his heart, and when it has entered his heart it will attract his mind. Then he will perform her *sādhana*. This is the *sādhana-mantra: śrlīṃ premamayi rasabatī dehi māma śaraṇāgata.*[33] This mantra is to be repeated 108 times. He should utter the first 25, and then make an offering [*añjali*] of flowers and sandalwood. In this way, there will be four *añjalis*, then the last eight mantras, and another *añjali*. Thus in all there are 108 mantras and 5 *añjalis*. Then the first part [*purbapakṣa*] of the *sādhana*[34] of the body, followed by meditation upon the rasa of the union of the divine pair.[35]

[2. *smaraṇa:*] This is the mantra for the united divine pair [*yugala-mantra*]: *śrlīṃ klīṃ rasa prema nama nama.*[36] Then, before *sādhana*, he will present a seat [*āsana*] to the *nāyikā*. (f.2.) The *āsana* will be eleven and a quarter [measures].[37] Then he will seat the *nāyikā* full of rasa on the *āsana* and, concentrating his full at-

32 *Rūpa gune samāna se adbhūta se nārī.*

33 [*Bīja*]. "Give me her who is full of prema, container of rasa, brought by my meditation." I have transcribed the mantras as accurately as I can; there are many spelling and grammatical mistakes throughout.

34 *Sādhana* is also a technical term for the male genital; see Vatsyāyana, *Kāma-sūtra: samprayoga adhi kāraṇe.*

35 *Pare smaraṇa yugala-rasa.*

36 "[*Bīja*]; obeisance to the *prema-rasa.*"

37 The meaning is unclear; the text reads *egāra poyāsana karibek. Āsana* is either a mat or, more usually, a low wooden stool. The *āsana* is of great importance to the Tāntrics, as physical comfort is necessary for extreme concentration. *Āsana* can also be a yogic posture, and *poyā āsana* could conceivably be a type of posture, though it is not among the usual ones.

tention upon her, he will wash her feet. Then he will begin the service [*sevā*] with sandalwood, thus: *etat candana śrīśrīrasamayica nama nama.*[38] Then [he will present] an *añjali* of flowers and sandalwood, and reflect on [*smaraṇa*] the *yugala-mantra* 109 times.

[3. *āropa:*] Then [to] the *nāyikā* full of rasa: *he he śrlīṃ rasamayi tava saraṇāgata mamāsteva svāhāya.*[39] This is the *āropa-mantra* of the *rasamayi* [*nāyikā*], and should be reflected upon 25 times. Having closed his eyes, [the *nāyaka*] will repeat this mantra in his inner mind. Then he will open his eyes and repeat the mantra again 5 times. Then, with another *añjali* of flowers and sandalwood, he should make the presentation of himself.[40] This is the *mantra* of presentation: *etat candanaṃ puṣpaṃ śrīśrīrasamayi nama nama.*[41] This is the presentation-mantra, and with this mantra 25 *añjalis* are made.

[4. *manana:*] Then the *manana.*[42] When the *manana* takes place, the *nāyikā* is unseen. In the mind [*manana*] the *rūpa* of the *nāyikā* is seen everywhere; she is present by means of bhāva. This is the *bhāvanāstava: he he rasamayi he rasanā-garī he he rasavilāsināḥ vilāsiniḥ he sundarī rasaullāsiniḥ he he mama prāṇa śiromaniḥ tava caraṇesa śaraṇaṃ nama nama.*[43] He will

[38] "Praise be to this sandalwood and the Śrīśrīrasamayi [*nāyikā*]."

[39] "[*Bīja*] O *rasamayī,* may I take refuge at your [feet]; homage to you."

[40] *Āpana nibedayet.*

[41] "Homage to this sandalwood and these flowers, O Śrīśrīrasamayī."

[42] Activity entirely within the mind.

[43] "O woman full of rasa, knower of all the depths and subtleties of rasa, who delights in the rasa of love, O beautiful woman, rejoicing in rasa, the crest-jewel of my life, my refuge is at your feet."

repeat this prayer, and then the *āropa-mantra* is to be uttered. (f.3.) Then the mantra of Śrīrūpamuñjari[44] and of Rādhā-Kṛṣṇa, these three, is to be uttered. The mantra is: *drlīṃ śrlīṃ klīṃ bhāva ullāsa rasaprema nama nama.*[45] This mantra should be uttered 103 times. Then, in bhāva, he will seat the *rasamayi* in the lotus of his heart.[46] Thus, the *pūja-bhāvanā.*

[5. *dhyāna:*] The *nāyaka* will meditate upon the *nāyikā* in the following way; let all hear of it. Taking the *nāyikā,* he will seat her on his left. Kissing her on the lips, he will touch her. At the touch, [his ?] heart is fulfilled. Then silently, within his mind, he will meditate on the *rasa-gāyatrī.* This is the *rasa-gāyatrī: śrlīṃ rasamayi tava caraṇe saranaṃ mamāste.*[47] He will utter this mantra 25 times. Kissing her on the lips, he will drink the *rasa.* Then he will meditate on the *rasa-bīja.* This is the *rasa-bīja: klīṃ rasarājā rasadānaṃ dehi mamāste.*[48] This mantra will be repeated 8 times. Then there will be meditation on the mantra on the *sādhana* of [i.e., to] Kandarpa, which is: *hlīṃ kandarpa kroṭi matumātaṅgī svāhāya.*[49] This mantra is [for] the worship of Kandarpa, and [the worshipper] will utter it 130 times. Kandarpa will be attracted by it. Then the

[44] The term *muñjari* is an obscure one, literally meaning the filament of a flower; it is possible that the term here refers to the sexual organs, possibly the sexual organs in union.

[45] "[*Bījas*]; Glory to the *rasaprema,* delighting in *bhāva.*"

[46] *Hridapadme baiśaibe.*

[47] "[*Bīja*]: O *rasamayī,* let my refuge be at your feet."

[48] "[*Bīja*]; O ruler of rasa, may the gift of rasa be given to me."

[49] The meaning of this mantra is unclear; *matumātaṅgī* is a maddened female elephant (also the name of a poetic meter).

nāyikā will perform[50] the worship of Kandarpa, with this mantra: *he he kandarpa he prāṇanātha he he rasarājā he rasa ullāsa tava dāsī mamāste.*[51] Before the prayer she will arrange the wooden seat.[52]

[6. *pūjā*:] Then the *pūjā*. This is the mantra: *klīṃ kandarpāya nama nama.*[53] First let this mantra be repeated nineteen times. Then there will be the presentation of an *añjali* to the *nāyaka*, and in this way, five *añjalis* should be presented. Because of this, Kandarpa will remain in his [i.e., the *nāyaka's*] own rasa.[54] Then the *nāyikā-pūjā*, which the *nāyaka* will perform. These are the necessary articles: incense, sandalwood, and flowers. First, these articles should be arranged. Then he will make an eleven and a quarter [measure] *āsana*. Then the *āsana-pūjā*, thus: *etat candanaṃ sthita āsanaṃ nama nama.*[55] After the sandalwood, the flowers [should be presented]: *etat gandhapuṣpam sthita āsanaṃ nama nama.*[56] Then he will seat the *rasamayi nāyikā* on the *āsana*. Then the bathing of the *nāyikā* [with this *mantra*]: *etat jalasnānaṃ śrīśrīrasamayī nama nama.*[57] After the bath comes the *pūjā*. First he will utter the *prema-gāyatrī* of the *rasamayī* 25 times. This is the *prema-gāyatrī*: *klīṃ premarasamayī śrlīṃ*

[50] It is interesting that the honorific verbal form is used: *pujā kariben.*

[51] "O Kandarpa, lord of my life, ruler of rasa, delighting in rasa, may I be your slave."

[52] *Ei stava āge pāṭa karibek.*

[53] "[*Bīja*]; hail Kandarpa."

[54] It is fairly certain that rasa here means semen.

[55] "Obeisance to the *āsana*, with this sandalwood."

[56] "Obeisance to the *āsana*, with these sweet-smelling flowers."

[57] "Obeisance to her, full of rasa, with this bath of water."

rasasindhubinduhi klīṃ rasavilāsinī svāhāyat.[58] After the uttering of the *prema-gāyatrī* comes the *pūjā*. The mantra of the *pūjā* is: *śrlīṃ rasamayī etat gandhapuṣpa tava caraṇe nama nama.*[59] He will utter this *mantra* 3 times. Then he will bow down in a *pranāma*, with another *añjali*-offering of flowers. And in this way there will be 19 *añjalis*. Then he will hold out before her on a banana-leaf those sweet things which have been prepared. On another leaf he will present to her water with camphor, with this mantra of presentation: *etat subhāṣita* [*sic*] *jalaṃ śrīrasamayica nama nama.*[60] He will utter this mantra three times. Then he will offer her another leaf, with *tulasī*. In this way, he will offer [her] five leaves. (f.5.) Then she will assume the *sajya āsana* [i.e., she will lie down], and having placed the *nāyikā* there, he will repeat the *āropayugala-mantra* 21 times. Then the *yugala* worship with the *gāyatrī-bīja*, in the bhāva of great joy [*ullāsa-bhāva*], thus: *śrlīṃ drlīṃ klīṃ yugala kiśora bhāva ullāsa nama nama.*[61] He will repeat this mantra 19 times. Then, on the *āsana*, having seated the *nāyikā* on his left thigh, the *nāyaka* will worship Kandarpa. This is the mantra for the worship of Kandarpa: *hlīṃ klīṃ kandarpa sāhā* [*sic*].[62] He will

[58] "[*Bīja*]; you, full of *premarasa*, [*bīja*], drop of the sea of rasa, [*bīja*], delighting in rasa, hail."

[59] "[*Bīja*]; *rasamayī*, with these sweet flowers, obeisance to your feet."

[60] Obviously, *subhāṣita* is a scribal error for *subāsita*, "perfumed, or sweet-smelling." The mantra means: "Glory to you, woman full of rasa, with this perfumed water."

[61] "[*Bīja*]; glory to the youth, united [with Rādhā] in highest joy."

[62] The text is full of spelling peculiarities of this kind; the scribe, of course, means *svāhāya*.

utter this mantra for the worship of Kandarpa 25 times. Then he will cause the *rasamayī nāyikā* to stand on the *āsana* [i.e., the bed], and raise her arms high. Naked, the *nāyaka* will gaze into her moon-like face, then slowly, with pleasure, at her breasts and at the place of rasa. Slowly his gaze will move down to her feet, and he will make a *pranāma*. Then the *nāyaka* and *nāyikā* [will] lie down, and, according to their desire, will have coition.[63] Coition should be according to the desire of the *nāyaka* or of the *nāyika*.[64] At the time of coition, the *yugala-mantra* will be repeated 19 times. This is the *yugala-mantra: klīṃ śrlīṃ yugala kiśorāya sāhā* [*sic*].[65] What is the purpose of this? By this the *nāyaka* and *nāyikā* become united with *mahārasa*.[66]

There are three tubular passages [*naḍi*]: *īḍā*, *piṅgalā*, and *susumnā*. People call them wind [*bāi*], bile [*pitti*], and phlegm [*slesmā*]. When it passes along the *bāi* passage, the rasa flows along the path to emptiness [*śunya*].[67] Then all men call [the *nāyaka*] sterile.[68] When it enters into *pitti*, the *nāyaka* and *nāyikā* remain [merely] full of pleasure [rasa]. (f.6.) But when it enters into the *slesmā*, the semen [*dhātu*] is fused

[63] *Sayana pare ramaṇa byābahāra he secchā pūrbbaka tāhā karibek.*

[64] *Yadyāpi ramaṇa bañca haya nāyikā icchā ki saba* [?] *nāeka icchā je haya tāhāte ramaṇa karibek.* Part of the line can be read another way, *Nāyikā icchā kinā eka icchā je haya,* which can be interpreted as, "if the wish of the *nāyikā* is at one with that [of the *nāyaka*]."

[65] "[*Bīja*]; to the youth, joined [with *Rādhā*], hail."

[66] Or, "*mahārasa* will be in the union of the *nāyaka* and *nāyikā*": *ihāte nāeka nāyikā mahārasa samyoga haibek.*

[67] That is, the semen is not discharged. The line reads: *bāi gata haile rasa śunya pathe jāya/tāhāre sakala loka bandhya bali kaya.*

[68] The end of this path is mere avoidance of procreation.

with the *jīvātmā*. Then he remains in this world, performing the worship [appropriate to] the jīva.[69] This is the reason that the *yugala-mantra* is uttered at the time of coition. Because of this mantra, *mahārasa* will be gained, through the *naḍis*. While [the mantra] is being uttered, the rasa moves along the path, inwardly, to the highest point,[70] and remains mingled with the *paramātmā*. The description of the age of that rasa which is mingled with the *paramātmā* should be heard.[71] Its age is twelve years and fifteen days.

Only our own people know the truth of this rasa, and Śrīgilimuñjari is chief amongst them.[72] It has been given as a gift to Nālimuñjari.[73] When Śrīnālimuñjari is present there is a perfect mingling in union. When there is union in *yugala-rasa*, at that time he comes to see [?]. What is *yugala-rasa* and how does it come to be? The *nāyaka* and *nāyikā* are completely absorbed in their *vilāsa* [līlā].[74] In body, mind, and speech, the *nāyaka* and *nāyikā* are one. This is called "burning love" [*ujjvala śṛṅgāra*]. This is the reason that, at the time of coition, there is worship with the *yugala-mantra*.

[7. *japana:*] Then the *jāpa*. In these ways the night

[69] That he is released while living.

[70] The thousand-petalled lotus of the brain.

[71] Assumedly, this is a statement of the relativity of time.

[72] It is unclear who or what *gilimuñjari* is. One suggestion is that Śrīgilimuñjari, and Śrīnalimuñjari in the next line, are Sahajiyā gurus. The two names are not found among those of the eight *sakhīs* or *mañjaris* of Rādhā. A second and better possibility is that the terms are esoteric, standing for the male and female (*nāli*) sexual organs respectively. The line then suggests the valid position that the true Sahajiyā finds the ultimate pleasure within himself, as if both male and female were within his own body.

[73] *Gilimuñjari haite nālimuñjari upadān.*

[74] *Vilāsa* is a term frequently used for the līlā of Rādhā and Kṛṣṇa. The union of Rādhā and Kṛṣṇa in svarūpa has been realized by the *sādhaka*.

will be passed. Then the *nāyaka* and *nāyikā* will arise, and go to their own homes. When they go to their own homes, they both become restless, and they begin to utter mantras, one to the other. These are their mantras. *Klīṃ rasarājā punamilitaṃ svāhā:*[75] this is the mantra of the *nāyikā;* she will utter it. The mantra for [the recall of] the *nāyikā* is: *śrlīṃ rasamayī punaḥ militaṃ svāhā.*[76] This is the mantra which the *nāyaka* will utter.

Thus I have spoken at length of the profound *nāyikā-sādhana.* The man who is a knower of rasa will understand, but the fool will not. I have spoken of Śrīgilimuñjari; let me expand on it. Let me speak of where he [she ?] stays, and what his [her ?] activities are. The union of lingam and vagina is called [?] Gilimuñjari; in the vagina-lingam is his dwelling-place. (f.7.) He desires [*itsā kare*], and by means of the vagina he causes the śakti which is contained at the base of the lingam [to rise to] *mahānanda,* in līlā [*vilāsa*]. Thus I have spoken briefly concerning Śrīgilimuñjari. Let me speak of Śrīnālimuñjari in a similar way. When there is coition between the *nāyaka* and *nāyikā,* then the two will be united in *mahārasa.* This is called Nālimuñjari. Where does Nālimuñjari stay? In the thousand-petalled lotus of the brain is the *parama-mānuṣa:*[77] [Nālimuñjari] stays in union with him. He assists in

75 "[*Bīja*]; [to] reunion with the lord of rasa, hail."

76 "[*Bīja*]; [to] reunion with her who is full of rasa, hail."

77 *Marjjāte sahasradala-padme parama mānusa* [*sic*]. The term *marjjā* is difficult, and presents three possibilities. The first, which I have chosen, is *majjā,* "marrow." The second, semantically related, is *madhyā,* "inner" or "within." The third is *marjji,* "desire" or "wish."

the rasa-pleasure of the *parama-mānuṣa* and nourishes the rasa of the *sahaja-mānuṣa*. Because of this, the name of Nālimuñjari is *niṣṭa*.[78]

So the essence of the truth of the *nāyaka* and *nāyikā* has been explained. Whoever makes it known to other than our own people is, I know for certain, lost, and will go to hell. He will never gain the feet of Śrīrūpa. He who reveals these things to other than our own people will not gain Kṛṣṇa, despite his prayers. [These secrets] should never be revealed to *paṇḍits* who are followers of other paths, or to those who believe in the Vedas. He who reveals them, not knowing who is a proper receptacle and who is not,[79] and shows them to an unworthy person—he and everything of his will be totally destroyed. If an improper person sees the book, he will doubt and if he doubts he will reveal it to others. *Paṇḍits* who are followers of the Vedas will not be able to understand it all; only Vaiṣṇava *paṇḍits* will understand its inner meaning. If anyone speaks ill of Vaiṣṇavas,. . . .[80] But those Vaiṣṇavas who worship with the Viṣṇu-mantra do not understand the inner meaning of it.[81] Among the people of Śrīśrīrūpa, those whose hearts he has made his refuge know the essence of the truth of it; they become eternal followers [of Kṛṣṇa—*parikara*] in Vṛndāvana. (f.8.) The highest

[78] *Niṣṭha* (?)—"firm, stable, disciplined."

[79] *Pātrāpātra nā bujhiyā prakāsa* [*sic*] *karibe*.

[80] The scribe seems to have left out half a verse here; there is no completion of the conditional clause.

[81] Assumedly, those Vaiṣṇavas who are worshippers of Viṣṇu, rather than Kṛṣṇa.

truth of all is the refuge of the perfected one [*siddha*] in Vraja. He makes known the *mantra* of his worship to no one, and he knows only those who are the most beloved companions of Rūpa. He knows the cause, and has taken shelter in [Kṛṣṇa]. He remains in the highest place,[82] in the lotus-refuge, in enjoyment. A thousand mouths could not tell of his bliss. Worship is in the twenty-four truths [?]. Know this for certain: when he takes refuge, he is [Kṛṣṇa's] own. Having taken refuge in the sahaja, that man will know and gain the [company of the] eternal *siddhas* in Vraja.

Thus has been described the *sādhana* of the eternal *siddha*. When one takes refuge in him, that is the *rasarati sādhana*. Thus have been described the rites of rasa,[83] as Rūpānuga-dāsa speaks the *Nāyikā-sādhana-ṭīkā*, and thus the *Nāyikā-sādhana-ṭīkā* is completed. With obeisance to the feet of Śrīrūpa. Signed, Śrīgopināth Mitra, dated the 22d Pouṣ, in the year 1266 *sāla*.[84]

EPILOGUE. It is a little difficult to remain detached, when confronted with teachings such as these, and most people who know anything about the Sahajiyās at all seem to hold strong opinions on the subject. Some would say that the whole Sahajiyā system is little more than an elaborate metaphor of the simple statement that sexual intercourse is a somewhat awesome, time-defying act. "Time enters only the unsteady mind," says the *caryā*-writer: time is relative.

[82] *Mahāsthāne thāke.*
[83] *Eita kahila rasa sārddhera uddesa* [*sic*].
[84] The date of the manuscript, not necessarily that of the original text.

Some would say that the whole Sahajiyā system is little more than a somewhat distasteful metaphysical justification for a mechanical, though impressive, act of yoga, a coitus reservatus par excellence. It is certain that the body, when trained and disciplined, is capable of the most extraordinary feats. Some, reacting more personally, would say that the mysteries of love and of faith are too full of beauty thus to reduce to system, or that the Sahajiyā attempt at immortality is too poignant a comment on the puniness and futility of man's striving. Mark Twain, in his satirical and irreverent *Letters from Earth*, has Satan write:

> [Human beings] thus prize [sexual intercourse] highly; yet like all their so-called "boons," it is a poor thing. At its very best and longest the act is brief beyond imagination—the imagination of an immortal, I mean. In the matter of repetition the man is limited—oh, quite beyond immortal conception. We who continue the act and its supremest ecstasies unbroken and without withdrawal for centuries, will never be able to understand or adequately pity the awful poverty of these people in that rich gift which, possessed as we possess it, makes all other possessions trivial and not worth the trouble of invoicing.[85]

Some would say that the Sahajiyā system should be viewed, not as an abasement, but as a recognition of the mysterious capacity of man for love, both spiritual and physical—a welcome hint of immortality in a very mortal, hate-filled world. Indeed, as M. M. Basu has said, "there is much in all these systems which attracts wise and religious minds."[86]

Perhaps the truth lies somewhere among all of these. It

[85] "Letter II."

[86] *Sahajiyā sāhitya, bhūmikā*, p. 1.

does not behoove us to judge. As Paracelsus, a man capable, among other things, of wisdom, has aptly written: "We know that a lover will go far to meet the woman he adores; how much more will the lover of wisdom be tempted to go in search of his divine mistress. . . . We look for knowledge where we expect to find it, and why should a man be despised, who goes in search of it." Man tries; perhaps for a time, he can escape his primeval, and appropriate, pain. Maybe Yeats, under that wild moon of his, knew whereof he spoke:

Solomon and the Witch[87]

And thus declared that Arab lady:
"Last night, where under the wild moon
On grassy mattress I had laid me,
Within my arms great Solomon,
I suddenly cried out in a strange tongue
"Not his, not mine."
Who understood
Whatever has been said, sighed, sung,
Howled, miau-d, barked, brayed, belled, yelled, cried,
crowed,
Thereon replied: "A cockerel
Crew from a blossoming apple bough
Three hundred years before the Fall,
And never crew again till now,
And would not now but that he thought,

[87] Reprinted from *Collected Poems of W. B. Yeats* (London: Macmillan & Co., Ltd., 1952 and A. P. Watt & Son; New York: Macmillan, 1952) by permission of the publishers. Copyright 1952 by Macmillan & Co., Ltd., and 1952 by Macmillan. The poem was called to my attention by my friend Dr. Naresh Guha of Jadavapur University. For a discussion of the influence of the Tāntric tradition on Yeats, see Dr. Guha's doctoral dissertation (Northwestern University, 1962), called "W. B. Yeats—An Indian View."

Chance being at one with Choice at last,
All that the brigand apple brought
And this foul world were dead at last.
He that crowed out eternity
Thought to have crowed it in again.
For though love has a spider's eye
To find out some appropriate pain—
Aye, though all passion's in the glance—
For every nerve, and tests a lover
With cruelties of Choice and Chance;
And when at last that murder's over
Maybe the bride-bed brings despair,
For each an imagined image brings
And finds a real image there;
Yet the world ends when these two things,
Though several, are a single light,
When oil and wick are burned in one;
Therefore a blessed moon last night
Gave Sheba to her Solomon."

"Yet the world stays."
"If that be so,
Your cockerel found us in the wrong
Although he thought it worth a crow
Maybe an image is too strong
Or maybe is not strong enough."

"The night has fallen; not a sound
In the forbidden sacred grove
Unless a petal hit the ground,
Nor any human sight within it
But the crushed grass where we have lain;
And the moon is wilder every minute.
O Solomon! let us try again."

8

The Bāuls of Bengal

THROUGHOUT THE BOOK, I have referred to the Sahajiyās in the past tense. Some people in Bengal say, with what I think is more wish than truth and certainly with more shame than necessary, that the Sahajiyā cult no longer exists. A non-initiate foreigner can neither prove nor disprove this, but he can have his suspicions. Mine are that, like the so-called *laja-dharma* of Rajasthan discussed by Carstairs,[1] the Sahajiyā cult, though no longer tolerated by civil law, continues to be followed secretly. Civil legislation is rarely strong enough to thwart belief. Nor, indeed, has the contempt of society ever meant very much to the Sahajiyās: it is, if anything, to be courted.

And some scholars say, as Winternitz has said, that the

[1] *The Twice-born*, p. 104.

"novel, monistic doctrines" propounded by the royal Lakṣmīmkarā of Orissa are "even at the present day prevalent among the Bāuls of Bengal."[2] There is an eternal borrowing and reborrowing of ideas and doctrines that goes on and has always gone on among religious sects in India, until the lines of derivation become very blurred indeed. The doctrines and the poetic language of the unusual sect known as the Bāuls are indeed in some respects similar to those of the Sahajiyās. But I do not think it can be said that the majority of those who are called Bāuls are Sahajiyās, if a Sahajiyā can be defined as a follower of that strange ritual of which we have had a glimpse.

The image which the Bāul presents to the world is, like that of the pure Sahajiyā, that of a madman, a man who tolerates no stricture of society, who goes deliberately against society to prove his independence of it. The very word *bāul*, in fact, means "mad." Dasgupta feels that the word can be derived in three ways.[3] It can be derived from the Sanskrit *vātula*, "infected with the wind disease," i.e., mad, or from the Sanskrit *vyākula*, "confused, disordered." Or, Dasgupta says, it can be derived from the Arabic *āuliya*, a term used for "friend" or "devotee." Although there is some reason to consider the latter possibility, the Bāuls being associated in some ways with Islam, there is no etymological reason to go so far afield. The derivations from *vātula* and *vyākula* seem clear, and both are equally possible. In Magadhi and in most dialects of eastern Hindi, as well as in Bengali, the Sanskrit intervocalic consonant is often lost. Thus, *vātula*

[2] *History of Indian Literature*, II, 393.
[3] *ORC*, pp. 83–84.

would be *vāula,* and *vyākula* would be *vyāula.* Further, initial *vy-* cluster becomes *v-,* and *vyāula* also yields *vāula.* Sanskrit "v" becomes "b" in eastern Hindi and consistently in Bengali, thus leaving us with the form *bāula.* If additional proof were needed, taking into account the fact of free variation in many dialects of eastern Hindi and Bengali between "r" and "l," we find that the term *bāur* occurs in one of the poems of Vidyāpati, a Maithili poet of the late fourteenth or early fifteenth centuries. In describing Śiva, the poet writes that "the lord of the three worlds is quite mad [*ṭhik bāur*]."[4]

Although in modern Bengal the term *bāul* is no longer used in its generalized sense, but exclusively to refer to a special group of people, the connotation of madness is still there. A Bāul is one who, dressed in tattered cast-off garments deliberately made up of remnants of clothing previously worn by both Hindus and Muslims, wanders incessantly, living on whatever those who listen to his songs, which are his only form of worship, choose to give him. The rags on his shoulders are reminiscent of those of the *durueś,* the saint of Sufi Islam, to whom the Bāul is similar in other respects as well. He plays a primitive but haunting one-stringed instrument, called *ek-tāra,* and the songs he sings are beautiful in melody and thought, as gentle and as stirring as the wind which is his home. The Bāul is thought mad because he goes deliberately and powerfully against the current of custom. As Dasgupta says: "[The Bāuls] refuse to be guided by any canon or convention, social or religious.

[4] *Vidyāpati,* ed. Khagendranāth Mitra and Bimanbihari Majumdār, p. 787.

. . . They proceed in a direction opposite to that followed by the general run of people. . . . It is for this reason that the Bāuls would call their path *ulṭa* [i.e., the contrary] path and would call the process of their spiritual advance as the process of proceeding against the current. It is said in a beautiful song—'Reverse are the modes and manners of the man who is a real appreciator of the true emotional life.' "[5] The praise or condemnation of the world mean nothing to the Bāul. Lālan Phakir sings: "As the lightning hiding in the cloud cannot be sought out, so I have lost that Black Jewel, that beauty seen as in a dream. When I remember, I have no fear of shame before the world."[6]

The Bāul cannot help his madness; he is maddened by the sound of Kṛṣṇa's flute, and, like a Gopī, caring nothing for home or for the respect of the world, he follows it: "I hear its sound, and maddened I leave everything and run to hear. . . . I leave my house and run away, abandoning my house and home."[7] In short, the Bāul is dead to every pain and sorrow, every joy and regret, that the world can cause: "Free from desire, indifferent to the world, dead while yet alive, he will have these credits in the ledger-book."[8] Such iconoclastic attitudes, of course, made the

[5] *ORC*, p. 185; cf. *SS* pada 24, signed "Kavi-vidyāpati": "The actions of the *sahaja-mānuṣa* are strongly adverse."

[6] A song of Lālan Phakir, *Lālan-gītikā*, ed. Motilāl Dāś, Calcutta University, 1958, no. 362, p. 248.

[7] A song of the Bāul Padmalocana, collected by Kṣitimohan Sen, published in *Pravāsī*, B.S. 1322, p. 323, and in Rabindranath Tagore's anthology *Bāṅglā kāvya paricaya*, p. 72.

[8] A song of Lālan Phakir, in *Pravāsī*, p. 193. The phrase is *khātāy oyāśilā*: *oāśila* is literally a statement of credit and debit, a financial account, and *khātā* the ledger in which the entry is made. The reference is to the Muslim belief in the book of good or evil that each man has, the totals being made on the Day of Judgment; see H. A. R. Gibb, *Mohammedanism*, p. 61.

Bāuls, at least in the days before Rabindranath Tagore, a laughing stock. To one writer they seemed nothing more than a species of buffoon: "Not only their dress, but their musical instruments, their dancing, and their songs are all characterized by a kind of queerness which makes them very amusing. The quaint allegories and rustic philosophy of their songs are highly appreciated by the lower classes. Their exhibitions are upon the whole so enjoyable that, in most of the important towns of Bengal, amateur parties of Bāuls have been organised, who cause great merriment on festive occasions by their mimicry."[9] Modern Bengalis do not feel this way. Rabindranath Tagore put the Bāuls on a higher-than-respectable level by his praise of the beauty of their songs and spirit, and by his frank and proud acknowledgment of his own poetic debt to them.[10] Besides, the Bāuls themselves were not to be troubled by the mocking parodies of their verses so in vogue among sophisticates. In fact, one Bāul sings one such parody, ending it with either great wit or charming ingenuousness (or maybe both), "Haripada says, How wonderful all this is to hear! He who has the power to understand these things goes beyond the Vedas."[11] Today, some Bāuls sing on concert stages to large audiences. Their brothers, perhaps more true to their avowed contempt for the glitter of the world, wander the countryside, as Bāuls have done for centuries.

The history of the sect is quite obscure, since until the

[9] Bhattacharjee, *Hindu Castes and Sects,* quoted by Kennedy, *CM,* p. 215.

[10] See my paper "Rabindranāth Tagore—'Greatest of the Bāuls of Bengal,'" in *Journal of Asian Studies,* XIX, No. 1 (November, 1959).

[11] From my own collection.

present century it had no written literature of its own. In medieval literature such as the *Padmāvatī* of Alāol and in the CC and *CBh*, the term *bāul* appears frequently in such contexts as "I am mad [*ami ta bāula*] . . . floating in the stream of the nectar of the sweetness of Kṛṣṇa."[12] But it is not at all clear whether or not the term had begun to assume its sectarian significance at the time when these texts were written. The usage of the word is ambiguous, as it continues to be in the seventeenth century *Prema-vilāsa* of Nityānandadāsa, where it is said that Śrīnivāsa, almost mad with grief, "fell and twisted on the earth as if mad [or, 'like a Bāul']."[13] Kṣitimohan Sen tries to show that the roots of the sect lie in the Vedas and Upaniṣads, and does succeed in suggesting that there is nothing new under the sun.[14] But whether *RV* 7:88:3, which suggests, in an image also used by the Bāuls, God as friend is indicative of the origin of the Bāuls is at least questionable. A more modern and, it might be said, perceptive scholar, Sukumār Sen, recognizes the existence of the Bāuls as a definable group in the early sixteenth century, saying that in the reign of Husein Shah there was a tendency of various religious groups, "including the Bāuls," toward the Vaiṣṇava movement of Caitanya.[15] Brajendranāth Śīl feels that "the birth of the Bāuls" took place toward the end of the fourteenth century or the beginning of the fifteenth and that after the sixteenth century they began to spread rapidly and widely.[16] One thing

[12] CC *Madhya* 21:124; see also *Madhya* 2:43, *Antya* 19:19–20.
[13] P. 59.
[14] *Bāṅglār Bāul*, pp. 6 ff.
[15] *BSI*, I, 396.
[16] Quoted in *Hārāmaṇi*, p. 5.

seems certain, and that is that the Bāuls drew upon the same spirit of iconoclastic bhakti which swept across northern India between the fourteenth and the seventeenth centuries, inspiring Rāmānanda, Tukurām, Kabīr, Nānak, Dādū, and Caitanya, the so-called *santa*-cults through which the effects of Sufi Islam show clearly.

The question of whether the origins of the Bāuls lie in these cults of bhakti, though of considerable academic interest, is not one that need detain us unduly. But it is relevant to note a few points of similarity between the Bāuls and other sects around them. It is characteristic that to the Bāuls worldly trappings and show are like weights around the neck and are to be scorned by the true men of God. And Sheikh Sā'dī of Shīrāz, in his pithy Sufi vein, tells us that

> There was a holy man, who saw in a dream that an emperor was in paradise, and a pious man in hell. He asked, "What is the reason for this changeabout? People say that it is just the opposite." A voice from heaven came, "This king has been close to saints, and is in paradise; the pious man has sought the company of kings, and is in hell."

> What use is a saint's tattered dress, or string of beads, or pious face? Keep yourself from evil works.

> What is the need of a costly cap of felt? Be like a *durueś*, with a cap of simple cloth.[17]

The Bāul called Kāngāli Bāul feels much the same: "O my mind, can you not see the falsity in this world? She wears fine

[17] *Gul-i-stān* 2:15.

clothes and ornaments, but underneath the finery, she is but a beggar-woman."[18]

The famous Baul Lālan Phakir sings of a "mirrored city":

> I have never seen him,
> though he is my neighbor,
> though he dwells in a mirrored city
> near my house.
> For around that city is a moat,
> bottomless and endless;
> there is no way to reach the farther shore.
> My heart yearns to see him,
> but I can never reach his city.[19]

This is the mirror in the heart, of which the Sufi poet Jalaluddin Rumi writes: "In the mirror of the heart is the reflection of your Friend; bow your head a moment, and see it there."[20] The nightingale singing in the Shīrāzī garden of the great Sufi poet Ḥāfiẓ becomes the elusive bird of the heart of the Bāul, trapped within the rib cage of his body, yet unknown. And it becomes again the bird of God of Rabindranath Tagore:

> Even though slow and sluggish
> evening comes,
> and stops as with a gesture
> your song;
> even though you are alone
> in the infinite sky,
> and your body weary,
> and in terror you utter

[18] *Pravāsī,* p. 640.
[19] Quoted in *BSI,* p. 994.
[20] *Hārāmaṇi bhumikā,* p. 16.

a silent *mantra*
to horizons hidden by the veil—
bird, O my bird,
though it is darkening,
do not fold your wings.[21]

And there is abundant use of Sufi technical terminology in the Bāul songs.[22]

That there was considerable interaction between the Sufis and the Bāuls is undeniable. A brief sketch of the life of Lālan Phakir or Lālan Shah, one of the Bāuls who had a profound effect upon Rabindranath, might indicate a way in which such mingling came about. It is interesting that the story is much the same as that of the Hindi bhakta and poet Kabīr.[23]

Lālan was born in Nadiyā district in Bengal, not far from Navadvip, sometime early in the nineteenth century. His family was Hindu, Kāyastha in caste, and the name given him was Lālancandra Rāya. He was married young, and very shortly after his marriage he went, some say with his mother, some say with a group of friends, to Navadvip to bathe in the Ganges. While he was there, he contracted a severe case of smallpox and was left for dead on the river bank. He lay there, more dead than alive, the lower part of his body immersed in the river, for several days. Finally, he regained

[21] Rabindranath's *Duḥsamaya*, in *Kalpanā* (no. 1.).

[22] See *Hārāmaṇi*, songs 43, 58, and 61, for example. For a discussion of the occupation of the middle ground between Islam and Hinduism by the *santa* cults, see Humayun Kabir, "Islam in India," in *CHI*, pp. 579–92, and F. E. Keay, *Kabir and His Followers*, pp. 89 ff. Suggestive reading is Roma Chaudhuri, *Sūfism and Vedānta*, Part I, pp. 4–40.

[23] One legend is that Kabīr was the bastard son of a Brahman widow, abandoned by his mother and picked up and raised by a childless Muslim couple. For other stories, see Keay, *op. cit.*, p. 10.

consciousness, and his cry for water was heard by a Muslim woman who was passing by. She brought him water, took him home with her, and she and her husband slowly nursed him back to health. But the disease had taken one of his eyes. When he was well, he attempted to return to his village, but, painfully, his wife and his family refused to take him back, because of his association with Muslims. So he returned to the house of his benefactors, and from his adopted father he learned much about the Muslim scriptures and the teachings of the Sufis. He abandoned the world and became a mendicant, some say accompanied by his new father, wandering and learning all he could of the writings of both the Hindus and the Muslims. Finally, a great number of pupils around him, he died, some time in the late nineteenth century.[24]

The doctrinal and poetic similarities between Bāuls and Sufis are plentiful. But whether it is fair to conclude that Sufi Islam influenced the Bāuls in the areas of the religious usage of song and dance, the importance of the guru (the Sufi *murśid*), opposition to external religious practices, the conception of man as the microcosm and the connecting link between the divine and phenomenal creation, and the conception of God as the Beloved, is at least doubtful.[25] For we have seen that most of these characteristics are present also in the very old Sahajiyā tradition. And, if the Bāul songs teem with Sufi terminology, there are in them equally

[24] Upendranāth Bhaṭṭācārya, *Bāṅglār bāul o bāul gān,* Part II, pp. 1–13; see also *Hārāmaṇi,* pp. 176 ff.

[25] For a discussion of such "influences," see *ORC*, pp. 193 ff.

many words special to the Sahajiyās and to the Tāntric tradition. Frequent use is made of such terms as svarūpa and *tripināle* or *tribenī*, the place where three rivers meet, the symbol of the place at the base of the spine where in the Tāntric physiology the three tubes or "nerves" come together.[26] Bāul songs use the imagery of the *cakras* of the Tāntric system also,[27] and often the "unknown bird," the Bāul (and Sufi) symbol for God within the human heart, is described as imprisoned in a cage made of eight sticks, the eight *sakhīs* or the eight members of the Tāntric circle. Much Bāul poetic imagery is the same as that of the Vaiṣṇava-sahajiyās. The Sahajiyās, we have seen, recognize Caitanya as the embodiment of all that they believe to be possible. The Bāuls also see him so and see him in addition as a support for their contempt for such orthodoxies as caste. Lālan Phakir sings: "O Gaurā, what law is this which you have brought to Nadiyā? It cannot be an earthly being's work. . . . 'Piety-impiety' to you is empty, you sing instead the qualities of love. . . . The impossible you make possible, and you do not shrink, in hatred, from the touch of any living thing."[28] To both Bāuls and Sahajiyās the six senses are dangerous if uncontrolled, thieves who seek to rob the traveler on the way of all his purpose. It seems to Ākiñcana-dāsa that "on the road to bhakti there are highwaymen who bind with ropes of kāma him who is on his way to *siddhi*."[29] And the Bāul sings: "I went to the bazaar that is

[26] *Hārāmaṇi*, pp. 16–19.
[27] *Hārāmaṇi, bhumikā*, p. 6 f.
[28] Lālan Phakir; *Lālan-gītikā*, no. 312 (p. 214).
[29] VV, p. 141.

the world. Six thieves were there. They stole from me, and bound me, and by a trick they bound me up and fled away."[30]

The body is a frail craft, laden with sin, in which the traveler sets out upon the wild and stormy river of life. The senses are drunken ferrymen, who in their stupor let the boat drive down upon the rocks. The only hope is the guru, the helmsman who, with steady hand, steers through the storm until the battered boat at last touches on the farther shore. A *caryā-pada* says: "Make the five *tathāgatas*, the oars, O Kānha, and steer the body on."[31] And, more subtly, Lālan: "What I do I do, and my boat is laden deep with sin. And Lālan cries, The waves ahead are high and heavy."[32] The image is not limited, incidentally, to Bengal, the land of rivers. The poet Dādū writes: "O Govinda, how can I reach the other shore? No boat have I, nor oarsman. . . . There is no landing-place, no path where I might set my foot. Adrift in a shoreless sea, Dādū is sore afraid."[33]

In some points of doctrine too the Bāuls are related to the Sahajiyās. The body is the world, in which the Lord's līlā is taking place: "He who knows the secret meaning of the Vedas knows in what form the līlā of the Sāi is in this body-world."[34] The presence of the divine is known to the Bāuls sometimes as svarūpa and often as the "man of the heart" (*maner mānuṣa*) or the "unknown bird" that dwells in the

[30] Anonymous song from my collection.

[31] A song of Kānhu-pā, quoted *ORC*, p. 105; the translation is Dasgupta's. See also *caryā* no. 38.

[32] Lālan Phakir, in *Bhaṭṭācārya, Bāul gān*, no. 12.

[33] *Śabda* 81 of Dādū, given in translation in W. G. Orr, *A Sixteenth-century Indian Mystic*, p. 59.

[34] Lālan Phakir, collected by Rabindranath and published in *Pravāsī*, p. 404.

body's cage. The Bāul feels a presence within him, and, tormented by it, seeks to know it:

Within the cage the unknown bird comes and goes.
If I could catch him, I would clamp the iron of my
mind upon his feet.
My whole life long I have nourished that bird,
and still he evades me. I do not understand—
I have given you bananas and the milk of my breast,
O bird, and still you ignore my coaxing.[35]

When will I find him, that man of my heart?
He is lost. In my search I have wandered near and far . . .
He distracts my mind. But when I find him
at last my mind will be at peace. . . .
if you know where he is hiding, be kind—
tell me of it.[36]

The bird is elusive:

The bird has flown away.
An evil wind has struck and smashed his cage.
His perch is fallen, and no more will be his rest.
The bird of my desire has flown away, and left an empty cage,
and I have no friend more,
and no companion.[37]

Like the Sahajiyās, the Bāuls feel that man cannot know the God within because he is trapped in māyā, enmeshed in intellectual knowledge, infatuated with self, dazzled by the glittering of the cheap baubles of the world:

[35] Lālan Phakir, quoted in *BSI*, I, 993. Sen says that "this song of Lālan had the effect of a *dīkṣā-mantra* on the mind of the young Rabindranāth."

[36] Song of Gagana Harakara, collected by Rabindranath and published in *Pravāsī*, XV (B.S. 1322 [A.D. 1917]), 154.

[37] Lālan Phakir, in Bhaṭṭācārya, *Bāul gān*, no. 32.

When you deal in the market of the world,
you think you buy rich rubies, diamonds, pearls—
you really only buy brass beads, my friend.
If you can profit by such a bargain,
your skill will make you famous in all the earth.[38]

Keep your name in my heart's mouth, Gosāi;
I am wretched. Where else lies my hope?
Whether he is disciple of a Hindu or a Muslim,
know and guide him, the traveller on the road,
at every turn of which there lurks a shadow—
there may be danger any time, my brother.

"My house," "my goods"—like this our days go echoing by.
We eat the poison of possession,
and when our wealth is lost, we weep.
What good will weeping do when it is lost, my brother?
The wealth of Sāi alone is always safe, my brother,
but my mind was deluded and did not see.
Lālan says, no matter where you store your earthly wealth
your hands will still be empty at the end, my brother.[39]

As to the Sahajiyās, the Vedas and the Vedānta are to the Bāuls not only uprofitable ways, but delusive and downright dangerous: "Read the Vedas and Vedānta, but you will find no sign of truth."[40] "The Vedic cloud casts a fearful darkness, and the day's jewel cannot rise."[41] "As much as you read the Vedas and Vedānta, so much will your delusion grow."[42] But—and here they differ from the Sahajiyā belief and are closer to the spirit of Sufism—to the Bāuls *all* ex-

[38] Lālan Phakir, *Hārāmaṇi* no. 30 (p. 21).
[39] Lālan Phakir, in Bhaṭṭācārya, *Bāul gān*, no. 63.
[40] Lālan Phakir, in *Lālan-gītikā*, no. 4 (p. 5).
[41] *Ibid.*, no. 413 (p. 286).
[42] Lālan Phakir, quoted in *BSI*, p. 993.

ternal ritual, Vaiṣṇava or Tāntric, Hindu or Muslim, is meaningless and foolish.

The path is blocked by the temple and the mosque.
Though I hear you call, O Sāi, I cannot find the way.
Against me, angry, stand my guru and *murśid*. . . .
On the gate are many locks—Purāṇas, Qurān, *tasbi*, *mālā*;
all this outward show makes Madana weep, in sorrow.[43]

And, in one of the nicer statements of its kind:

Some say that praying to Hari instead of Kālī is an error.
Some say that praying to Kālī instead of Hari is an error.
I have thought much upon these things,
and have gone mad. There seems to be no meaning in it.
I used to make a show . . . :
bathing in the Ganges thrice a day, reciting many mantras;
I performed my Yogic exercises constantly,
and all I got was out of breath.
I fasted, day after day,
and the result was a pain in my belly.[44]

The Vaiṣṇavas, Sahajiyās, and indeed Tāntrics in general, condemn caste, at least in the context of religion. The Bāuls go even further and condemn it outright as an evil.

Go once to see Jagannātha. See there how caste is kept.
A Caṇḍāla brings a Brahman's food, and the Brahman takes
and eats.
Kabīr was a Jolā . . .

[43] Madana Bāul, in Rabindranath's *Bāṅglā kāvya paricaya*, p. 70. Cf. Keay, *op. cit.*, p. 14, who quotes Kabīr, *Bījak*, *śabda* 113: "Devotion, sacrifice and rosary, piety, pilgrimage, fasting and alms, the nine bhaktis, the Vedas, the Book, all these are cloaks of falsehood." See also Yusuf Husain, *L'Inde mystique au moyen age*, pp. 70 ff. *Murśid* is the Islamic equivalent of guru, as *tasbi* is the Islamic equivalent of *mālā*, a string of beads counted while repeating the names of God.

[44] A song of Āli Khān Munśi of Noakhāli: *Pravāsī*, p. 541.

In such measure as one lives by caste, in that measure
he is evil. . . .
Do not sing the eulogies of caste, saying "Do not touch
him . . ."
Lālan says, If I could take caste into my hands,
I would hurl it into the fire![45]

Like the Sufi, who, from the heights of wisdom, sees all men as the same, to the Bāul there is no difference between Hindu and Muslim. A godly man is neither.

Hindu, Muslim—there is no difference,
nor are there differences in caste.
Kabir the bhakta was by caste a Jolā, but
drunk with *prema-bhakti* he seized the Black Jewel's feet.
One moon is lantern to this world,
and from one seed is the whole creation sprung.[46]

A man deluded by ritual, by social custom, by māyā, may search for God. But however much and in whatever different ways such a man may search about the world, he finds no trace; God, hidden, is within. The closer a man is to the world, the less is his perspective on truth. So say the Sahajiyās, and so, somewhat more strikingly, say the Bāuls:

Though you are near the Sāi, you look toward the
distant hills.
I grope from Dacca to Delhi, but cannot find my way,
in the twilight of my mind. . . .
The god Hari is within me!

[45] Lālan Pharkir, *Lālan-gītikā,* no. 446 (p. 307). The reference is to the temple of Jagannāth in Puri, where Caitanya spent his last years. The temple was supposedly originally Buddhist, though for many centuries it has been Vaiṣṇava, and from time immemorial has had no caste barriers, every individual (except, interestingly, Europeans) being allowed to enter and to worship without discrimination. Jolā is a caste of weavers, mostly Muslim.

[46] *Ibid.,* no. 53 (p. 37). The Black Jewel is of course Kṛṣṇa.

If my mind would but be still,
I would search him out. . . .[47]

In his search the Bāul goes alone, in the darkness. The world of men holds no comfort for him. He sits alone in the twilight on the shore of the river, having to embark in his frail boat, yet fearful of the river's wildness and the danger:

> I was sitting, alone on the landing place,
> when the sun was setting in the west.
> I was alone, without you,
> and in the darkness there was danger.
> I was afraid, for I could not see the way. . . .[48]

And, like the Sahajiyās and the Tāntrics, and indeed like the Vaiṣṇavas and Sufis also, the Bāul needs the strong hand of the guru-helmsman upon the tiller to steer him safely across:

> An unknown one is calling, at the river's bend—
> I hear him call!
> But let me stand and rest upon the bank a little time,
> for once I start across that shoreless stream,
> I will not rest again.
> The river rolls, resistless and profound.
> It rolls
> and pulls my boat adrift—
> my mind awhirl—
> O guru! Hold fast to the helm!
> The river rolls, and waits in moving darkness
> for Jāgā.[49]

[47] Lālan Phakir, quoted in *BSI*, I, 993. See also the song of Padmalocana in *Pravāsī*, p. 640. The term *sāi* is a form of *gosāi* or *gosvāmi*, "lord" (perhaps "lord of cows"), a term of great reverence among Vaiṣṇavas. Here the reference may be either to Kṛṣṇa or guru indwelling in man.
[48] Lālan Phakir, in Bhaṭṭācārya, *Bāul gān*, no. 16.
[49] Jāgā Kaivarta, in *Bāṅglā kāvya paricaya*, p. 68.

The waves are deep, the night is dark,
and I am dying, filled with dread.
Where are you,
boatman of this infinite sea?[50]

Come, O merciful one, and take me from this worldly *ghāṭ*
across to the other shore
You are the helmsman, for him
who flees in terror from this world.[51]

For him whose helmsman you are,
steering steady,
there is no terror in the storm.
Dancing and singing he will cross
to the other shore.[52]

In the Bāul songs, the river is not always the swirling, pulling, resistless, dangerous river of life. It sometimes moves calmly and deeply toward the infinite sea, toward God. The sea is the end of the journey, the soothing water in which the flame of life, with its searing pain and passion, is extinguished.

My heart is a lamp, moving in the current,
drifting to some landing-place I do not know.
Darkness moves before me on the river,
it moves again behind,
and in the moving darkness
only ripples' sounds are heard,
for underneath the ripples moves
the current of the quiet night.
My lamp, as if to seek a friend, goes drifting
by the shore. Both day and night
my drifting lamp moves searching

[50] Lālan Phakir, in Bhaṭṭācārya, *Bāul gān*, no. 2.
[51] *Ibid.*, no. 20.
[52] *Ibid.*, no. 70.

by the shore. My Friend is ocean to this river,
my Friend is the shore to this shoreless river.
The current bends again.
At one such bending he will call to me,
and I will look upon his face,
and he will catch me up in his embrace,
and then my flame, my pain, will be extinguished.
And on his breast will be extinguished, in my joy,
my flame.[53]

And sometimes, as with the Sahajiyās, the river is the river of rasa, the river of pure bliss that flows in man:

My eyelids were closed by the darkness of rasa,
closed leaves of the lotus on the shore of darkness.
In bottomless black roll the waves of the Jamnā,
the darkness rolls on in the waves of the Jamnā,
the black waves of rasa in the waves of the Jamnā,
and over them floats the flute-sound of rasa,
over them sounds the sweet flute of the Sāi.[54]

Given all this, it is quite possible, and even probable, that some Bāuls, as some troubadours, carry things to their Sahajiyā conclusion, and despite their antagonism to ritual worship, follow the sexual *sādhana*. It would not be hard, especially for a foreigner, to confuse Bāuls as a whole with Sahajiyās, as Kennedy—and, it might be added, some Bengali scholars—did; in the same way, and for the same reasons, Vaiṣṇavas were confused with Vaiṣṇava-sahajiyās. Kennedy writes: "Their main doctrine, summed up in the term *dehatattva* [i.e., truth, known within the body] is the presence of God within the human body and the sufficiency

[53] Bāul Gaṅgārām, in *Bāṅglā kāvya paricaya*, p. 68.
[54] Padmalocana, in *Bāṅglā kāvya paricaya*, p. 72.

of self-worship. . . . This is best achieved through sex-love and the worship of woman. Female companions are therefore essential."[55] Bāgchi also says that Bāul worship is "derived from Sahajiyā *sādhanā*," though he does not point directly to the use of women in worship.[56] But although it does seem as though the end which the Bāuls seek is essentially that of the Sahajiyās, a condition of bliss eternal, in life making no distinction between pleasure and pain, quality or stain, good or evil, their means are different.[57] Dasgupta's statement of the case seems accurate:

> The earlier Sahajiyā cult underwent a notable transformation in the hands of the Bāuls. . . . The Buddhist Sahajiyās conceived Sahaja as Mahā-sukha which is the unity of the duality represented by man and woman as Upāya and Prajñā. The method for the realisation of this Mahā-sukha consisted, therefore, essentially of sexo-yogic practice. To this, the Vaiṣṇavas supplied the element of love. . . . In all their theories of love and speculations on the lover and beloved, the Vaiṣṇava-sahajiyās never speak of any love beyond the purest and most perfect form of human love . . . [of] man and woman, who are themselves incarnations of the eternal Lover and Beloved. But the Bāuls conceived Sahaja as the innermost eternal Beloved who is the "Man of the Heart.". . . The Bāuls also speak of love and union, but this love means the love between the human personality and the Divine Beloved within, and in this love man realises his union with the divine.[58]

The difference between the Bāuls and the Sahajiyās is brought out in their poetry. The music and the poetry of the

[55] *CM*, p. 214; see also *Hārāmaṇi, bhumikā*, p. 10.
[56] *Hārāmaṇi*, p. 11.
[57] Bāgchi, quoted in *Hārāmaṇi*, p. 10.
[58] *ORC*, p. 189.

orthodox Vaiṣṇavas is lyrical, sensual, and full of enthusiasm, even at its most poignant. That of the Sahajiyās is doctrinal, obscure, and, with some notable exceptions, dry—especially to one who cannot fully understand the code. The Bāul songs are more in the Vaiṣṇava spirit, emotional and full of earthly imagery. And, while the Sahajiyā poems are confident, the songs of the Bāuls are often sad, filled with longing and a profound consciousness of human frailty. A beautiful Bāul song says:

O false and cheating builder, what joke is this
that you have built my house a frame of bones,
and wrapped it in a husk of skin?
This is no house. The watchman of my mind remains within,
but still the thieves break in and steal.
In my childhood, how I ran and laughed, and played,
and in my youth. But now
my last days pass in dream and meditation.
My teeth fall out, my hair is turning white,
my last youth ebbs away.
The days go by,
and my once gaily decorated house, built of the earth,
returns slowly to the earth.
But the garden of flowers at my house
still spreads its scent—
I will pick the flowers, and weave of them a garland
for my Friend.[59]

And Bāul songs are sometimes songs of pure joy, when the Bāul has rolled back the veil of māyā that hides Him who dwells in the heart, when he has seen His true reflection in the mirror.

[59] *Pravāsī,* p. 154.

I am forever blessed!
For I am his own breath, within his flute!
And if that breath is used up, in one song,
I shall not mourn.
The joy of all the worlds is in his flute,
and I his breath!
Let my song be good or evil,
let it be played with joy or sorrow,
I will sound it in the morning,
and in the evening it will sound,
and I will play it, softly muffled, in the night.
I will play it in the spring,
I will play it in the fall,
and when his breath is used up, in his song,
I shall not mourn.
My song will be the loveliest of songs.
What more could I want?[60]

While not quite Sahajiyās, the Bāuls are fitting hybrids; the Vaiṣṇava, Sahajiyā, and Sufi strains yield beauty, sympathy, and strength. From the Vaiṣṇavas, and from the Sufis, comes the Bāul vision of the warmth and humanness and love of God. From the Sahajiyās comes their conviction of His compelling immediacy. The mysteries of love and God, hinted at by Vaiṣṇava poets, explained by Vaiṣṇava theologians, attempted by Sahajiyā practitioners, perhaps find their truest expression in the songs of the Bāuls. In these there is an awe and understanding not often found in the poetry or thought of their Vaiṣṇava, Sahajiyā, or Vaiṣṇava-sahajiyā forebears. In the songs of the Bāuls is felt the power of divine love, here graced with human dignity.

[60] Īśan Yugi, in *Bāṅglā kāvya paricaya,* p. 66.

Bibliography

NOTE: In Sections I and II, which list source material, the titles of texts are arranged alphabetically. In Sections III and IV, books and articles are entered according to the name of the author.

Some texts in Bengali and Sanskrit give dates according to the Bengali calendar (signified by the initials B.S. for one system and the term *Gaurābda* for another); in such cases, the Bengali dates are preserved, with the approximate year according to the Christian calendar in parentheses.

I. Bengali and Sanskrit Sources

Advaita-prakāśa of Īśāna-nāgara. Edited by Mṛṇālakānti Ghoṣ. Calcutta: Amṛta-bājār patrikā Office, 1339 B.S. (1933).

Āgama-grantha of Yugalera-dāsa (Yugala-dāsa). See *Sahajiyā-sāhitya* under "Anthologies."

Amṛtarasāvalī of Mathurā-dāsa. See *Sahajiyā-sāhitya* under "Anthologies."

Ānanda-bhairava of Prema-dāsa. See *Sahajiyā-sāhitya* under "Anthologies."

Anurāgavallī of Manohara-dāsa. Edited by Mṛṇālakānti Ghoṣ. Calcutta: Amṛta-bājār patrikā Office, *Gaurābda* 445 (1931).

Ātma-tattva. See *Vaiṣṇava granthāvalī* under "Anthologies."

Bhagavad gītā. Edited and translated by Franklin Edgerton. Vol. I, text and translation. Cambridge: Harvard University Press, 1952.

Bhāgavata purāṇa. Murshidabad edition. 5 vols. Berhampur: Rādhāramaṇ Press, 1294 B.S. (1888). With the commentaries of Śrīdharasvāmin, Sanātana Gosvāmin, Jīva Gosvāmin, and Viśvanātha Cakravartī.

Bhāgavata purāṇa (Śrīmadbhāgavatam), *daśama skandha* only. Edited by Kuñjabihāri Vidyābhūṣaṇa. Calcutta: Gauḍīya maṭh, *Gaurābda* 446 (1932). With the commentary of Viśvanātha Cakravartī.

The Srimad Bhagavatam. Translated by J. M. Sanyal. 5 vols. 2d ed. Calcutta: Oriental Publishing Company, n.d. (date of foreword, 1952).

Bhakti-ratnākara of Narahari Cakravarti. Edited by Navīnakṛṣṇa Paravidyālaṁkāra. Calcutta: Gauḍīya maṭh, 1940.

Brahma-saṃhitā. Book V. Vṛndāvana: Ravīndranātha Bandyopādhyāya, n.d. With the commentary of Jīva Gosvāmin.

Brahmavaivarta purāṇa. Bengali version of Subodhacandra Majumdār. Calcutta: Deva-sāhitya-kuṭi, 1360 B.S. (1954).

Bṛhadbhāgavatāmṛtaṃ of Sanātana Gosvāmin. Edited by Praṇodagopāla Bhaktiśāstri. Calcutta, *Gaurābda* 469 (1955).

Bṛhattantrasāraḥ of Kṛṣṇānanda Āgamavāgīśa. Edited by Upendranāth Mukhopādhyāya and Satīścandra Mukhopādyāya. Calcutta: Basumati sāhitya mandir, 1341 B.S. (1935).

Caitanya-bhāgavata of Vṛndāvana-dāsa. Edited by Bhaktisiddhānta Sarasvatī Gosvāmi. 3d ed. Calcutta: Gauḍīya maṭh, *Gaurābda* 448 (1934).

———. Edited by Rasabihāri Bhāgavatabhūṣaṇa. Murshidabad edition. Berhampur: Rādhā-ramaṇ Press, 1320 B.S. (1914).

Caitanya-candrāmṛtaṃ of Prabodhānanda. Murshidabad edition. Berhampur: Rādhā-ramaṇ Press, 1333 B.S. (1927).

Caitanyacandrodaya-kaumudī of Prema-dāsa. Calcutta University MS No. 2145.

Caitanya-caritāmṛta of Kṛṣṇadāsa Kavirāja. Edited with the commentary *Gaurā-kṛpā-taraṅginī* by Rādhāgovinda Nāth. 6 vols. Calcutta: Bhakti-pracāra-bhāṇḍar, 1355 B.S. (1949–50). Four volumes of text and commentary, two of introductory essays and notes.

———. Calcutta: Gauḍīya maṭh, 1364 B.S. (1958). With the commentaries of Saccidāndana Bhaktivinod Ṭhākur and Bārṣobhānabīdayita-dāsa.

———. Murshidabad edition. Berhampur: Rādhā-ramaṇ Press, 1334 B.S. (1928). With the commentary of Jaganmohana-dāsa.

Caitanya maṅgala of Locana-dāsa. Edited by Mṛṇālakānti Ghoṣ. Calcutta: Amṛta-bājār patrikā Office, 1354 B.S. (1948). With the padas of Locana-dāsa.

Caitanya-maṅgala of Jayānanda. Edited by Nāgendranāth Basu and Kālidāsa Nāth. Calcutta: Baṅgiya sāhitya pariṣad, 1312 B.S. (1906).

Campaka-kalikā of Nareśvara-dāsa. See *Vaṅga sāhitya paricaya* under "Anthologies."

Durlabhasāra of Locana-dāsa. See *Vaiṣṇava-granthāvalī* under "Anthologies."

Gauragaṇoddeśa-dīpikā of Kavi-karṇapūra. Edited by Rāmanārāyaṇa Vidyāratna. Murshidabad edition. Berhampur: Rādhā-ramaṇ Press, 1329 B.S. (1923).

Haribhakti-vilāsa of Gopala Bhaṭṭa. Murshidabed edition. Berhampur: Rādhā-ramaṇ Press, 1344 B.S. (1938).

Jñānādi- sādhana. See *Vaṅga sāhitya paricaya* under "Anthologies."

Karacā of Govinda-dāsa. Edited by Dīneścandra Sen and Vanoyārīlāl Gosvāmī. Calcutta: University of Calcutta, 1926.

Karṇānanda of Yadunandana-dāsa. Edited by Rāmanārāyaṇa Vidyāratna. Murshidabad edition. Berhampur: Rādhā-ramaṇ Press, 1335 B.S. (1929).

Kṛṣnacaitanya-caritāmṛtam of Murāri Gupta. Edited by Haridās Dās. Navadvīp: Haribol kuṭī, *Gaurābda* 459 (1945).

Manasā-vijaya of Vipra-dāsa. Edited by Sukumār Sen. Calcutta: Asiatic Society of Bengal, 1953.

Muralī-vilāsa (or *Vaṃśī-vilāsa*) of Rājavallabha; text partially given

in the *Nityānanda-vamśāvallī* of Kṣīrodabihāri Gosvāmī. Calcutta: Kṣīrodabihāri Gosvāmī, 1337 B.S. (1931).
Narottama-vilāsa of Narahari-dāsa. Edited by Rāmanārāyaṇa Vidyāratna. Murshidabad edition. Berhampur: Rādhā-ramaṇ Press, 1328 B.S. (1918).
Nāyikā-sādhana-ṭīkā of Rūpānuga-dāsa. Calcutta University MS No. 3906.
Padyāvalī of Rūpa Gosvāmin. Edited by Suśilkumār De. Dacca: Dacca University, 1934.
Pāṣaṇḍa-dalana of Rāmacandra Gosvāmī (sometimes attributed to Narottama-dāsa). See *Vaiṣṇava granthāvalī* under "Anthologies."
Prācīna-dalila (two early legal MSS having to do with the *svakīyā-parakīyā* controversy). See *Vaṅga sāhitya paricaya* under "Anthologies."
Prameya-ratnāvalī of Baladeva Vidyābhūṣaṇa. Edited by Akṣayakumār Śāstrī. Calcutta: Sanskrit sāhitya pariṣad, 1927.
Prema-vilāsa of Nityānanda-dāsa. Murshidabad edition. Berhampur: Rādhā-ramaṇ Press, 1318 B.S. (1912).
Prema-vilāsa of Yugala-kiśora-dāsa. See *Vaṅga sāhitya paricaya* under "Anthologies."
Rādhārasa-karikā, anonymous in the text used, but occurring with the *bhaṇitā* "Mukunda-dāsa" (Sen, *BSI*, p. 419). See *Vaṅga sāhitya paricaya* under "Anthologies."
Sādhana-mālā. Edited by B. Bhaṭṭācāryya. Baroda: Gaekwad's Oriental Series. Nos. XXVI, XLI (1925–28).
Sahaja-tattva of Rādhāvallabha-dāsa. See *Vaṅga-sāhitya paricaya* under "Anthologies."
Ṣat-saṃdarbha of Jīva Gosvāmin (*Bhakti-saṃdarbha* and *Kṛṣṇa-saṃdarbha* only), with commentary of Baladeve Vidyābhūṣaṇa. Murshidabad edition. Berhampur: Rādhā-ramaṇ Press, 1362 B.S. (1957).
Śrīkṛṣṇa-kīrtana, attributed to Baḍu Caṇḍīdāsa. Edited by Vasantarañjan Rāy. Calcutta: Baṅgīya sāhitya pariṣad, 1323 B.S. (1917).
Śrīśrīrāmakṛṣṇa-kathāmṛta. 5 vols. Calcutta: Kathāmṛta bhavan, 1310–39 B.S. (1904–33).
Ujjvala-nīlamaṇi of Rūpa Gosvāmin. Edited by Rāmanārāyaṇa

Vidyāratna. Murshidabad edition. Berhampur: Rādhā-ramaṇ Press, 1341 B.S. (1935). With commentaries of Jīva Gosvāmin and Baladeva Vidyābhūṣaṇa.

Vivarta-vilāsa of Ākiñcana-dāsa. Calcutta: Tārācānd Dās, 1354 B.S. (1948).

Vraja-maṅgala of Uddhava-dāsa. Calcutta University MS No. 1022.

II. Anthologies and Journals That Include Bengali Source Material

Bāṅglār bāul o bāul gān, by Upendranāth Bhaṭṭācāryya. Calcutta: Oriental Book Company, 1364 B.S. (1958). Part I of the book is expository; Part II is a collection of Bāul songs.

Balarāmadāser padāvalī. Edited by Brahmacārī Amāracaitanya, with an introduction by Sukumār Sen. Calcutta: Nababhārata Publishers, 1362 B.S. (1956).

Basumati. Monthly journal. Calcutta.

Bāṅglā kāvya paricaya. Collected and edited by Rabīndranāth Ṭhākur (Rabindranāth Tagore). Calcutta: Viśvabhārati, 1345 B.S. (1939–40).

Bauddhagān o dohā. Edited by Satiścandra Mukhopādhyāy. Calcutta: Basumati sāhitya mandir, 1340 B.S. (1934).

Caryāgīti-padāvalī. Edited by Sukumār Sen. Burdwan: Sāhitya sabhā, 1956.

Dīna-caṇḍīdāser padāvalī. Edited by Manindramohan Basu (Bose). Two vols. Calcutta: University of Calcutta, 1341 B.S. (1935).

Gaurapada-taraṅginī. Compiled by Jagadbandhu Bhadra. Edited by Mṛṇālakānti Ghoṣ. Calcutta: Baṅgīya sāhitya pariṣad, 1341 B.S. (1935).

Hārāmaṇi (loka saṅgīta saṃgraha). Edited by Muhammad Mansur Uddin. Calcutta: University of Calcutta, 1942.

Kalpanā, by Rabīndranāth Thākur (Rabindranāth Tagore). In *Rabīndra-racanāvalī*. 26 vols. Viśvabhārati, 1353–55 B.S. (1947–49).

Kṣaṇadāgīta-cintāmaṇi. Compiled by Viśvanātha Cakravartī. Edited by Rādhānātha Kābāsī. Calcutta: Madanamohana mandir, *Gaurābda* 439 (1925).

Lālana-gītikā. Edited by Matilāl Dās and Pīyūṣakānti Mahāpatra. Calcutta: University of Calcutta, 1958.

Padakalpataru. Compiled by Vaiṣṇava-dāsa. Edited by Satiścandra Rāya. 5 vols. Calcutta: Baṅgīya sāhitya pariṣad, 1322–38 B.S. (1916–32).

Pravāsī. Quarterly journal. Calcutta. All references in the book are to vol. 15 (1322 B.S., 1916), four parts, paging consecutive.

Sahajiyā sāhitya. Edited by Manindramohan Basu (Bose). Calcutta: University of Calcutta, 1932. The anthology includes one hundred Sahajiyā padas plus complete texts of the *Āgama, Amṛtrarsāvalī,* and *Ānandabhairava.*

Sāhitya pariṣad patrikā. Quarterly journal of the Baṅgīya sāhitya pariṣad. Calcutta.

Vaṅga sāhitya paricaya. Compiled and edited by Dineścandra Sen. 2 vols. Calcutta: University of Calcutta, 1914. The anthology includes incomplete texts of *Campaka-kalikā, Jñānādi-sādhana, Prema-vilāsa, Rādhārasakarikā, Rasabhakti-candrika, and Sahajatattva,* and complete texts of the two legal works collectively entitled by the editor *Prācīna-dalila.*

Vaiṣṇava-granthāvalī. Edited by Satyendranāth Basu. Calcutta: Basumati sāhitya mandir, 1342 B.S. (1936). Together with a number of orthodox Vaiṣṇava texts, the anthology includes the Sahajiyā works *Ātma-tattva* and *Durlabhasāra.*

Vaiṣṇava-padāvalī. Edited by Khagendranāth Mitra, Sukumār Sen, Viśyapati Caudhuri, and Śyāmaprasād Cakravartī. Calcutta: University of Calcutta, 1952.

———. Edited by Harekṛṣṇa Mukhopādhyāya. Calcutta: Sāhitya saṃsad, 1961.

———. Edited by Sukumār Sen. New Delhi: Sahitya Akademi, 1957.

Vidyāpati. Edited by Khagendranāth Mitra and Bimānbihārī Majumdār. Calcutta: Saratkumār Mitra, 1359 B.S. (1953).

III. Other Materials: Bengali

Bandyopādhyāya, Jitendranāth. *Pañcopāsana.* Calcutta: K. L. Mukhopādhyāya, 1960.

Basu, Rameś. "Bauddha o śaiva ḍakinī o yoginīdiger kathā," *Sāhitya pariṣad patrikā,* No. 1 (1333 B.S. [1927]).

Bhaṭṭaśālī, Nalinīkānta: "Gopāladāser Rasakalpāvalī," in *Sāhitya pariṣad patrikā,* Vol. 38, No. 3 (1338 B.S. [1932]).

Caṭṭopādhyāya (Chatterji), Sunitikumār. *Bāṅgalā bhāṣātattver bhūmikā.* Calcutta: University of Calcutta, 1950.

Dāsgupta, Śaśibhūṣan. *Śrīrādhār kramavikāśa—darśane o sāhitye.* Calcutta: E. Mukherji, 1359 B.S. (1953).

Gauḍīya vaiṣṇava abhidhāna. Compiled and edited by Haridās Dās. First of 3 vols. Navadvīp: Haribol kuṭī, *Gaurābda* 470 (1957).

Majumdār, Bimānbihāri. *Śrīcaitanyacariter upādān.* Calcutta: University of Calcutta, 1939.

Mitra, Amalendu. "Bolāna gān," *Sāhitya pariṣad patrikā,* No. 2 (1362 B.S. [1956]).

Mukhopādhyāya, Harekṛṣṇa. *Kavijayadeva o śrīgītagovinda.* Calcutta: Gurudās Mukhopādhyāya and Sons, 1362 B.S. (1956).

Śāstrī, M. M. Haraprasād. "Caṇḍīdāsa," *Haraprasād racanāvalī.* Vol. I, edited by Sunītikumār Caṭṭopādhyāya and Anilkumār Kañjilāl. Calcutta: Eastern Printing Co., 1363 B.S. (1957).

Sen, Kṣitimohan. *Bāṅglār bāul.* Calcutta: University of Calcutta, 1951.

Sen, Sukumār. *Bāṅgalār sāhityer itihāsa.* 3 vols. Calcutta: Modern Book Agency, 1940. Volume I deals with the period of this study's concern. References are to this edition, unless otherwise noted.

———. *Ibid.* Vol. I. 2d ed. Calcutta: Eastern Publishers, 1959.

———. "Śrīkhaṇḍa sampradāya o caṇḍīdāsa," *Vicitra sāhitya.* Calcutta: East End Book Co., 1956.

———. *Bāṅgālār sāhitye gadya.* Calcutta: Modern Book Agency, 1356 B.S. (1950).

IV. Other Materials, Non-Bengali

Aquinas, St. Thomas. *Summa Theologica.* Edited, annotated, and with an introduction by Anton G. Pegis. Vol. I. New York: Random House, 1945.

Arnobius. *Adversus nationes.* Edited by C. Marchesi. "Corpus Scriptorum Latinorum Paravianum," No. 62. I. B. Paraviae and Sociorum. Augustae Taurinorum (n.d.).

Bagchi, Prabodh Chandra. "Development of Religious Ideas," *History of Bengal.* Vol. I. Edited by R. C. Majumdar. Dacca: Dacca University, 1942.

Bagchi, Prabodh Chandra. *Studies in the Tantras.* Part I. Calcutta: University of Calcutta, 1939.

Bhandarkar, Sir R. G. *Vaiṣṇavism, Śaivism, and Minor Religious Systems* (Volume IV of the *Collected Works*). Edited by N. B. Utgikar. Poona: Bhandarkar Oriental Research Institute, 1929.

Bharati, Agehananda. "Intentional Language in the Tantras," *Journal of the American Oriental Society,* 81 (1961): 261–70.

Bhatt, Govindlal Hargovind. "The School of Vallabha," *The Philosophies,* Vol. III of *The Cultural Heritage of India.* Calcutta: Ramakrishna Mission, 1953.

Bhattacharya, Benoytosh. *An Introduction to Buddhist Esoterism.* Oxford: Oxford University Press, 1932.

Bhaṭṭācārya, Siddheśvara. *The Philosophy of the Śrīmad-Bhāgavata.* 2 vols. Śantiniketan: Viśvabhārati, 1960.

Bose (Basu), Manindra Mohan. *The Post-Chaitanya Sahajiya Cult of Bengal.* Calcutta: University of Calcutta, 1930.

Bose, Nirmal Kumar. *My Days with Gandhi.* Calcutta: Nishana, 1953.

Carstairs, G. Morris. *The Twice-Born, Study of a Community of High-caste Hindus.* London: Hogarth Press, 1961.

Chakravarti, Chintaharan. *The Tantras: Studies on Their Religion and Literature.* Calcutta: Punthi Pustak, 1963.

Chatterji (Caṭṭopādhyāya), Sunitikumar. *The Origin and Development of the Bengali Language.* 2 vols. Calcutta: University of Calcutta, 1926.

———. "Islamic Mysticism," *Indo-Iranica,* 1, No. 2 (Calcutta, 1946).

Chaudhuri, Roma. *Sūfīsm and Vedānta.* 2 parts. Calcutta: Prācyavāṇī mandir, 1945–48.

———. "The Nimbārka School of Vedānta," *The Philosophies,* Vol. III of *The Cultural Heritage of India.* Calcutta: Ramakrishna Mission, 1953.

Dasgupta, Shashibhusan. *Obscure Religious Cults as a Background to Bengali Literature.* Calcutta: University of Calcutta, 1946. References are to this, the first edition, unless otherwise noted.

———. *Obscure Religious Cults.* 2d ed. Calcutta: K. L. Mukhopādhyāya, 1962.

Dasgupta, Shashibhusan. *An Introduction to Tantric Buddhism.* Calcutta: University of Calcutta, 1950.

———. *A History of Indian Philosophy.* 5 vols. Cambridge: Cambridge University, 1951–62.

Datta, Phulrenu. *La societé bengalie au XVIᵉ siecle.* Paris: Editions litteraires de France, 1938.

De, Sushil Kumar. *Early History of the Vaiṣṇava Faith and Movement in Bengal.* Calcutta: General Printers and Publishers, 1942. References are to this, the first edition, unless otherwise noted.

———. *Early History of the Vaiṣṇava Faith and Movement in Bengal.* 2d ed. Calcutta: K. L. Mukhopādhyāya, 1961.

———. "The Doctrine of Avatāra in Bengal Vaiṣṇavism," *Kuppaswāmī Śāstrī Commemoration Volume.* Madras, n.d.

———. *History of Bengali Literature in the Nineteenth Century.* Calcutta: University of Calcutta, 1919. 2d ed. Calcutta: K. L. Mukhopādhyāy, 1962.

———. *History of Sanskrit Poetics.* 2d ed. Calcutta: K. L. Mukhopādhyāya, 1960.

Dikshit, K. N. *Excavations at Paharpur, Bengal* (*Memoirs of the Archeological Survey of India,* No. 55). Delhi: Office of the Superintendent of Government Printing, 1939.

Dimock, Edward C. "The Place of Gauracandrikā in Bengali Vaiṣṇava Lyrics," *Journal of the American Oriental Society,* 78, No. 3: 153–69.

———. "Rabindranath Tagore—'The Greatest of the Bāuls of Bengal,' " *Journal of Asian Studies,* 19, No. 1: 33–51.

Eliade, Mircea. *Patterns in Comparative Religion.* New York: Sheed and Ward, 1958.

———. *Yoga: Immortality and Freedom.* New York: Pantheon Books (Bollingen Series), 1958.

———. *The Sacred and the Profane.* New York: Harper, 1959.

Fowler, Murray. "Ṛg-veda 10.27.14—bṛhánn achāyó apalāśó árvā," *Journal of the American Oriental Society,* No. 4 (1947).

Gibb, H. A. R. *Mohammedanism.* Oxford: Oxford University Press, 1949.

Gonda, J. *Aspects of Early Viṣṇuism.* Utrecht: N.V.A. Oosthoek's Uitgevers Mij, 1954.

Ghose, Shishir Kumar. *Lord Gauranga*. 2 vols. 3d ed. Calcutta: Amṛta bājār patrikā Office, 1923.

Ghosh, J. C. *Bengali Literature*. Oxford: Oxford University Press, 1949.

Ghoshal, Satyendranath. "Jāyasī and Alāol," *Chatterji Jubilee Volume*, Vol. 16 of *Indian Linguistics*. November, 1955.

Graves, Robert. *The Greek Myths*. 2 vols. Middlesex, England: Penguin, 1955.

Griffith, R. T. H. *Hymns of the Rig-veda*. Benares: E. J. Lazarus, 1896–97.

Guha, Naresh. *W. B. Yeats: An Indian Approach*. Unpublished doctoral dissertation, Northwestern University, 1962.

Hauer, J. W. *Die Dhāraṇī im nordlichen Buddhismus und ihre Parallelen in der sogennanten Mithrasliturgie*. Stuttgart: W. H. Kohlhammer, 1927.

Hiriyanna, M. "The Sāṃkhya," *The Philosophies*, Vol. III of *The Cultural Heritage of India*. Calcutta: Ramakrishna Mission, Calcutta, 1953.

History of Religions. Semi-annual journal, edited by Mircea Eliade, J. Kitagawa, and C. Long. Chicago: University of Chicago Press.

Hoebel, S. Adamson. *The Cheyennes*. New York: Holt, Rinehart, and Winston, 1960.

Hopkins, Thomas J. *Vaiṣṇava Bhakti Movement in the Bhāgavata Purāṇa*. Unpublished doctoral dissertation, Yale University, 1960.

———. "Social Teachings of the Bhāgavata Purāṇa," *Krishna: Myths, Rites, and Attitudes*, edited by Milton Singer. Honolulu: East-West Center, 1965.

Hume, Robert E. *The Thirteen Principal Upanishads*. Indian edition. Madras: Oxford University Press, 1949.

Husain, Yusuf. *L'Inde Mystique au moyen age*. Paris: A. Maisonneuve, 1929.

Jeanroy, Alfred. *Anthologie des troubadours*. Paris: Renaissance du livre, 1927.

Indian Folklore. 1st series. Quarterly journal. Edited by P. C. Pal and Gopinath Sen. Calcutta.

Indian Linguistics. Journal of the Linguistics Society of India. Poona. Edited by Sukumār Sen.

Journal of the American Oriental Society. Published quarterly by the American Oriental Society at Baltimore, Maryland.

Ingalls, Daniel H. H. *An Anthology of Sanskrit Court Poetry* ("Harvard Oriental Series", No. 44). Cambridge: Harvard University Press, 1965.

———. "A Sanskrit Poetry of Village and Field: Yogeśvara and his Fellow Poets," *Journal of the American Oriental Society*, 74, No. 3 (1954).

———. "Cynics and Pāśupatas: The Seeking of Dishonor," *Harvard Theological Review*, 55, No. 4 (1962).

Jung, Carl G. *Psychology and Religion, East and West* (Vol. XI of Jung's *Collected Works*). New York: Pantheon Books, 1958.

Kabir, Humayun. "Islam in India," *The Religions*, Vol. IV of *The Cultural Heritage of India.* Calcutta: Ramakrishna Mission, 1956.

Kardiner, Abram. *The Psychological Frontiers of Society.* New York: Columbia University Press, 1945.

Keay, F. E. *Kabir and His Followers.* Calcutta: Association Press, 1931.

Kennedy, Melville. *The Chaitanya Movement: A Study of the Vaishnavism of Bengal.* Calcutta: Association Press, 1925.

Kripalani, Krishna. *Rabindranath Tagore: A Life.* New York: Grove Press, 1962.

Lazar, Moshe. *Amour Courtois et Fin' Amors dans la litterature du XIIe sieclè.* Paris: Librairie C. Klincksieck, 1964.

Malinowski, Bronislaw. *Magic, Science, and Religion.* Boston: Beacon Press, 1948.

Majumdar, Ramesh Chandra (ed.) *History of Bengal.* Vol. I. Dacca: Dacca University, 1942.

Maspero, Henri. "Les procédés de 'nourir le principe vital' dans la religion taoiste ancienne," *Journal Asiatique*, vol. 299 (1937).

Moore, George Foote. *Judaism.* 2 vols. Cambridge: Harvard University Press, 1946.

Mukherji, Tarapada. *The Old Bengali Language and Text.* Calcutta: University of Calcutta, 1963.

Nāth, Rādhāgovinda. "The Acintya-bhedābheda School," *The Phi-*

losophies, Vol. III of *The Cultural Heritage of India*. Calcutta: Ramakrishna Mission, 1953.

Nims, John Frederick. *The Poems of St. John of the Cross*. New York: Grove Press, 1959.

Olson, Elder. *The Poetry of Dylan Thomas*. Chicago: University of Chicago Press, 1961.

Orr, W. G. *A Sixteenth-Century Indian Mystic*. London: Lutterworth Press, 1947.

Orwell, George. "The Art of Donald McGill," *A Collection of Essays*. Garden City, N.Y.: Doubleday, 1954.

Payne, Ernest A. *The Śāktas*. Calcutta: Association Press, 1933.

Plato. *Dialogues*. Translated by B. Jowett. 2 vols. New York: Random House, 1937.

Radhakrishnan, Sarvapelli. *Indian Philosophy*. 2 vols. 2d ed. London: George Allen and Unwin, 1929.

Raghavan, V. *Prayers, Praises, and Psalms* (*Selections from the Vedas, Upanishads, etc.*). 2d ed. Madras: G. A. Nateson, n.d.

Raychaudhuri, Hemchandra. *Materials for the Study of the Early History of the Vaiṣṇava Sect*. Calcutta: University of Calcutta, 1936.

Read, Herbert. *Collected Essays in Literary Criticism*. 2d ed. London: Faber and Faber, 1950.

Renou, Louis and Filliozat, Jean. *L'Inde classique*. Vol. I. Paris: Payot, 1947. Vol. II. Paris: Imprimerie nationale, 1953.

De Rougemont, Denis. *Love in the Western World*. New York: Doubleday, 1956.

Rowbotham, John Frederick. *The Troubadours and Courts of Love*. London: S. Sonnenschein and Co., 1895.

Sa'dī (Shekh Sa'dī Shīrāzī). *Gul-i-stān*. Delhi, 1960.

Sen, Dinesh Chandra. *History of Bengali Language and Literature*. 2d ed. Calcutta: University of Calcutta, 1954.

———. *Chaitanya and His Companions*. Calcutta: University of Calcutta, 1917.

———. *Chaitanya and His Age*. Calcutta: University of Calcutta, 1924.

Sen, Sukumār. *History of Brajabuli Literature*. Calcutta: University of Calcutta, 1935. Includes Brajabuli and Bengali texts in roman type.

———. *A History of Bengali Literature.* New Delhi: Sahitya Akademi, 1960.

Shastri (Śāstrī), M. M. Haraprasad. *A Descriptive Catalogue of the Vernacular Manuscripts in the Collection of the Royal Asiatic Society of Bengal.* Revised and edited by Yogendra Nath Gupta. Calcutta: Asiatic Society, 1941.

Singer, Milton B. "The Rādhā-Krishna Bhajanas of Madras City," *Krishna: Myths, Rites, and Attitudes,* edited by Milton B. Singer. Honolulu: East-West Center Press, 1965. Also in *History of Religions,* Winter, 1963.

Singer, Milton B. (ed.). *Krishna: Myths, Rites, and Attitudes.* Honolulu: East-West Center Press, 1965.

Sinha, Jadanāth. "Bhāgavata Religion: The Cult of Bhakti," *The Religions,* Vol. IV of *Cultural Heritage of India.* Calcutta: Ramakrishna Mission, 1956.

Swain, Anam Charan. *A Study of Saṃkara's Concept of Creation.* Unpublished doctoral dissertation, Harvard University, 1957.

Tagore, Rabindranath, and Evelyn Underhill (trans.). *One Hundred Poems of Kabir.* New York: Macmillan, 1915.

Tillich, Paul. *Systematic Theology.* Vol. I. Chicago: University of Chicago, 1951.

Tillyard, Eustace M. W. *Shakespeare's History Plays.* London: Chatto and Windus, 1944.

Thompson, Edward J. and A. M. Spencer (trans.). *Bengali Religious Lyrics, Shākta.* Calcutta: Association Press, 1923.

Twain, Mark (Samuel Clemens). *Letters from the Earth.* Edited by Bernard De Voto. New York: Harper and Row, 1963.

Valency, Maurice. *In Praise of Love, an Introduction to the Love Poetry of the Renaissance.* New York: Macmillan, 1961.

Winternitz, Maurice. *History of Indian Literature.* Vol. II. Calcutta: University of Calcutta, 1933.

Woordoffe, Sir John (Arthur Avalon, pseudonym). *Shakti and Shākta.* Madras: Ganesh and Co., 1951.

Yeats, William Butler. *The Collected Poems of W. B. Yeats.* New York: Macmillan, 1952.

Zimmer, Heinrich. *The Art of Indian Asia.* Edited by Joseph Campbell. 2 vols. New York: Pantheon Books, 1955.

Index

Abhisārikā, defined, 25
Acintya, quality of relation of *jīva* to Bhagavat, 129
Acintya-bhedābheda: orthodox theory of, 129–34; reinterpretation of by Sahajiyās, 130, 134. *See also* Sameness; Duality
Ādi-caṇḍīdāsa. *See* Caṇḍīdāsa, multiple identity of
Advaita Ācārya: alleged defection of, 89; conflict of with Nityānanda, 88, 89; summons Caitanya *avatāra* of Kṛṣṇa, 136
Advaita philosophy, Vaiṣṇava view of, 126, 126 n., 127 n.
Āgamas, defined, 43 n.
Aiśvarya, synonym for *vaidhi,* 193
Amṛtaṛasāvalī, allegory of, 144
Ānanda. See Svarūpa, components of
Añjali, in Sahajiyā sādhana, 236, 237
Anubhāva, function in Sanskrit poetics, 21
Anupama, father of Jīva Gosvāmin, 73, 74
Āropa: definition of, 164; function in Sahajiyā worship and doctrine, 164, 198, 214, 223, 234, 237. *See also Bhāva;* Kāma; Prema
Asceticism, of Avadhūtas, 47, 48; of Caitanya, 153–55; in Sahajiyā practice, 53, 155–57; of Gandhi, 156
Ātmārāma, quality and function of, in Sahajiyā and Tantric doctrine, 172
Ātmārāmeśvara: dwelling place of, 172; quality and function of, in Tantric and Sahajiyā doctrine, 173